The Balkan Route

The Balkan Route

Historical Transformations from Via Militaris to Autoput

Edited by
Florian Riedler and Nenad Stefanov

DE GRUYTER

ISBN 978-3-11-061682-8
e-ISBN (PDF) 978-3-11-061856-3
e-ISBN (EPUB) 978-3-11-061706-1

Library of Congress Control Number: 2020951363

Bibliographic information published by the Deutsche Nationalbibliothek
The Deutsche Nationalbibliothek lists this publication in the Deutsche Nationalbibliografie;
detailed bibliographic data are available on the Internet at http://dnb.dnb.de.

© 2021 Walter de Gruyter GmbH, Berlin/Boston
Printing and binding: CPI books GmbH, Leck

www.degruyter.com

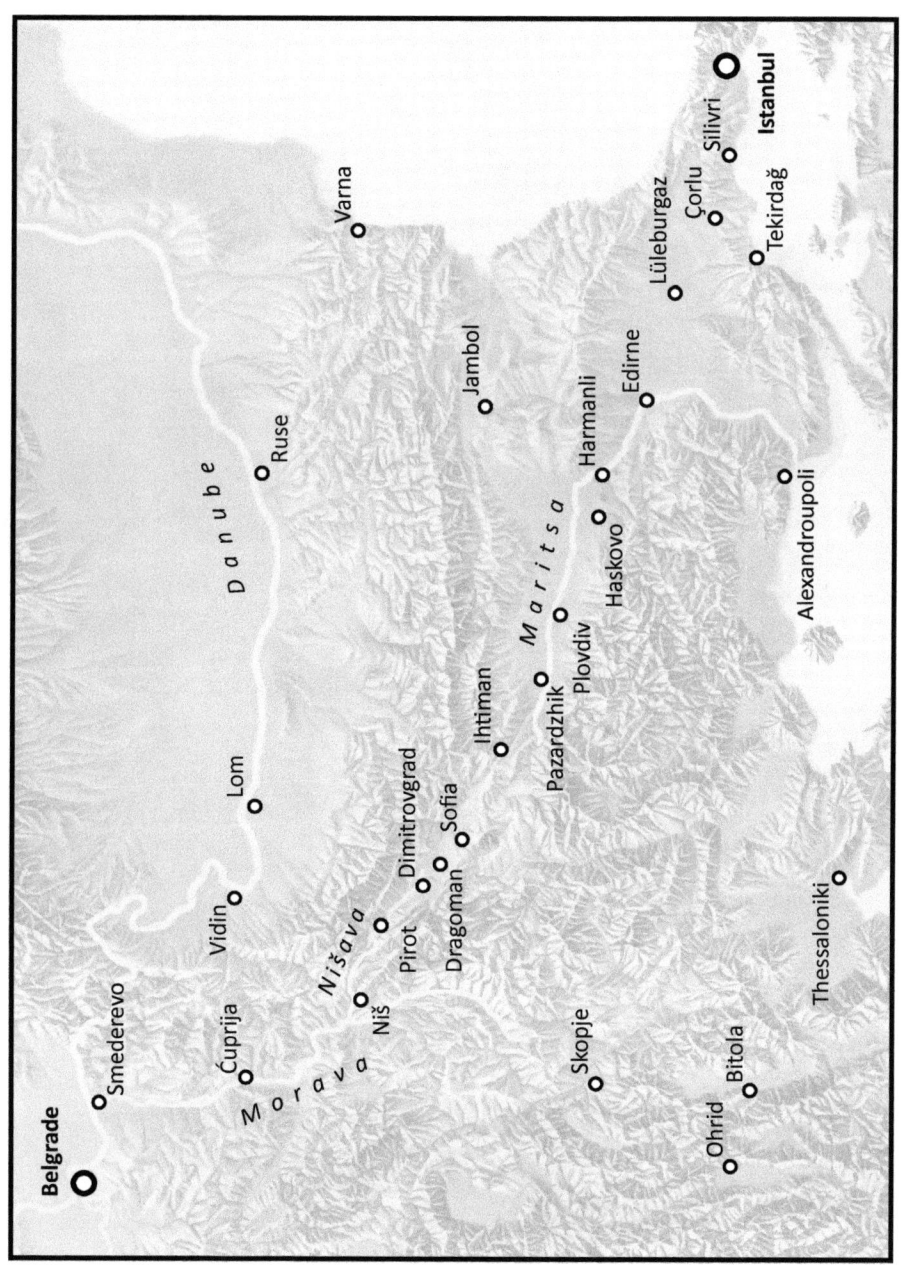

Fig. 1: The main cities on the Istanbul–Belgrade route together with other places mentioned in the book. Cartography by Florian Riedler using a relief map available at http://www.shadedreliefarchive.com/Balkans_CIA.html.

Acknowledgements

The idea for this volume goes back to two workshops organized by the editors in 2016 and 2018. The intial workshop took place in the framework of the research network "Phantom Borders in East Central Europe" funded by the German Federal Ministry of Education and Research (01UC1504 A–D). The follow-up workshop was hosted by the Interdisciplinary Centre of the Humboldt Universität zu Berlin "Border Crossings – Crossing Borders. Berlin Centre for Transnational Border Research." We like to express our thanks to both institutions for their material support. This volume is also the beginning of a series of publications by the Berlin Center for Transnational Border Research, which will focus on the topic of the societal production of borders.

Academically, the volume profited from the discussions with the participants of the original workshops and our colleagues and friends such as Prof. Hannes Grandits, Dr. Andreas Helmedach, and PD Dr. Nora Lafi, who offered advice and help in numerous ways. In particular, we like to single out Prof. Stefan Rohdewald for reading and commenting on a draft version of the book.

In the preparation of the manuscript, Dr. Philip Jacobs prudently brushed up our language and Julian Sandhagen assisted in the editing. Finally, our thanks go to Dr. Sophie Wagenhofer and Dr. Eva Frantz from the De Gruyter publishing house for their continuous assistance.

Nowawes, 19 September 2020
Florian Riedler (florian.riedler@uni-leipzig.de)
Nenad Stefanov (nenad.stefanov@hu-berlin.de)

Table of Contents

Acknowledgements —— VII

Florian Riedler and Nenad Stefanov
Bordering and Mobility as an Approach to the History of the Balkan Route —— 1

Matthew Larnach
The Via Militaris in Transition: From Late Rome to the Crusades —— 21

Vladimir Aleksić
Continuity of Travel and Transport Infrastructures from Antiquity to the Middle Ages: The Case of Via Militaris in the Morava and Nišava Regions —— 53

Tatjana Katić
Transforming the Landscape of the Constantinople Road in the Fifteenth and Sixteenth Centuries (Section Niš–Dragoman) —— 81

Florian Riedler
The Istanbul–Belgrade Route in the Ottoman Empire: Continuity and Discontinuity of an Imperial Mobility Space —— 103

Dobrinka Parusheva
Cities along the Route: Plovdiv Becoming "Modern" at the End of the Nineteenth Century —— 121

Nenad Stefanov
Tsaribrod, a Dot on the Line: A Microhistorical Approach to Societal Change along the Route in the Nineteenth and Twentieth Centuries —— 139

Nenad Stefanov
Park ve Restoran: About Oblivion, Obstinate Mobility and Temporary Infrastructures on the Road —— 183

Sandra King-Savić
Voices of the Via Egnatia: Deliberating Migratory Pull-Factors along the Roman Road in the Western Balkans —— 201

Florian Riedler and Nenad Stefanov
Balkan Transit: Conclusion and Outlook —— 229

List of Contributors —— 235

Index —— 237

Florian Riedler and Nenad Stefanov
Bordering and Mobility as an Approach to the History of the Balkan Route

1 The Balkan Route in Summer 2015

In 2015, Nenad Stefanov, one of the authors, spent much of his research time in the Serbian town of Dimitrovgrad, located on the border to Bulgaria. Beginning in April there was a change in the everyday life of the small town and its surroundings. Frequently, small groups of young men were passing through the city; they had obviously already travelled a long distance and they seemed to still have a long way ahead of them. Usually they had a short rest in the town and then walked along the E-80, the modern name of the Roman road, referred to today usually as the Via Militaris, at least up to Pirot, the district city to the north, where one could get a seat on a bus to the Serbian capital, Belgrade.

The small groups walking one behind the other next to the ditch running along the road created a strange impression, as if these people, on their way to the next larger city, were separated from the mobility of all the others by an invisible membrane. Nobody seemed to notice these people, be it the farmer driving his *motocultivator* at walking speed on the field next to them, or the cyclists, not to mention the car drivers on the road. Everyone seemed to be traveling in his/her own invisible tunnel.

That changed as summer approached. More and more people: women, children and men arrived by the almost impassable mountain paths to Dimitrovgrad, which is situated in a valley right next to one of the most frequented crossings on the Serbian-Bulgarian border. Here, too, the contrast seemed absurd: since June, the border crossing in the valley was being used by large numbers of Turkish migrant workers from Germany heading southeast, as has usually been the case during the summer season over the last fifty years. In their expensive cars they were on the way to their summer holidays in Turkey. On the mountain slopes in the immediate vicinity of the border crossing, the refugees from Pakistan, Afghanistan, Iran, Iraq and Syria were on their laborious way in the opposite direction, along paths mostly forgotten by even the locals themselves.

But now the separated worlds of mobility started to intermingle and there was interaction between, on the one hand, those locals who thought they were particularly shrewd and who put up billboards in Arabic letters in abandoned shops in Dimitrovgrad to advertise quick transport to Hungary, and on the other, the refugees who were actually hoping to make the journey as rapidly as possible. Meanwhile, the individual groups of refugees had united into a small society with the most diverse backgrounds—rich and poor, exhausted and confident. As they came down from the mountains, they had to stop at the former barracks of Dimitrovgrad where the border police is housed on a hill above the city in order to be "processed for identification purposes," as it is called in the language of bureaucracy.

In the September heat of 2015, many people huddled truly exhausted on the roadside of the settlement located adjacent to the military barracks. This was also the case in the street where the author lived, just opposite the entrance to the barracks. He could see young families with their children who had fled from Kobane on the Syrian-Turkish border; they were looking for shade along the roadside and locals occasionally offered them some refreshments.

At first, it might seem as if very different worlds were coming into contact with each other here, each with very different experiences of involuntary migration. But that was not quite true: exactly twenty years earlier, in August 1995, the people in Serbia had witnessed a similar exodus, but at that time the refugees were coming from the west. The motorways then were clogged with small tractors and their trailers, on which many people were fleeing from Croatia. They were coming from the Serb-populated areas of Krajina in Croatia and were fleeing from the Croatian army, which had re-captured these areas from the Serbian nationalist militias who had temporarily occupied Krajina. In 2015, this simultaneity of new refugees from the Syrian war encountering a local society that had only slowly and with great effort begun to overcome the traumas of the Yugoslavian wars of the 1990s was a disturbing moment for many.

Less than 130 years ago, Damascus, Kobane, Sofia and Dimitrovgrad all belonged to the Ottoman Empire. In that past, the fate of the refugees would have been just as tragic, their journey just as exhausting, but at that time they would not have had to cross state borders with the attendant control facilities on what would become known as the Balkan Route. In 2015, these borders had become particularly impermeable. Those refugees who sought to avoid such borders, choosing instead to go via Greece and Macedonia to Serbia, faced the danger of drowning in the Aegean Sea. Those who went along the land route and on their way passed through Dimitrovgrad had to cross the highly secured border between Turkey and Bulgaria. In Bulgaria, they had to put up with the violence of the Bulgarian authorities and others who exacted large sums of money from them for the passage across the mountainous border into Serbia. By contrast, until 1878 there was no border on this route from Syria to Serbia. For centuries it had been one of the most important transit routes from the Ottoman Middle East to Central Europe. With the formation of new nation-states in the nineteenth century, new borders were drawn and their function as barriers intensified over time, culminating in the Cold War. However, the desire to shut or at least tightly control this route has always been challenged by mobile actors, as was once again the case in the summer of 2015.

In Western media, the Balkans are associated with borders and violence. For Maria Todorova, the genesis of the term Balkans at the end of the nineteenth century is inextricably linked with stigmatizing attributions, such as small states and war.[1] This nexus was revitalized in the 1990s when in Western Europe the disintegration of Yugoslavia and the subsequent wars over ethnically homogeneous territories were often interpreted in the traditional essentializing categories of the nineteenth century. By externalizing responsibility, the rest of Europe assigned otherness and heterogeneity to the Balkans—a region that was governed by myth not reason; a region of invisible borders and violence, where hermetically sealed-off communities remained trapped in the past. In contrast, Western Europe styled itself as an open civil society, in which borders had seemingly become less and less relevant. Since 2015 at least, this normative mental map has begun to lose its significance. The present debates about new walls and borders in Europe, at least in retrospect, convey the anachronistic and ahistorical nature of the binary characteristics of civility and violence mentioned above.

In the summer of 2015, the appellation Balkan Route, much used by the media, flipped around the previous attributions: now what the Balkans represented was precisely the lack of efficient control and "protective" borders against the refugees, who were passing on their way from the EU-member state Greece to the EU-states in the northwest by way of this territorial "gap" called the Balkans. The border crossing between Idomeni in Greece and Gevgelija in Macedonia showed a "loss of control," which disturbed Western European spectators, for whom the earlier wars in Yugoslavia had still seemed reassuringly remote. The Balkans continued to convey a negative image and so did the route, which was now perceived less as a line of communication connecting people and different cultures, but instead was associated with paths for illegal smuggling. Topics such as human trafficking and drug smuggling in East and Southeast Europe were overlaid now with the so-called refugee crisis. In the media, the refugees themselves were no longer addressed as fleeing individuals, but as an anonymous, dangerous mass that used an already infamous route for its equally infamous goals, i.e., "economic migration." Slogans such as *antemurale christianitatis*, a term coined in the early modern wars against the Ottoman Empire, began to circulate again among modern nationalist actors in some of the Balkan states and formed the background of this generally negative discourse about refugees.

---

1 Maria Todorova, *Imagining the Balkans* (New York: Oxford University Press, 1997).

Some scholars discussed the way migrants on the Balkan Route were being likened to the Ottomans armies, which had conquered Central Europe in the sixteenth and seventeenth centuries.[2]

Eventually, the Balkan Route was shut down (soon after the events described above) through a tightening of the border regimes by the enforcing of legal restrictions as well as constructing physical barriers at certain strategic points along the passage. Most impressive are the installations on the Greek-Turkish border close to Edirne, which now consist of a fence and a ditch; there are also barbed-wire fences along the borders between Bulgaria and Turkey, Greece and Macedonia, and between Serbia and Hungary. Still today, those refugees who did not make it to Western Europe prior to these borders being closed are trapped in camps in Idomeni, in Belgrade and elsewhere.

At least in public discourse, borders as well as routes—both of them being opposing concepts that are quite normatively charged and emotionally loaded—were always used with a negative connotation when talking about the Balkans and their societies. This becomes very apparent in the intense and controversial discussions about the refugees on the Balkan Route that appeared in the press and other media. The slogan of "loss of control" became one of the triggers for the growth of new authoritarian and xenophobic attitudes in the societies of the EU.

At the same time, the events of summer 2015 and the subsequent discussions have also sharpened our own attention to the historical dimension of communication and mobility in the societies of the Balkans. Our ongoing historical research on the route has gained a sense of urgency, which in turn supplemented the various conceptual approaches which we will spell out in the next section. In a final step of this introduction, we make a case for connecting our work to the tradition of historical research on mobility in the Balkans and particular research on the Istanbul–Belgrade route.

2 Mobility, Borders and Microregions: Approaching the Road

This volume examines the lines of communication, roads and routes of trade and traffic in the Balkans from a historical perspective. More precisely, it focuses on

---

2 Catherine Baker, *Race and the Yugoslav Region: Postsocialist, Post-conflict, Postcolonial?* (Manchester: Manchester University Press, 2018), http://library.oapen.org/handle/20.500.12657/28907, last accessed 7 September 2020.

the historical development of the land route from Istanbul to Belgrade, reaching from the Middle Ages to the second half of the twentieth century. Our examination includes various topics such as how historical actors experienced mobility, what kind of infrastructural networks sustained it, and what changes it engendered in the relationship between power and society. We think that a focus on routes is particularly useful for establishing a new understanding of the history of the Balkans by connecting it to questions and approaches of the "mobility turn,"[3] which has been shaping the social sciences since the turn of the millennium. We not only seek to correct the above-mentioned stereotypical views on the Balkans prevalent in Western media and academia, but we also take a position against the nationalist historiography from within the region with its narrow focus on bounded and isolated national communities. Instead, our approach on routes will stress the long-term connectivity within the region and beyond. In this, we are following a growing scholarship that examines the history of migration and entanglements in the Balkans.[4] However, in order not to fall into a one-dimensional romanticization of connectivity, we will also include the aspect of immobility in our discussion of the route. As the contemporary example of refugees and migration shows quite vividly, it is particularly at borders that immobility becomes visible. The contributions to this volume will take up this issue, which has been thematized in mobility studies, but this time will do so from a historical perspective.[5]

The central topic of this volume, the relationship between borders and lines of communication, emerged from discussions in the research network "Phantom Borders in East Central Europe."[6] In this network, we examined the persistence of spatial orders, the main example being "phantom borders," i.e., historical border lines which had disappeared but then reappeared situationally under completely changed societal conditions. Such revivals of old spatial orders can be observed in architecture, settlement structures, but also in representations such as statistics or maps as well as in social practices:

---

[3] Mimi Sheller and John Urry, "The New Mobilities Paradigm," *Environment and Planning A: Economy and Space* 38, no. 2 (2006): 207–26.
[4] Ulf Brunnbauer, *Transnational Societies, Transterritorial Politics: Migrations in the (Post-)Yugoslav Region, 19th–21th Century* (Munich: Oldenbourg, 2009); Marie-Janine Calic, *The Great Cauldron: A History of Southeastern Europe* (Cambridge: Harvard University Press, 2019).
[5] Tim Richardson, "Borders and Mobilities: Introduction to the Special Issue," *Mobilities* 8, no. 1 (2013): 1–6.
[6] See the website of the research network at www.phantomgrenzen.eu, last accessed 7 September 2020.

> In the study of phantom borders and phantom spaces, the primary question is how and why varied social, historical, and imagined heritages mutually influence each other. Here, they not only can combine to create something new, but also persist over a more or less extended period of time. We underscore the ephemeral and non-deterministic nature of the examined regions: their 'phantom-like' nature.[7]

In discussions about the persistence of spatial demarcations, we posed the question as to how *connections,* and especially materialized lines of communication such as roads, also disappear and reappear again. As a first empirical example, we chose the road connection from Istanbul to Belgrade and focused on the urban centers Niš and Pirot situated in its middle section. In this volume, we will now extend this discussion to include the transformation of the entire route from the Ottoman to the Yugoslavian period. The three dimensions of the "social production of space" which determine phantom borders and spaces—namely, perception, experience and structuring—will help us to analyze the continuities and discontinuities of the Istanbul–Belgrade route.[8]

The concept of a conduit of communication, such as the Istanbul–Belgrade route, can meaningfully integrate micro-studies into a larger framework. That is why we asked colleagues to provide case studies which focus on different regions and also on different actors and their experience on and with the road. As Dimitris Dalakoglou, the author of an influential anthropological study of a road which connects Greece with Albania, puts it: "The meanings of the road as a product are open to those who use it, experience its existence, and are simply aware of its existence."[9] However, also from a perspective which focuses on the appropriation of the road by the local actors, it is essential to keep in mind the factors that literally produced it. This is even more crucial for historical studies, where the varying availability of sources often make an actor-centered approach difficult.[10] Therefore, in addition, the infrastructures built by the states that governed the route will also be a recurring topic. Particularly for the time since the nineteenth century, it can be argued that railways and motorways have become one of the most paradigmatic material infrastructures that shape

---

[7] Béatrice von Hirschhausen et al., "Phantom Borders in Eastern Europe: A New Concept for Regional Research," *Slavic Review* 78, no. 2 (2019): 371–2.
[8] Béatrice von Hirschhausen and Michael G. Esch, eds., *Wahrnehmen, Erfahren, Gestalten: Phantomgrenzen und soziale Raumproduktion,* (Göttingen: Wallstein, 2017), 13.
[9] Dimitris Dalakoglou, *The Road: An Ethnography of (Im)Mobility, Space, and Cross-Border Infrastructures in the Balkans* (Manchester: Manchester University Press, 2017), 13.
[10] Colin Divall, "Mobilities and Transport History," in *The Routledge Handbook of Mobilities,* ed. Peter Adey, David Bissell, and Kevin Hannam (London: Routledge, 2014), 36–44.

our societies and cultures up to the present day.¹¹ Such infrastructure is "not simply objectively or rationally created, but involve complex sociocultural, historical, and especially political dynamics, while simultaneously encapsulating what Michel Foucault called the micro-physics of power within their materiality."¹²

The overall aim of a historical study like ours is to provide a genealogy of modern mobilities that can root mobility studies in a new way. By acting as a "corridor through time,"¹³ routes and roads can connect present-day with historical concerns, thus offering an excellent vantage point from which to study phenomena of long duration. We seek to detect the different rhythms of disappearance and reappearance of the route resulting from different constellations of dominion, infrastructure and communication. The collective effort of a long-term history of the road aims at providing a first step towards an integrated history of mobility, which pays equal attention to the aspect of power, to the mobile actors, the infrastructures (which enable mobility), as well as the cultural representation of mobility. The issue at stake is to show in which constellation these elements constituting mobility come together in shaping social life in the particular case of the Istanbul–Belgrade road.¹⁴

Additionally, we think that our approach is justified by its ability to integrate different scales of analysis. In particular, the relationship between the micro-perspective of the road and its individual concrete connecting points (such as cities, villages, guesthouses, horse change stations or border crossings), and the overarching reach as projected from the perspective of the state becomes clear. Many of the contributions to the volume do not look at the whole of this line of communication by taking a bird's eye view, as it were, from a retrospective perspective of the state. State and society and infrastructure and their practical appropriation are always localized, i.e., discussed in a concrete local and regional frame of reference. In this way, what can be analyzed are the relations between state and society in their practical presence in the imperial/national state space, then the forms of participation of local society in them, and finally the relationship between the local and the transregional, especially with regard to the division of labor along the route. The focus is on the effects of this translocal dimension of mobility as well as the impact of dominion on different localities.

---

11 Dalakoglou, *The Road*, 5.
12 Ibid., 13.
13 Richard Cuttler, Andrew Davidson, and Gwilym Hughes, *A Corridor through Time: The Archaeology of the A55 Anglesey Road Scheme* (Oxford: Oxbow, 2011).
14 Colin Divall and George Revill, "Cultures of Transport: Representation, Practice and Technology," *The Journal of Transport History* 26, no. 1 (2005): 99–111.

We chose to focus on specific local contexts, because the route itself only functioned as a seamless connection between two points at very specific historical moments; at other times it was highly fragmented. Research in the history of infrastructures has frequently stressed the importance of technologies of transport and communication for both the empires from antiquity and the colonial empires in the modern age.[15] In a similar manner, the Istanbul–Belgrade road as a whole was a significant means for imperial powers such as the Roman, the Byzantine and the Ottoman Empires to control and penetrate their territories. These *imperia* became the great infrastructure builders on the route, fitting it with inns, post stations, bridges and secure mountain passes. However, when the central power was weak, the route became fragmented and served at best to integrate smaller regions. The national states that were established in the region beginning at the end of the nineteenth century are a case in point. Also, for these states technological and infrastructural development of communication and transport were crucial, but in contrast to empires they tried to isolate themselves from their neighbors and were not interested in the route as a whole.

The dialectics between integration and fragmentation continued into the twentieth century. On the one hand, the border between the eastern and western block, the Iron Curtain, overwrote the national borders. On the other hand, traffic on the route between Turkey and Central Europe rose and, at the same time, was transformed by auto-mobility. Not only goods but also people, e.g., the Turkish "guest workers" in Germany were beginning to use the route, despite the frictions and decelerations imposed by borders.

Ultimately, this long-term history of the route suggests the dialectics of bordering and mobility as an overarching perspective for the volume. As sources of friction, deceleration or blockage, state borders are relatively new phenomena on the route from Istanbul to Central Europe. They appeared during the nineteenth century, but since then they have become accepted as a "natural" condition of our modern world. We are interested in the way they function as barriers structuring mobility as the expression of a power relation, in this case between states and subjects. Also, the relationship between blockage and mobility always has to be examined in a concrete local context, particularly at the intersections between borders and lines of communication and passage. Here, on the microscale and in relation to the local society, the relationship between power and mobility becomes apparent.

---

15 Daniel R. Headrick, *The Tools of Empire: Technology and European Imperialism in the Nineteenth Century* (Oxford: Oxford University Press, 1981).

Such intersections can also help in developing a more precise definition of the local not as an essentialized bounded territory, but as part of a line of communication. Especially the work of the cultural anthropologist Sarah Green on the Pogoni region along the Albanian-Greek border is a case in point since it shows the strong interconnection between the local and the global in defining a place. It is particularly the critique of essentializing "places" that is productive for our analysis; as Sarah Green puts it: "It is now widely argued that the earlier habit of depicting peoples as 'belonging' to certain places as if they were rooted in the soil, and focusing on the separations rather than interconnections between differing peoples/places [...] generated a range of difficulties in understanding the construction of place."[16]

Especially the specific character of micro-regions located in border areas can best be explained when lines of communication that run through them are taken into account. Mobility along such a conduit can break up a static understanding of center-periphery relations in which the regional is often equated with the periphery. Phenomena such as labor migration or trade networks, which connect different micro-regions, are not directly related to and controlled from the center. From a perspective, which is not that of the center, we can understand a region as more than just a periphery. We propose that every micro-history of a region should include elements of mobility to show its multi-dimensional character. Especially in contexts like the Balkans, where nation states with their new national centers have fundamentally reshaped spatial relations, this is important for any historical analysis that seeks to look beyond the national period. In this volume, several contributions focus on the section of the route between Sofia and Niš. By positioning this micro-region in relation to different and changing centers at different periods of time, these chapters make an attempt at redefining locality in relation to mobility.

3 The Historiography of the Route

A work which examines the history of the Istanbul–Belgrade route from a longterm perspective cannot but acknowledge the pioneering role of Konstantin Jireček's first monograph on the topic: *Die Heerstraße von Belgrad nach Constantinopel/The Military Road from Belgrade to Constantinople*, published in 1877. In this work, which deals with the Roman road, its significance in the Middle

---

16 Sarah F. Green, *Notes from the Balkans: Locating Marginality and Ambiguity on the Greek-Albanian Border* (Princeton: Princeton University Press, 2005), 90.

Ages as a crusaders' route, and, briefly, with its transformation in the Ottoman period, Jireček establishes the narrative that would dominate until the middle of the twentieth century about this "most important traffic artery of the Balkan peninsula." For Jireček, the road was rather a line of confrontation than one of communication: "Especially the crusades awarded [this route] a role in world history: The Turks began their conquests in Europe in this direction and were also forced to partially give up their domination of the peninsula there."[17] For us, Jireček's work has an appeal even today, not so much because of the author's conclusions, but more so because of his general approach which views collectively all the epochs through which the route perdured.

The first part of Jireček's book is dedicated to the route as a Roman road from the time of the incorporation of the Balkans into the Roman Empire in the first century CE until the end of Roman rule in the seventh. Jireček, as a compiler of the contemporary classicist knowledge about the route, relied on a long tradition of research. Roman roads have been the focus of scholarly attention at least since the seventeenth century, when Nicolas Bergier published his *Histoire des grands chemins de l'Empire romain*. This erudite work used the classical authors, inscriptions on Roman milestones, as well as the received itineraries such as the *Tabula Peutingeriana* and was republished several times up through the eighteenth century. Like Bergier and subsequent works, Jireček continues a reconstruction of the itinerary of the Roman road by using the classical sources, but he also frequently mentions travel writers of the early modern period, who encountered remains of the Roman road along their way.[18]

Roman roads as a topic have stayed popular even today.[19] However, from among the Roman road connections of Southeast Europe, the Via Egnatia, the road from Byzantium to the Adriatic, has attracted more scholarly attention than the connection through the Central Balkans to Singidunum (today's Belgrade). In contrast to Via Egnatia, the latter route did not even have a proper name. Via Militaris, as it is usually referred to, is a general categorization of a

---

[17] Constantin Jireček, *Die Heerstrasse von Belgrad nach Constantinopel und die Balkanpässe: Eine historisch-geographische Studie*, (Prague: Tempsky, 1877), 3, all translations are ours.
[18] Michael W. Weithmann, "Zur Geschichte der Erforschung der Römerstraßen in Südosteuropa: Eine Übersicht der älteren Forschung," in *Serta Balcanica-Orientalia Monacensia: In Honorem Rudolphi Trofenik Septuagenarii*, ed. Hans-Joachim Kißling (Munich: Trofenik, 1981): 17–31.
[19] For an overview of the state of scholarship cf. the following articles of *Brill's New Pauly:* Hans Lohmann, Josef Wiesehöfer, and Michael Rathmann, "Roads"; Michael Rathmann, "Viae publicae"; Christoph Höcker, "Roads and bridges, construction of"; Georges Raepsaet, "Land transport," in *Brill's New Pauly*, antiquity volumes ed. Hubert Cancik and Helmuth Schneider, English edition ed. Christine F. Salazar, consulted online on 2 July 2020.

Fig. 1a: Part of the excavated Via Militaris near Dimitrovgrad. Photo by Nicole Münnich, 2011.

particular road type in the Roman Empire. These roads connected the postal stations of the individual provinces and were a sub-category of the *viae publicae*. They differed in layout and construction from those of the lower categories, the *viae vicinales*, which connected smaller places in the provinces.[20]

It is not known when exactly the route between Byzantium and Singidunum was constructed as a Roman road. Most archaeologists assume that the different sections of the road were built in the first century CE to integrate the region into the Roman Empire. Most probably our route was already used in pre-Roman times as a transregional line of communication.[21]

Recently, the study of Roman roads on the Istanbul–Belgrade route has been given a new push by excavations in connection with the construction of the new

---

20 Matthew Larnach, "All Roads Lead to Constantinople: Exploring the Via Militaris in the Medieval Balkans, 600–1204" (PhD diss., University of Sydney, 2016), 25–6.
21 Gavro Škrivanić, "Roman Roads and Settlements in the Balkans," in *An Historical Geography of the Balkans*, ed. Francis W. Carter (London: Academic Press, 1977): 115–46; Mitko Madžarov, *Rimski pătišta v Bălgarija: prinos v razvitieto na rimskata pătna sistema v provinciite Mizija i Trakija* (Veliko Tarnovo: Faber, 2009).

E-80 motorway in Serbia and Bulgaria. For example, the Roman remains discovered near Dimitrovgrad close to the Serbian-Bulgarian border offer new insight into the ancient history of the road. The excavation shows quite vividly that the Roman road was not only part of an overarching imperial system (which itself has fascinated scholars since the early modern period), it was also a permanent work in progress and was being adapted to local contexts. The section mentioned, which dates to the middle of the second century and which probably replaced the original road, does not correspond to the general norm. It has a different layering and is missing the obligatory ditches; moreover, with 7.5 meters it is unusually wide. Archaeologists have concluded that it was constructed very quickly, perhaps in preparation for an important military campaign.[22]

Fig. 1b: Part of the excavated Via Militaris near Dimitrovgrad. Photo by Nicole Münnich, 2011.

---

22 Miroslav Lazić, "Rimski put Via militaris i Malo kale kod Dimitrovgrada kao primer devastacije istraženih arheoloških nalazišta na koridoru E-80," *Glasnik Srpskog arheološkog društva* 30 (2014): 340–3.

Moreover, in the same excavation, a wide variety of other finds, from nails to horseshoes, have come to light, dating back to the eleventh and twelfth centuries CE. They attest to the long continuity of the route after the end of the Roman Empire. The question of how the Roman road network continued from Late Antiquity into the Middle Ages has been a constant reference point for research on the Roman West.[23] In respect to Southeast Europe, the first two contributions to this volume take up this question from two different perspectives. In his chapter "The Via Militaris in Transition: From Late Rome to the Crusades," Mathew Larnach examines if and how the route still functioned as one continuous route during the Middle Ages. In the eleventh century, the Byzantines were the first who united the entire route under their single authority after the fall of the Roman Empire. Byzantine building activities and settlement policies in the cities along the road, most notably in Philippopolis (today Plovdiv), prove the importance of the route for the state and its stability. So does the fact that the crusader armies were able to pass along it relatively easily.

In contrast to this imperial perspective, Vladimir Aleksić in his chapter "Continuity of Travel and Transport Infrastructures from Antiquity to the Middle Ages: The Case of Via Militaris in the Morava and Nišava Regions" examines the route from a local point of view. The chapter focuses on the question how a certain section of the route functioned and was integrated into different medieval states, most notably the emerging Serbian state. Relying on local chronicles and toponyms, the author reconstructs the changing itinerary of the route and connects it to the regional settlement structure. Chronologically, the chapter examines the road up until the conquest by the Ottomans at the turn from the fourteenth to the fifteenth century.

After the Byzantines in the eleventh and twelfth centuries, the Ottomans from the beginning of the sixteenth century brought the route yet again under one authority. Regarding the Ottoman period, the imperial governance of the route has been the prevalent topic of research. Jireček himself acknowledged the central role that the Istanbul–Belgrade route had for the Ottoman domination of the Balkans. However, from his late-nineteenth century perspective, the role of the Ottomans was rather negative, and his judgement was clearly guided by orientalistic prejudice:

---

23 Georges Livet, *Histoire des routes et des transports en Europe: Des chemins de Saint-Jacques à l'âge d'or des diligences* (Strasbourg: Presses universitaires de Strasbourg, 2003), 81–4; Gertrud Blaschitz, "Von der 'Via publica' zur mittelalterlichen Heeresstraße: Zur Kontinuität der Römerstraßen in literarischen Quellen," in *Der umkämpfte Ort – von der Antike zum Mittelalter*, ed. Olaf Wagener (Frankfurt: Peter Lang, 2009): 85–103.

> Since the fall of the Roman Empire no state in Europe [except the Ottomans] has given so much care to its road system. However, between the Roman and the Turkish institutions there is a big difference. The Roman monuments have withstood more than one and a half millennia and their remains will continue to be respected by future generations. The buildings of the old Turks are already mostly gone even during the time when the Turkish Empire still exists. The Romans built themselves. The Turks, according to Gerlach's report (1573), had 'the stone buildings constructed by captured Christians.' Another traveler from the same time, Salomon Schweigger, remarked that even Selim's Mosque in Adrianople was not built by the Turks 'because they are not able to do so,' but by Italian prisoners of war.[24]

As this quote shows, Jireček reconstructed the early modern history of the route almost exclusively from the rich corpus of European travel literature produced by diplomats and also by merchants who went from Central Europe to the capital of the sultan. This approach has been taken up by Mihailo Popović in one of the few books on the route published in recent decades.[25] But scholars also have examined Ottoman sources in order to close the gap in Jireček's study. In the 1970s, Olga Zirojević devoted two volumes to the road, first, from Belgrade to Istanbul and then from Belgrade to Budapest during the sixteenth and seventeenth centuries.[26] Despite the recent interest in the route from a regional historical perspective,[27] Zirojević's work has remained authoritative to the present day when it comes to dealing with the infrastructure of the road in the Ottoman epoch.

Although not dealing with the Istanbul–Belgrade road, but with the connection between Istanbul and the Adriatic, Elisabeth Zachariadou's collection on the

---

24 Jireček, *Heerstrasse*, 114.
25 Mihailo Popović, *Von Budapest nach Istanbul: Die Via Traiana im Spiegel der Reiseliteratur des 14. bis 16. Jahrhunderts* (Leipzig: Eudora, 2006).
26 Olga Zirojević, *Carigradski drum od Beograda do Sofije (1459–1683)* (Belgrade: Istorijski muzej Srbije, 1970); ead., *Carigradski drum od Beograda do Budima u XVI i XVII veku*, (Novi Sad: Štampa Forum, 1976); translated to German as "Zur historischen Topographie der Heerstraße nach Konstantinopel zur Zeit der osmanischen Herrschaft," *Études Balkaniques* 23, no. 1–2 (1987): 81–106, 46–64 and "Das türkische Straßennetz (Land und Wasserstraßen) auf dem Gebiet der heutigen Vojvodina und Slawoniens," *Acta Historica Academiae Scientiarum Hungaricae* 33, no. 2–4 (n.d.).
27 Aleksandăr Antonov, "Kervansaraite kato element ot pătnata infrastruktura v balkanskite provincii na Osmanskata imperija prez XVI–XVIII v.," in *Balkanite: Ezik, istorija, kultura* (Sofia: Veliktotărnovski Universitet Sv. Sv. Kiril i Metodij, Universitetsko Izdatelstvo, 2013), 3:104–22; Aleksandăr Antonov, "Infrastrukturata na ovladjanoto prostrantstvo: Osmanski Dokumenti za pătnite stancii po dijagonalnija păt (Orta Kol) ot 16., 17., 18. Vek," in *Etničeski i kulturni prostranstva na Balkanite: Sbornik v čest na prof. d.i.n. Cvetana Georgieva*, vol. 2, ed. Svetlana Ivanova (Sofia: Universitetsko. izdatelstvo. Sv. Kliment Ohridski, 2008).

Via Egnatia has to be mentioned for its specific focus on the Ottoman period.[28] The volume includes many topics which are also relevant for the present volume, such as migration, religious networks, road infrastructure and urban settlements along the route. However, Zachariadou's volume somehow arbitrarily stops at the end of the seventeenth century and does not follow the history of the Via Egnatia up to the end of the Ottoman period.

Two chapters in the present volume seek in particular to make a contribution to the scholarship on the Ottoman period of the route. In her piece, "Transforming the Landscape of the Constantinople Road in the Fifteenth and Sixteenth Centuries (Section Niš–Dragoman)," Tatjana Katić focuses on the division of labor between local actors and the central administration in maintaining the road. The author pays special attention to the watchmen at mountain passes (*derbendžije/derbentçi*) and their villages as part of the Ottoman security infrastructure for the route. By analyzing the population structure along the route using Ottoman tax registers, the chapter maps the economic and cultural influence the Ottoman infrastructure had in a local setting.

The following chapter "The Istanbul–Belgrade Route in the Ottoman Empire: Continuity and Discontinuity of an Imperial Mobility Space" by Florian Riedler gives an overview of the long-term role of the route. It focuses on the route as an imperial infrastructure, which was not only a means of practical dominion, but also shaped the mental maps of the Ottoman elite, as geographical literature and campaign itineraries show. The contribution includes the history of the decline of the route up until the nineteenth century and its subsequent revival as a consequence of the modernization efforts of the Ottoman government.

In the historiography on eighteenth-century Europe, various scholars have explored the theme of state formation through infrastructure development. It has been shown that in Britain and Scotland but also in the absolutist states on the continent such as France, Austria, Prussia, and Russia, better roads gave the central state access to the provinces and the ability to spread its authority. Road construction not only involved central officials, but also created new groups of experts such as engineers who were closely interlinked with the state. As a consequence, the "infrastructure state" emerged, a declension of the modern state that created or regulated important infrastructures of mobility,

---

[28] Elisabeth Zachariadou, ed., *The Via Egnatia under Ottoman Rule (1380–1699)* (Rethymnon: Crete University Press, 1996).

welfare and so on, and thereby gained a hitherto unknown leverage of control over the lives of its citizens.²⁹

In the nineteenth century, Ottoman, Balkan and European travelers as well as geographers such as Ami Boué (1794–1881) and Felix Kanitz (1829–1904), who began to explore the Balkans around the middle of the century, all directly experienced and documented the lack of good roads—an impression which fitted well into a general discourse of Ottoman under-development. Jireček also recognizes the loss of importance of the route due to the introduction of steam shipping both on the Danube and between Trieste and Constantinople in the 1830s. But he was also a contemporary observer of the revitalization of the route: "Recently, the Turkish government reconstructed the military highway and numerous byways and, on that occasion, reused many remains from Antiquity as building material."³⁰ In his eyes even more significant than this reconstruction of the road was the construction of the railway that was completed in 1871 for the 560 kilometer section from Istanbul up to Belovo in today's Bulgaria. Jireček predicted a bright future for the route: "Presently, the road is in ruins and has been forgotten, but it will be revived when Constantinople, which until now can almost only be reached by ship, will link up with the Occident by a railway along the old Roman and Crusader road."³¹ He linked the railway with a civilizing mission to the European Orient and joined the discourse, which Ami Boué had initiated already in the 1850s: It predicted a profound modernization of "European Turkey" through an acceleration of mobility by the railway.³²

Compared to its contemporary popular appeal, the railway line, which was constructed in the 1870s and '80s along the course of the Istanbul–Belgrade route, has attracted little scholarly attention. Under the name "Orient Express,"

---

29 Jo Guldi, *Roads to Power* (Cambridge, MA: Harvard University Press, 2012); Andreas Helmedach, *Das Verkehrssystem als Modernisierungsfaktor: Straßen, Post, Fuhrwesen und Reisen nach Triest und Fiume vom Beginn des 18. Jahrhunderts bis zum Eisenbahnzeitalter* (Munich: Oldenbourg 2002); Uwe Müller, "Der Beitrag des Chausseebaus zum Modernisierungsprozess in Preußen," in *Die moderne Straße: Planung, Bau und Verkehr vom 18. bis zum 20. Jahrhundert*, ed. Hans-Liudger Dienel (Frankfurt: Campus, 2010): 49–75; Herbert Knittler, "Das Verkehrswesen als Ausgangspunkt einer staatlichen Infrastrukturpolitik," in *Von der Glückseligkeit des Staates: Staat, Wirtschaft und Gesellschaft in Österreich im Zeitalter des aufgeklärten Absolutismus*, ed. Herbert Matis (Berlin: Duncker & Humblot, 1981): 137–60; Tracy Nichols Busch, "Connecting an Empire: Eighteenth-Century Russian Roads, from Peter to Catherine," *The Journal of Transport History* 29, no. 2 (2008): 240–58.
30 Jireček, *Heerstrasse*, 137.
31 Ibid., III.
32 Ami Boué, *Sur l'établissement de bonnes routes et surtout de chemins de fer dans la Turquie d'Europe* (Vienna: Braumüller, 1852).

this railway has been examined by railway and travel historians almost exclusively from a European perspective. Only very few publications focus on the contribution of the Ottomans or the local Balkan societies when examining the transformation in mobility that the railway brought about.[33]

From among the contributions to this volume, Dobrinka Paruševa's chapter "Cities along the Route: Plovdiv Becoming 'Modern' at the End of the Nineteenth Century," deals most directly with the effect the railway had on the city at the time when it was integrated into Bulgaria. The author examines how in a new national context, communication networks were modernized and adapted to new circumstances. Her contribution also demonstrates the effects of the railway on everyday life and culture for the city populations, which was more and more modeled on examples and objects from Europe that were finding their way to the city along the new conduits.

In Nenad Stefanov's chapter, "Tsaribrod, a Dot on the Line: A Microhistorical Approach to Societal Change along the Route in the Nineteenth and Twentieth Centuries," the railway is also used to analyze a special microregion. The author focuses on Tsaribrod, which turned from an insignificant village into a city when it became a railway border station in the late nineteenth century. The railway together with the corresponding road stood in a dialectical relation with the border representing an obstacle to mobility. The chapter contrasts the local and transregional functions of mobility as it was supported or hindered by Serbia and Bulgaria under different regimes from the time when they became independent nation states in 1878 to the socialist period in the 1960s. Also, the different transport technologies, from the railway to the motor car, left an imprint on this relationship as the chapter shows.

In recent decades, auto-mobility has become an important subject that has been instrumental in introducing all kinds of innovative cultural, social and political questions and approaches to transport history. Together with the car, roads have become part of the history of motorization and the new emerging identities of its users; likewise, motorways have been in the focus of studies on urban history, the history of technology, as well as studies on modern landscape formation. Many of these perspectives come together in Peter Merriman's study on the history of the M1, the motorway connecting London and Leeds. It not only

---

33 Vahdettin Engin, *Rumeli Demiryollan* (Istanbul: Eren, 1993); Bülent Bilmez, "European Investments in the Ottoman Railways, 1850–1914," in *Across the Borders: Financing the World's Railways in the Nineteenth and Twentieth Centruies*, ed. Ralf Roth and Günter Dinhobl (Aldershot: Ashgate, 2008): 183–206; Peter Mentzel, "Networks, Railroads, and Small Cities in the Ottoman Balkans," in *The Growth of Non-Western Cities: Primary and Secondary Urban Networking*, c. 900–1900, ed. Kenneth R. Hall (Plymouth: Lexington Books, 2011): 271–87.

introduced innovative questions of mobility culture to transport history, but can also count as an example of a study on one particular road that was built largely in the 1960s.[34]

Other recent studies on motorways have remained attentive to the social and political framework of road planning and construction and have also examined the tensions between local and central governments regarding road construction. Another prominent issue is the interaction of the state with different groups of experts such as engineers and traffic planners. In this research there was an early focus on the US highway system and the German *autobahn*;[35] later it was complemented by studies that examined road networks in many European countries, in particular, from a transnational perspective.[36] Recently, also the function of car roads in socialist Bulgaria and Yugoslavia has been examined.[37]

Nenad Stefanov's chapter "Park ve Restoran: About Oblivion, Obstinate Mobility and Temporary Infrastructures on the Road" focuses on the infrastructure for auto-mobility that was created beginning in the 1980s on the Serbian part of the route. He uses it as the starting point for a larger reflection on the persistence of certain structures and practices connected with mobility from the late nineteenth century until today. International car traffic (mainly that of Turkish workers from Germany) have re-activated patterns of mobility that reach back to Ottoman times. The chapter analyzes this persistence as a process situationally revived by actors and expressed in structures and symbolizations.

As mentioned before, most recently this route was again in the headlines as the Balkan Route used by refugees from the Middle East whose fate mobilized solidarity as well as generated fear among the people living along this route. Against this background, Sandra King-Savić examines contemporary migration and the way it is understood and practiced. Transregional mobility, labor migration between south-eastern and western Europe is opened up in a "decelerated way," so to speak, by the author as she walks along the old Via Egnatia. In her encounters with the people along this route, who at the same time are them-

---

34 Peter Merriman, *Driving Spaces* (Malden, MA: Blackwell, 2007).
35 Mark H. Rose, *Interstate* (Knoxville: University of Tennessee Press, 1990); Bruce Edsall Seely, *Building the American Highway System* (Philadelphia: Temple University Press, 1987); Richard Vahrenkamp, *The German Autobahn 1920–1945* (Lohmar: Eul, 2010).
36 Gijs Mom, *Road History* (Neuchatel: Alphil, 2007); Hans-Liudger Dienel, *Die moderne Straße* (Frankfurt: Campus, 2010); Frank Schipper, *Driving Europe* (Amsterdam: Amsterdam University Press, 2008).
37 Lyubomir Pozharliev, *The Road to Socialism: Transport Infrastructure in Socialist Bulgaria and Yugoslavia (1945–1989)* (Göttingen: V&R unipress, 2021).

selves traveling between different worlds as labor migrants, King-Savić explores the subjective side of mobility.

Matthew Larnach
The Via Militaris in Transition: From Late Rome to the Crusades

1 Introduction

Once considered a subject of somewhat dubious historical import, at least amongst English language historians, the study of Byzantine history has advanced enormously in the past few decades. This renaissance, expedited by the fall of communism in Eastern Europe and the subsequent easing of access to the region for eager historians and archaeologists alike, has led to a surge in new research on the topic. And yet, for all the progress that has been made, Byzantine history still frequently labors under some of the pejorative associations established by Edward Gibbon; in particular, that the history of the empire is essentially one of prolonged decline from a pre-established highpoint of Roman greatness. The enormous empire carved out by the strength of Roman armies, and its astonishing accomplishments in the fields of science, engineering, medicine and the arts, all subsequently crumbled in the inept hands of inferior Byzantines.

Is this characterization fair? Of course many, if not all, Byzantinists would argue it is not and point to the manifold, yet relatively uncelebrated, achievements of the Byzantine state. However, when it comes to the topic of roads, conclusions are not so easy to draw. Did Roman roads universally decline in Byzantine hands, or was the empire able to actively maintain the extensive road network that it inherited? It is an unfortunate reflection of the paucity of available literary and archaeological sources pertaining to the topic that it is impossible to answer this question definitively. Available evidence is scanty. Direct literary references to road work dwindle to almost nothing after the extensive building programs of the Emperors Athanasius and Justinian in the sixth century. Similarly, archaeological remains are disappointingly poorly chronicled.

This absence of conclusive evidence has led to suppositions that Byzantium deliberately abandoned the Roman network, allowing it to fall into ruin owing to either neglect or ignorance.[1] Others, such Edward Luttwak, have mused that Byzantine generals typically preferred poor roads over good, as they offered the el-

---

[1] Lynn White, "Technology in the Middle Ages," in *Technology in Western Civilization*, ed. Melvin Kranzberg and Carroll W. Pursell Jr (New York: Oxford University Press, 1967), 66–7.

ement of surprise.² Similarly, Byzantium may have concluded that broad well paved roads provided overly easy ingress for the Empire's many enemies into its heartland, and therefore proved a greater liability than an asset.

And yet we are reminded that the Byzantine Empire was a highly bureaucratic and ferociously centralized state, with an administrative apparatus deliberately localized within the capital, Constantinople. Whilst the day to day function of these administrative bodies are sadly largely lost to us, they encompassed the governance and defense of an enormously large landmass which, in the eleventh century, stretched from the Danube to the Tigris. How could such a vast and unwieldy entity function without the assistance of even rudimentary infrastructure networks?

Reference is often made to the importance of naval linkages in sustaining the cohesion of the sprawling empire, but this overlooks those regions beyond the Mediterranean littoral where such access was not so easily obtained. This was especially the case in the Balkan hinterland. Imperial flotillas may have occasionally patrolled the Danube, and barges could potentially negotiate the Maritsa River as far as Philippopolis (today Plovdiv), but if imperial authority wished to penetrate the mountainous, densely forested interior it had only one option; it had to go by foot.

This chapter will argue that the fate of Roman roads in the Byzantine Empire was mixed. Some clearly, owing to demographic change and attendant centuries of neglect, declined to become little more than over-grown, half-forgotten tracks leading into a largely unpopulated wilderness. And yet other roads not only survived but appear to have thrived. Of these the Via Militaris stands apart. Encompassing a route millennia old, usage of which predates any Roman laid foundations, this road not only survived into the medieval era but, as will be demonstrated below, played a transformative role as a conduit along which trans-continental migrations of people, material and ideas flowed.

2 Byzantium and the Medieval World

To understand how the Via Militaris operated in the Middle Ages it is necessary to explore briefly the character of the Byzantine Empire, and the violent upheavals it endured in the early centuries of its existence. Upheavals which would play

---

2 Edward Luttwak, *The Grand Strategy of the Byzantine Empire* (Cambridge, MA: Belknap Press of Harvard University Press, 2009), 421.

a vital role in shaping its subsequent identity and how it came to utilize the infrastructure it inherited.[3]

The Byzantine state was defined by a seemingly contradictory duality that existed at its very core. On the one hand was its extraordinary conservatism. The empire would, throughout its long life, remain inherently wedded to a political and legal system that was founded upon Late Roman principles. Indeed, over time, this political structure became suffused with religious symbolism; the empire was a manifestation of God's will being enacted upon earth. Any change, any innovation, was therefore necessarily a move away from a model that was perceived to have already achieved divinely ordained perfection.

And yet, on the other hand, the Byzantine state could prove to be astonishingly pragmatic, in particular capable of quickly adapting militarily to new threats as they arose. It was this capability which allowed the empire to survive the seventh century, a period of unrelenting military disasters that would have undoubtedly overwhelmed a less self-assured state. Instead Byzantium not only survived, but subsequently flourished within a very different geo-strategic environment than that which had confronted Late Rome.

Byzantine military pragmatism was founded upon a fervent belief in the supernatural protection afforded to its capital by the divine grace of the Virgin Mother. Convinced of the invulnerability of Constantinople's formidable walls, evidence of which was amply demonstrated on numerous occasions throughout its long history, Byzantium was subsequently afforded the opportunity of adopting a long-term approach seldom available to its foes. The state, and especially the capital city which came to embody it, could endure all manner of military setbacks in the conviction that they were but momentary inconveniences that Byzantium would not only endure, but eventually overcome. The empire's extraordinary recovery in the ninth and tenth centuries suggests that this confidence was not misplaced.

This psychological outlook influenced how Byzantium reacted to the challenges of the seventh century, a period defined by mass migration, invasion, and plague. These factors dramatically altered the demographic constitution of the empire, leading to a rapid decline in urban settlements. Even Constantinople appears to have temporarily shrunk to a fraction of its former size, from a population of perhaps half a million to perhaps less than one hundred thousand. With regional cities diminishing in number and size, and Constantinople there-

---

[3] Some historians argue the Byzantine Empire, as an entity distinct from the Roman, did not properly emerge until the seventh century. See Mark Whittow, *The Making of Byzantium, 600–1025* (Berkeley: University of California Press, 1996), 97.

fore growing in relative importance, the relationship between the centralized empire and its periphery was unquestionably altered from that of the Late Roman era. This was emphasized by the loss of economic and political independence of formerly influential regional cities.[4] Only those cities which existed within Constantinople's substantial orbit continued to flourish.

3 Infrastructure in the Post-Roman World

The Roman world was famously overlaid by a spider web of interconnecting roads which all, ultimately, led to Rome. This matrix of roads not only serviced practical needs, but united the empire into a coherent whole, forming part of a recognizable landscape that emphasized a cultural unity across the empire, in contrast to those regions beyond it.[5] Itineraries, in particular the famous *Tabula Peutingeriana*, further emphasized this inherent unity, rendering the landscape in terms of an easily understandable depiction of stations and cities, and the distances which separated them. At least theoretically, this network enabled a traveler to journey from one corner of the empire to the other, taking advantage of conveniently sited inns and mansions en route.

We do not possess a similarly coherent image of how Byzantium perceived the world around it, or the manner in which travelers negotiated the vast expanse of its territory. Certainly the tradition of map-making and *itineraria* did not survive in a world increasingly fixated on the capital, Constantinople. And whilst we do possess scattered information on the journeys of saints and envoys across Byzantine territory, they were often at risk of losing their way and were indebted, as indeed Byzantine armies often were, to the assistance provided by local scouts who could guide their way.

As it faced the turmoil of the seventh century, not only did the empire change internally but its understanding of its position within the wider world also began to alter. It is notable that beyond the sixth century some of Byzantium's loftier ambitions, as demonstrated by Justinian's conquests of Italy and North Africa, were abandoned, although admittedly the dreams of Byzantine Italy were revived in the twelfth century, albeit briefly. Whittow nevertheless de-

---

4 John Haldon, *Byzantium in the Seventh Century: The Transformation of a Culture* (Cambridge: Cambridge University Press, 1990), 94.
5 Ray Laurence, "Travel and Empire," in *Travel and Geography in the Roman Empire*, ed. Colin Adams and Ray Laurence (London: Routledge, 2011), 172.

fines this transition as being one from a superpower to a medium sized regional state, one which was hereafter gripped in a dour and endless battle for survival.[6]

Although still rich in relative terms, certainly the resources of the medieval Byzantine state were far less than those previously enjoyed by Rome. The Byzantine Empire, whilst famed for its ostentatious displays of wealth, might be considered as typically money rich but cash poor. State revenues were dedicated to sustaining an impressively large standing army, paying a vast bureaucratic cohort, and funding an elaborate (and in Byzantine eyes, utterly necessary) court ceremonial. This enormous expense often left emperors, however, short on available reserves to meet immediate needs, leading to sometimes desperate measures to raise necessary funds to finance military campaigns. Given the inherently tumultuous nature of the Byzantine Empire, besieged by enemies from without and endemic domestic insurrection within, it is difficult to perceive how expensive long-term infrastructure projects could even be conceived, let alone enacted.

As a manifestation of this we observe the deliberate abandonment of the previously fortified frontier, and in particular the Danubian legionary barracks. As early as the eighth century, we also observe the systematic abandonment of threatened outlying regions, beginning in the Mesopotamian provinces increasingly exposed to endemic Arab raids.[7] In time, this approach would come to be employed elsewhere, including in the Balkans, involving the abandonment of much of the former province of Moesia Inferior, between the Danube and the Central Balkan Mountains. The Roman *limes*, the fortified frontier which had kept the empire's enemies at arm's length, was instead replaced with a new concept, the *limen*, a permeable region through which hostile forces could penetrate but were unable to find succor or permanent conquest.[8]

The intent, recognizing that most threats to the empire consisted of raids of short duration and typically involved a large proportion of horse mounted warriors, was that the depopulation of frontier regions would deny the enemy of both pillage and necessary dry fodder. Robbed of spoils, and facing a critical

---

6 Whittow, *The Making of Byzantium*, 96.
7 See Theophanes, *The Chronicle of Theophanes: An English Translation of anni mundi 6095– 6305 (A.D. 602–813)*, trans. Harry Turtledove (Philadelphia: University of Pennsylvania Press, 1982) 61, for the deliberate Byzantine depopulation of the Upper Tigris.
8 Dmitri Obolensky, "The Byzantine Frontier Zones and Cultural Exchanges," in *Actes du XIVe congrès international des études byzantines,* ed. Mihai Berza and Eugen Stinescu (Bucharest: Editura Academiei Republicii Socialiste România, 1974), 1:303–13.

shortage of provisions, a raiding party would have no choice but to withdraw.[9] Thus, Byzantium sought to establish a dynamic equilibrium with its often hostile neighbors. Raids could be suffered as short-term inconveniences, with the walls of Constantinople being sufficient to resist more serious incursions.

Byzantium further famously employed its stature and ostentatious wealth as a diplomatic tool to either impress or cow potential enemies, and through the granting of gifts, titles and tribute drew them within the orbit of what has been described as the Byzantine Commonwealth.[10] Against more tenacious opponents, stratagems and deceptions were encouraged as means of defeating a foe without resorting to the risk of pitched battle. This is not to say that Byzantine armies did not fight battles, only that the received wisdom of the age argued against them generally. Byzantine *taktika*, military manuals which drew upon the traditions inscribed in Late Roman texts (such as the *De re militari*), consistently cautioned against engagement in open battle except in cases of the utmost favorability.[11]

Byzantine military strategy was therefore grounded upon the principle that, whilst Constantinople itself occupied an envious position, the empire was surrounded on all sides by a sea of potential enemies. War was seldom absent in the Byzantine world, often occurring on both eastern and western frontiers simultaneously; a nightmarish scenario for any state to confront. Byzantine armies were likely consistently outnumbered by their foes and, moreover, victories tended to earn only short reprieves as defeated enemies were frequently replaced on the empire's borders by new, often more vigorous, opponents.[12] In short, Byzantium was confronted by a highly dynamic and threatening strategic context which required more subtle tools to overcome than simple brute force.

Thus, the extensive infrastructure networks constructed by the Roman Empire proved largely redundant in a world in which regional cities had dramatically shrunk in power and influence, and to a state that viewed warfare, and the world around it, in far different terms. This is not to say that all Roman roads were abandoned, rather that we can observe a gradual shift in their iden-

---

9 Jonathan Shepard, "Information, Disinformation and Delay in Byzantine Diplomacy," *Byzantinische Forschungen* 10 (1985): 251–3.
10 Dmitri Obolensky, *The Byzantine Commonwealth: Eastern Europe, 500–1453* (London: St. Vladimir's Seminary Press, 1971), 13–4.
11 John Haldon, *Warfare, State and Society in the Byzantine World, 565–1204* (London: UCL Press, 1999), 37.
12 The number of soldiers that Byzantium could call upon has been the subject of extensive debate. See Whittow, *The Making of Byzantium*, 181–93, and Haldon, *Warfare, State and Society in the Byzantine World*, 99–106.

tities. Roman roads designed exclusively to meet the needs of the Roman state subsequently became, over time, Byzantine as they were required to serve far different purposes. The challenge, in the face of the absence of definitive evidence, is to define the unique characteristics of Byzantine roads and demonstrate how they operated in practice.

4 Roads in the Late Roman Empire

The Romans had built their roads to suit a variety of different roles, but one of the main functions of the major arterial routes, and especially military highways such as the Via Militaris, was to accommodate large numbers of marching infantry and heavy four-wheeled wagons in all seasons of the year. In particular, those legions barracked along the frontiers required not only regular provisions and the means for rapid reinforcement, but also building materials and all the mundane staples of civilized life.[13] In remote regions, the road network was often the only reliable means of connecting these bulwarks with the rest of the Roman world.

As the Roman state struggled to overcome the crises of the third and fourth centuries, its ability to maintain its extensive infrastructure network understandably declined. The responsibility for its maintenance was accordingly increasingly decentralized. Literary evidence strongly suggests that, at least outside of Italy itself, local communities became progressively obliged to render essential services to the state in the form of *munera personalia* and *munera publica*, which typically involved physical labor such as road building or fortress construction. An inscription from Thrace dated to AD 202, for instance, mentions that villagers in the territory of Alexandroupolis and Traianopolis were required to repair a section of the Via Egnatia.[14]

The *Codex Theodosianus* of the fourth century further contains a number of references to the services provincial citizens were obligated to render to the state, and in particular mentions the construction and repair of roads.[15] In the sixth

---

[13] Florin Curta, "Peasants as 'Makeshift Soldiers for the Occasion': Sixth-century Settlement Patterns in the Balkans," in *Urban Centers and Rural Contexts in Late Antiquity*, ed. Thomas. S. Burns and John W. Eadie (Michigan: Michigan State University Press, 2001), 205–12.
[14] Theodor Kissel, "Road Building as a *munus publicus*," in *The Roman Army and the Economy*, ed. Paul Erdkamp (Amsterdam: Gieben, 2002), 140.
[15] *The Theodosian Code and Novels and the Sirmondian Constitutions: A Translation with Commentary, Glossary and Bibliography*, trans. Clyde Pharr (New York: Greenwood Press, 1969), 431–2.

century, during the reign of Justinian, these obligations were codified into law, becoming compulsory for all citizens and exemption from which could only be granted by special dispensation from the emperor.[16] These practices appear to have continued into at least the tenth century as seen in the references to exemption (*exkousseia*) from forms of compulsory labor, such as *hodostrosia* (road-repairing) and *gephyroktisia/gephyrosis* (bridge-building) recorded in the foundation *actes* of monasteries established during this period.[17]

Notably soldiers, who had formerly assumed much of the burden of road and fortification repairs, are seldom thereafter seen performing these roles and it cannot be simply assumed that they continued to do so.[18] Indeed in the early ninth century, when Emperor Nicephorus ordered forces under his command to repair the walls of Serdica, the soldiers promptly refused and threatened to revolt instead.[19] From this example it appears that such work had ceased to be considered a routine function of a soldier's life, and was instead shouldered by, effectively, chain-ganged citizens.

Theoretically, local populations would be reimbursed for their efforts, with the manual labor performed counting against tax obligations to the state.[20] The practice of requiring local populations to undertake manual labor to repair local roads, also known as *corvée*, has been adopted by numerous states across history, including nineteenth century France. Nevertheless, the quality of road repair achieved by an untrained labor force was likely quite low, as it certainly lacked the expertise to methodically rebuild the roads first constructed by skilled engineers.

In this sense the decay of Roman roads, a phenomenon often attributed wholly to the Byzantine era, commenced during the Late Roman period. As early as the fifth and sixth centuries we already find numerous references to the appalling state of Roman roads. The *Codex Theodosianus* refers to the "immense ruin of the highways."[21] Similarly the Via Egnatia was described by Malchos of Philadelphia in the late fifth century as being in such a state of disrepair

---

16 *The Digest of Justinian*, trans. Alan Watson (Philadelphia: University of Pennsylvania Press, 1985), 4:431.
17 John Haldon, "The Organization and Support of an Expeditionary Force: Manpower and Logistics in the Middle Byzantine Period," in *Byzantium at War (9th–12th c.)*, ed. Nikolaos Oikonomides (Athens: Idryma Goulandrē-Chorn, 1997), 143.
18 Haldon, *Warfare, State and Society in the Byzantine World*, 237.
19 Theophanes, *The Chronicle*, 166.
20 Nicolas Oikonomides, "The Role of the Byzantine State in the Economy," in *The Economic History of Byzantium: From the Seventh through the Fifteenth Century*, ed. Angeliki. E. Laiou (Washington, DC: Dumbarton Oaks Research Library and Collection, 2002), 1000.
21 *Codex Theodosianus*, trans. C. Pharr, 431.

that travelers could barely pass along it and furthermore described by Procopius as being (in the sixth century) "for the most part uneven; and if rain chanced to fall, it became a bog and was difficult for travelers to get through."²² This rapid collapse in quality of formerly important roads suggests an equally rapid collapse of imperial authority and administration.

5 The Byzantine Balkans

The fifth and sixth centuries were indeed periods of great upheaval in the Balkans. Subjected to Gothic, Hunnic and Alani depredations, archaeological evidence indicates widespread devastation. Settlements along the Struma River for instance, an important thoroughfare linking Thessalonica with the Central Balkans, appear to have been entirely overwhelmed, with all evidence of occupation abruptly vanishing in the sixth century.²³ This was exacerbated by the great plague of the same century which, according to Procopius, laid waste to the countryside.²⁴ The attendant collapse of imperial authority was exploited in the seventh century by waves of Slavic migrations which swept over the region, and further into the eighth when the Bulgars penetrated south of the Danube.

Byzantine control over the Balkan Peninsula was therefore largely lost during the tumultuous seventh century. The impact of these migrations on the demographic constitution of the region, and its subsequent administration, is a long-debated topic. Contemporary refugees to Thessalonica, likely from the Struma Valley, bewailed the damage wrought by the invaders, claiming that Thessalonica now stood alone in the Byzantine Balkans as "all the cities and provinces which had formerly been under its control had become uninhabited because of the Slavs."²⁵ This has been interpreted as meaning that the entire Balkan hin-

---

22 Malchos of Philadelphia, *The Fragmentary Classicising Historians of the Later Roman Empire: Eunapius, Olympiodorus, Priscus and Malchus*, trans. Roger C. Blockley, vol. 2, *Text, Translation and Historiographical Notes* (Liverpool: Cairns, 1983), 440; Procopius, *Buildings*, trans. Henry B. Dewing (London: Harvard University Press, 1940), 285.
23 Yordanka Yurukova, "Byzantine Fortresses to the South of the Hemus Mountain in the Light of Coin Finds from the last Decades of the Sixth Century," in *Church and State: Studies in Medieval Bulgaria and Byzantium*, ed. Vassil Gyuzelev and Kiril Petkov (Sofia: American Research Center in Sofia, 2011), 96.
24 Procopius, *The Secret History*, trans. Geoffrey A. Williamson (Harmondsworth: Penguin, 1981), 157.
25 *Hagiographic Sources for Byzantine Cities, 500–900 A.D.*, trans. David Abrahamse (Michigan City: University Microfilms, 1967), 70.

terland had been overrun by the Slavs, with the former cities abandoned, leaving behind a wasteland devoid of literate culture.²⁶

More recent analysis has cast serious doubt upon this interpretation, suggesting a continuity of urban settlement beyond the initial Slavic migration period. Important regional cities, such as Philippopolis, Serdica and Naissus (today Sofia and Niš) appear to have survived in at least diminished states, with small urban communes sheltering behind the safety offered by their impressive Late Roman fortifications. We cannot, however, derive much information on their subsequent existence from available sources. As Haldon notes, the survival of urban sites does not tell us anything of the economic and social relations that developed from the seventh century onwards, only that they offered more protection than life in the surrounding countryside, and that they likely continued to function as administrative and ecclesiastical centers, as is to be expected.²⁷ Curta likewise states that it is almost impossible, using the available evidence, to differentiate between smaller towns and larger cities in the medieval Balkans, and the inability to do so impacts upon our ability to trace economic and social developments over this period.²⁸

From the mid-ninth century, under the leadership of a succession of formidable soldier-emperors, Byzantium regained control over much of this entire region, culminating in Basil II's destruction of the First Bulgarian Empire in 1018. Although Basil was surprisingly lenient (especially giving his later reputation as the *Bulgaroktonos* – The Bulgar Slayer) in his treatment of the conquered Bulgars, the Empire still needed to impose active authority over this newly subjugated region and defend it from the encroachment of further enemies from beyond the Danube.

6 The Development of the Byzantine Road Network

Given the geographical context, the only means available for Byzantium to enforce and defend its hegemony over the Balkan hinterland was through the uti-

---

26 See, for instance, John V.A. Fine, *The Early Medieval Balkans: A Critical Survey from the Sixth to the Late Twelfth Century* (Ann Arbor: University of Michigan Press, 1983), 36.
27 Haldon, "Some Considerations on the Byzantine Society and Economy in the Seventh Century," 85.
28 Florin Curta, *Southeastern Europe in the Middle Ages, 500–1250* (Cambridge: Cambridge University Press, 2006), 430.

lization of road networks. The major cities named above, Philippopolis, Serdica and Naissus, all shared the distinction of lying along the pre-existing major Roman highway, the Via Militaris. To their number can also be added further important centers, such as Adrianople (today Edirne), Belgrade and, of course, Constantinople. All of these were, or would become, major cities during their life spans.

This is no coincidence. The Via Militaris traversed the most logical route geographically across the Balkan Peninsula, along the major river valleys. And it was alongside these major rivers, the Morava, the Nišava and the Maritsa, that the most arable land could be found. The soils along these rivers are enriched by nutrient deposits washed down from the surrounding mountains, resulting in remarkably fertile agricultural land. In comparison the heavily forested mountain slopes, which comprise much of the rest of the Balkans, are typically extremely poorly suited to agricultural activity as most of the nutrients have been leeched from the soils, leading to low levels of phosphates and nitrogen.[29] Urban settlement along the river valleys, exploiting these highly arable soils, accordingly long pre-dates Roman occupation (Philippopolis itself was first settled by Thracians as far back as 4,000 BC), and would subsequently long survive its fall.

Undoubtedly the Via Militaris of the medieval period bore little resemblance to that of the Roman, as the monumental roads of the Roman era were entirely unsuited to the needs of the contemporary Byzantine state. As noted above, the Danubian legionary barracks, with their large dependent populations, were abandoned by Byzantium. Within the Byzantine Empire there was, in consequence, a far greater emphasis on short-range transport, utilizing beasts of burden, rather than on the long-distance freight undertaken by wagons in the Roman era.[30] Moreover, medieval armies were typically much smaller than their Late Roman precedents, and supported by far less extensive logistical apparatus, typified by the move from oxen drawn wagons to the employment of pack animals.

In addition, the Byzantine state almost certainly lacked the finances, or likely even the technological expertise, necessary to sustain such surfaces. Procopius notes that Justinian rebuilt a section of the Via Militaris on such a scale that its tightly fitting paving stones appeared "not simply of being laid together

---

29 Zosia Archibald, *The Odrysian Kingdom of Thrace: Orpheus Unmasked* (Oxford: Clarendon Press, 1998), 17–8.
30 Michael McCormick, *Origins of European Economy: Communications and Commerce, A.D. 300–900* (Cambridge: Cambridge University Press, 2001), 76.

at the joints, or even of being exactly fitted, but they seem actually to have grown together."[31] However, this oft-quoted example was almost certainly exceptional, and in this instance concerned a stretch of the road near Rhegion, approaching the famed Golden Gate of Constantinople. The road here played a conspicuous role in imperial triumphs and subsequently in public veneration of the state. Similar literary references to equally extravagant road construction elsewhere in the empire are entirely absent.

Therefore, whatever road construction and maintenance within the empire that did occur, away from relatively well populated towns and cities that could provide the necessary labor, was almost certainly performed on an ad hoc basis. Formal repair work was likely only undertaken under the instruction of particularly diligent emperors to meet anticipated needs, such as the bridge construction and repair instigated by Constantine V ahead of his Balkan campaign of 775.[32] Well versed in Roman principles of military strategy and tactics, as conserved and re-examined in the broad corpus of Byzantine *taktika*, Byzantine generals were acutely aware of the importance of identifying suitable marching routes before the commencement of a campaign, and of ensuring good field intelligence of lines of advance and possible retreat.[33]

In particular, Byzantine *taktika* emphasized the necessity of maintaining ordered marching camps, much as the Roman legions had, and ensuring reliable lines of communication, with much stress placed on the employment of reliable scouts and guides. Scouting parties therefore ranged ahead of the army, tasked with intelligence gathering, ensuring the suitability of the road ahead and locating and preparing that evening's camp site. Where practicable they also likely engaged in expedient means of rendering the road surface usable, removing fallen trees or filling in dangerous potholes for instance. Where the road proved entirely unsuitable, alternate routes were to be identified. Such measures are, of course, rudimentary and limited, but typically served to meet the immediate needs of an army on campaign.

The practicality of such measures was enhanced through the greatest legacy of the roads constructed by the Romans, that is, not necessarily their surfaces but rather their foundations.[34] Long after the tight fitting *pavimentum* of the orig-

---

[31] Procopius, *Buildings*, 286–7.
[32] Cyril Mango, "Three Inscriptions of the Reign of Anastasius I and Constantine V," in *Byzantinische Zeitschrift* 65 (1973): 391.
[33] Constantine Porphyrogenitus, *Three Treatises on Imperial Military Expeditions*, trans. John Haldon (Vienna: Verlag der Österreichischen Akademie der Wissenschaften, 1990), 83–5.
[34] Robert Lopez, "The Evolution of Land Transport in the Middle Ages," *Past and Present* 9 (1956): 17.

inal roads had disintegrated (a process that could take from 50–100 years depending on maintenance, frequency of use and climatic conditions), the formidable foundations upon which these roads had been built remained. These foundations were typically impressively deep and built up in successive layers of substrata. The architect Vitruvius provides a detailed description of the process.[35] The initial trench was dug so deep at times its floor could lay upon the underlining bedrock. This floor (*ruderatio*) was then built up in successive layers of fist sized stones (*statumen*), then gravel and sand (*rudus*), before the surface was given a covering of paving stones (*pavimentum*).

Importantly, the necessity of locating these foundations on solid ground led the Romans to deliberately choose routes which avoided marshy or otherwise unsuitable land. These precautions played a fundamental role in the subsequent longevity of Roman roads and their continuing utility over, in some cases, millennia. The practice of building directly upon older Roman roads, and utilizing material found within embankments to rebuild the surface, is accordingly a well attested practice throughout Europe, including in eighteenth century England for instance.[36] The convenience provided by these foundations was reason enough alone for Byzantium to have little need to construct new roads of their own.

With the extensive infrastructure networks which it inherited, Byzantium was therefore well positioned to appropriate these foundations to meet their needs. Where repair work was required, for potholes and the like, spolia was used to refill any areas of degradation. This spolia could be sourced from the remains of the original *pavimentum*, which could be broken down and used to perform immediate repairs. Examples of this activity can be observed in well preserved Byzantine roads in Asia Minor.[37] Another source of material were the many fortresses which punctuated the route. These fortresses had been constructed in the Justinian era, often on the foundations of pre-existing Roman stations, but had been largely abandoned shortly thereafter and therefore made for extremely convenient quarries of readily available building material.

Such measures likely proved sufficient to keep important roads in at least a rudimentarily usable state. The Via Militaris, however, would prove far more capable than this. Not only does the road appear to have remained a viable route throughout this period, it was able to convey large pilgrim hosts such as the Ger-

---

35 Vitruvius, *Vitruvius: Ten Books on Architecture,* trans. Morris H. Morgan (London: Cambridge University Press, 1914), 202–3.
36 Thomas Codrington, *Roman Roads in Britain* (London: Sheldon, 1903), 15.
37 David French, "A Road Problem: Roman or Byzantine?," *Istanbuler Mitteilungen* 43 (1993): 447–8.

man Pilgrimage of 1064–65.³⁸ Ultimately, too, it would prove capable of accommodating the majority of the mass of human traffic which comprised the first three crusades. During the late eleventh and twelfth centuries the Via Militaris therefore accommodated likely no less than 100,000 crusaders, attendants and pilgrims en route to the Holy Land. No small accomplishment for a road already one millennium old.

7 The Via Militaris and the Decline of the Via Egnatia

What made the Via Militaris so exceptional that it could accomplish such a feat? Primarily it was a function of the geographically convenient route it followed, which allowed it to avoid a precipitous course like that followed by the Via Egnatia. The Via Egnatia, famously the first road built by the Romans outside of Italy itself, on its winding course over the Pindus Mountains encompasses inclines and descents which can occasionally reach gradients of 20 per cent or more.³⁹ This stands in stark contrast to the route of the Via Militaris which, at its highest point, in the Vakarel Pass, reaches an altitude of only 880 meters above sea level, whilst its steepest section, through the Gates of Trajan, barely reaches gradients of 10 per cent at its most precipitous, and averages closer to 5–6 per cent across the length of the pass.

As noted above, the road followed the most logical course across the Balkan Peninsula, along the relatively well populated river valleys. It was, moreover, extraordinarily well-made and broad. Roman roads tended to vary widely in width; the standard breadth of a vehicular road was approximately five and a half meters, which was sufficient to allow two vehicles to pass each other. In comparison the Via Egnatia, in parts, may have been only three meters wide.⁴⁰ A section of the Via Militaris, however, uncovered by road work in South-Eastern Serbia and

---

38 *The Crusades: A Documentary Survey*, trans. James Brundage (Milwaukee: Marquette University Press, 1962).
39 Georgios Xeidakis and Evgenia Varagouli, "Design and Construction of Roman Roads: The Case of Via Egnatia in the Aegean Thrace, Northern Greece," *Environmental & Engineering Geoscience*, March (1997): 128.
40 For further discussion of the medieval condition of the Via Egnatia see John Pryor, "Introduction: Modelling Bohemond's March to Thessalonike," in *Logistics of Warfare in the Age of the Crusades: Proceedings of a Workshop Held at the Centre for Medieval Studies, University of Sydney, 30 September to 4 October 2002*, ed. John Pryor (Aldershot: Ashgate, 2006), 1–24.

dated to the fourth century, revealed it was seven meters wide.[41] This is an astonishingly broad surface, and proof in itself of the acknowledged importance of this road in the Late Roman world as the primary land route connecting Northern Italy and Central Europe with the new capital of Constantinople.[42]

When required to appropriate difficult routes the Byzantine Empire made use of a technique for which evidence dates back to classical Peloponnesian roads. Here, in regions where roads were required to negotiate steep terrain, the surface was often actively cut away to form steps (*klimakes*, or *basmides*).[43] Stepping rendered the surface far easier to navigate for beasts of burden, especially in bad weather, however it obviously also made the road difficult to use for wheeled vehicles.[44] Given the preferred employment of pack animals over wheeled vehicles in Byzantine armies, this was a convenient compromise.

Evidence of stepping is subsequently pronounced along sections of Via Egnatia, however similar evidence along the Via Militaris is entirely lacking.[45] This is almost certainly owing to the fact that the Via Militaris, following a far less precipitous route, simply did not require such measures. This is an important distinction to draw, for the Via Egnatia was the only other practical major trans-Balkan route available in the Middle Ages. Whilst some elements of the first crusade travelled along this route in the late eleventh century, the entirety of land-based contingents of the second and third crusades travelled instead exclusively along the Via Militaris. In addition, large pilgrim hosts, such as one led by Henry the Lion in 1172, also took this latter route.

There are several possible reasons for why the Via Militaris appears to have been exclusively preferred over the Via Egnatia starting around the beginning of the twelfth century. Of particular importance was the fact that the Via Militaris avoided the necessity of porting men and material across the Straits of Otranto. A mundane passage today between Italy and Albania, this was a dangerous voyage in the medieval period, and during the first crusade it saw numerous ships capsize, with subsequent loss of life and material. The Via Militaris was also the

---

[41] Miroslav Lazic, "Via militaris: Rimski drum kod Caribroda," *Glasnik Društva konzervatora Srbije* 35 (2011): 69–73.
[42] Ronald Syme, *The Provincial at Rome and Rome and the Balkans, 80BC–AD14*, ed. Anthony Birley (Exeter: University of Exeter Press, 1999), 206.
[43] Robert Forbes, *Studies in Ancient Technology* (Leiden: Brill, 1972), 136.
[44] If the steps were wide enough apart it is possible wagons could have negotiated them, albeit with some difficulty.
[45] Nigel Hammond, "The Western Part of the Via Egnatia," *The Journal of Roman Studies* 64 (1974): 187.

most accessible route for forces originating in Central Europe, avoiding the need to negotiate the Alpine Passes and a long journey through Italy.[46]

However, by far the most important consideration was almost certainly the fact that the Via Militaris was far more capable of accommodating wheeled vehicles than the stepped Via Egnatia. We possess clear evidence within sources, pertaining to the first, second and third crusades, that wagons were used along this route, and in relatively large numbers. Certainly the going was not always easy, and during the passage of the second crusade Odo of Deuil remarked that the wagons employed offered more "hope than usefulness" and that in trying to avoid broken down carts, or long traffic jams, they "ran into more serious hindrances."[47] Further, in 1172, the pilgrim host led by Henry the Lion had to simply abandon its carts in the forests of Serbia owing to the poor condition of the road.[48]

Nevertheless, these complaints are surprisingly few, given the vast weight of men and material the Via Militaris conveyed during the eleventh and twelfth centuries. Pointedly, during the third crusade, Frederick Barbarossa made great use of wagons during the German's passage along the Via Militaris.[49] These wagons were used to convey essential material, injured and sick soldiers, but equally importantly the vast and bulky material wealth the crusaders had been instructed to bring along with them.[50] However, before the army reached Anatolia, as it was awaiting portage across the Bosporus, the wagons were abandoned. Clearly Barbarossa, who was familiar with the conditions to be expected en route to the Holy Land owing to his participation in the second crusade, well knew that the roads of Asia Minor were far less suitable for wagons than those of the Balkans.

---

46 Alan Murray, "Roads, Bridges and Shipping in the Passage of Crusade Armies by Overland Routes to the Bosporus 1096–1190," in *Die Vielschichtigkeit der Straße: Kontinuität und Wandel in Mittelalter und früher Neuzeit*, ed. Kornelia Holzner-Tobisch, Thomas Kuhtreiber and Gertrud Blaschitz (Vienna: Verlag der Österreichischen Akademie der Wissenschaften, 2012), 189.
47 Odo of Deuil, *De profectione Ludovici VII in orientem*, trans. Virginia G. Berry (New York: Columbia University Press, 1948), 31.
48 Arnold of Lübeck, *Arnoldi Chronica Slavorum*, in *Scriptores rerum Germanicarum in usum scholarum ex Monumentis Germaniae Historicis recudi fecit*, ed. Johann. M. Lappenberg (Hanover: Hannoverae Impensis bibliopolii Hahniani, 1868), 15.
49 *Chronicle of the Third Crusade: A Translation of the Itinerarium peregrinorum et gesta Regis Ricardi*, trans. Helen J. Nicholson (Aldershot: Ashgate, 1997), 55.
50 Alan Murray, "Finance and Logistics of the Crusade of Frederick Barbarossa," in *In laudem Hierosolymitani: Studies in Crusades and Medieval Culture in Honour of Benjamin Z. Kedar*, ed. Iris Shagir, Ronnie Ellenblum and Jonathon Riley-Smith (Aldershot: Ashgate, 2007), 364.

8 Philippopolis and Medieval Settlement along the Via Militaris

That the Via Militaris remained a viable route was therefore primarily a function of its immense foundations, which themselves were a direct consequence of its inherent strategic value. However, it was also a reflection of the fact that the road retained along its length populations which could be tasked with its maintenance. As noted above, many of the major urban population centers of the region, Belgrade, Naissus, Serdica, Philippopolis, Adrianople and finally Constantinople, all lay along its route. What lives some of these cities led after the seventh century is, unfortunately, extremely difficult to discern. Undoubtedly their populations declined to a mere fraction of their Late Roman heights. The city of Philippopolis, for instance, which had once drawn comparison to Rome by spreading over seven hills of the region, was by the seventh century clustered instead around the central acropolis.[51] By the eleventh century Anna Comnena could note that many Roman remains, including of the hippodrome, could barely be seen at all.[52]

Nevertheless, these cities would have remained important regional hubs. Rather than simply disappearing under the waves of migration and invasion which swept over the region, they likely forged new identities although, again owing to the scarcity of sources, details are maddeningly scarce. Serdica, for instance, almost disappears from the pages of history in the seventh and eighth centuries, however archaeological excavations of St. Sophia Church located there indicate it remained in use in the ninth century, suggesting the continuing presence of at least a small Christian population.[53] Further, one of the few examples of literary evidence available to us suggests that in Thessalonica, at least, a degree of reciprocal exchange may have been established between these vestig-

---

51 Ralph Hoddinott, *Bulgaria in Antiquity: An Archaeological Introduction* (London: Benn, 1975), 291.
52 Anna Comnena, *The Alexiad of the Princess Anna Comnena: Being the History of the Reign of Her Father, Alexius I, Emperor of the Romans, 1081–1118 A.D.*, trans. Elizabeth Dawes (London: Kegan Paul, Trench, Trubner, 1928), 463.
53 James D. Howard-Johnston, "Urban Continuity in the Balkans in the Early Middle Ages," in *Ancient Bulgaria: Papers Presented to the International Symposium on the Ancient History and Archaeology of Bulgaria*, ed. Andrew G. Poulter (Nottingham: University of Nottingham, 1981), 2:247–8.

ial urban communities and the largely agricultural "Slavic" population which settled elsewhere in the region.[54]

The Via Militaris itself may be used as a means for evaluating cultural change over space and time. In this respect the experiences of the "Paulician" community proves illuminating. This militant Christian community, originating in Armenia, was accused by the Byzantines of being monotheistic dualists. Under threat of persecution, members of the community commenced migrating to Thrace. This process was accelerated through forced resettlement.[55] Such resettlement was a common Byzantine tactic employed to simultaneously break up troublesome Asiatic "sects," and reinforce regions subjected to continued military depredations.

This process climaxed in the tenth century, after the city of Philippopolis was brutally sacked by armies of the Kievan Rus in 969. In response, Emperor John Tzimisces forcibly transferred what the sources claim to be as many as 200,000 Paulicians to the region, to repopulate the city and defend it against further invasions.[56] Whilst the number of people so displaced is clearly exaggerated, undoubtedly it was hoped that the disempowered Paulicians would eventually become absorbed into the local populace and perhaps even become good Orthodox citizens.

Instead the Paulicians remained a unique element within the city. Indeed, they seem to have thrived to the extent that by the late eleventh century Anna Comnena would complain that Philippopolis was overrun by them.[57] Throughout the twelfth century the Paulicians further instigated, or at least conspicuously contributed to, several major popular revolts. Intriguingly these uprisings were not limited to Philippopolis alone but broke out also in Serdica and Naissus,[58] cities, it hardly needs noting, which also lay along the Via Militaris.

The number of Paulicians in the region, and their influence, was no doubt exaggerated in contemporary sources, particularly by Anna Comnena, whose father was given no little trouble by the community. We, sadly, know little of their subsequent cultural identity, however evidence suggests that they persisted as a distinct group in the region long beyond the eleventh century. Paulicinism is also argued to have influenced the formation of Bogomilism, another dualist religious

---

54 *Hagiographic Sources for Byzantine Cities*, 79.
55 Dmitri Obolensky, *The Bogomils: A Study in Balkan Neo-manichaeism* (Middlesex: Anthony C. Hall, 1972), 59–63.
56 John Skylitzes, *A Synopsis of Byzantine History, 811–1057*, trans. John Whortley (Cambridge: Cambridge University Press, 2010), 273–4.
57 Anna Comnena, *The Alexiad*, 385.
58 Obolensky, *The Bogomils*, 189–90.

sect which quickly spread throughout the Balkans, and which in turn is sometimes claimed to have influenced the Cathar heresy which took root in southern France between the twelfth and fourteenth centuries.[59] The veracity of this link aside, it is tempting to reflect upon the role played by the Via Militaris in potentially spreading religious ideology, both within the Balkans and also to Central Europe and beyond.

In any event, the persistence of the Paulician community belies the easy categorization of Philippopolis as a "Byzantine," "Slav" or "Bulgarian" city. Equally tantalizing is a brief reference to a community of Latins outside the city who provided market services to participants of the second crusade. So, whilst the literary and archaeological records do not allow us to make more informed evaluations of the demography of Balkan cities in the Middle Ages, those which lay along the Via Militaris were clearly far from the homogenous entities they might otherwise be assumed to be.

9 The Roads of the Medieval Balkans: A Comparison

With additional references to life in the Balkans scarce, the primary means of evaluating the functionality of the Via Militaris comes from studying military campaigns, one of the few topics on which contemporary Byzantine historians were compelled to divert their gaze from Constantinople itself and, albeit usually only briefly, give consideration to life outside of the capital. The comparison of two Balkan campaigns in particular provides further compelling evidence of the unique status of the Via Militaris.

The first example concerns Emperor Basil II's campaign of 986. In the late tenth century, relations between the Byzantine and Bulgarian Empires reached a crisis point after the sack of Larissa by the Bulgarian general, and future emperor, Samuel. The Byzantine Emperor, Basil II, had possessed the throne for near a decade, but after a series of major revolts in Asia Minor had only achieved true autonomy of action in 985. Accordingly, in the following year, Basil determined to quash the upstart Bulgarian Empire, newly revitalized under a dynasty referred to in Constantinopolitan circles as the *Cometupoli*, owing to their meteoric ascent. Basil chose as the target of his campaign the host city of this dynasty, the then capital of the Bulgarian Empire, Serdica.

---

59 Ibid., 286–9.

What ensued was nothing short of a fiasco. The Byzantine army, after a twenty-day siege, proved incapable of overcoming the defenses of Serdica, in itself evidence of the impressive fortifications the city must have retained. With provisions running low, and the camp assailed by roving bands which captured their animals and set fire to their siege engines, the decision was made to withdraw. Here, whilst the Byzantines attempted to negotiate the Gates of Trajan, Samuel's army fell on them, routing the Byzantines and capturing their entire baggage train. Basil barely escaped the ambush alive.

This event, the Battle of the Gates of Trajan, has a long and rich legacy. In contemporary Bulgaria the battle is celebrated, with Samuel feted as a national hero who defended Bulgarian independence by driving out the foreign invaders. In Byzantine historiography the calamitous defeat is often credited with the making of Basil, turning an irresolute ruler into a fiercely determined soldier-Emperor, one who would ultimately conquer the Bulgarian Empire.

The veracity of the above depictions is open to debate, and historians are engaged in lively arguments over the battle, its import, and its influence on the personality of Basil. Such debates need not distract us here, other than to note that this emphasis on the legacy of the battle has left the campaign which preceded it relatively unstudied. The scale of Basil's defeat might suggest that the Gates of Trajan were an imposing physical obstacle for an army to overcome, a natural chokepoint in which to trap and annihilate an army, when upon reflection the reality is quite different.

What is important to note is not that Basil's army was ambushed on its return journey through the pass, but rather that it was able to make the outward passage at all. Bulgarian historians have claimed that Basil was leading an army of some 30,000 men, but even if a more realistic size of 10 – 15,000 is suggested, the attendant logistical strains were enormous.[60] This is especially so considering that according to Leo the Deacon, who accompanied the army, it carried with it enough supplies to have sustained itself at least for the duration of the twenty-day siege of Serdica.[61]

This necessitated the accompaniment of a massive number of attendant baggage animals. To sustain an army of 12,000 men in the field for twenty-four days, approximately 8,000 pack animals would be required. Added to this was the number of animals required to convey the imperial baggage which accompanied

---

60 Dimităr Simeonov Angelov and Boris Čolpanov, *Bălgarska voenna istorija prez srednovekovieto: (X–XV vek)* (Sofia: Izdatelstvo na Bălgarskata akademija na naukite, 1994), 39–41.
61 Leo the Deacon, *Historia*, trans. Alice-Mary Talbot and Denis Sullivan, *The History of Leo the Deacon: Byzantine Military Expansion in the Tenth Century* (Washington, DC: Dumbarton Oaks Research Library and Collection, 2005), 214.

an emperor on campaign. Finally, the Byzantine army was also accompanied by a siege train. The entire logistical apparatus which accompanied the army, even an army of only 10–15,000, was therefore enormous, and quite possibly involved the employment of over 10,000 pack animals.

It is instructive to relate Basil's experiences along this route to those encountered along another road in similar circumstances. In 599 a Byzantine general, Comentiolus, after campaigning along the Danube, attempted to find the road through the Central Balkan Mountains back to Constantinople before the onset of winter. But, as the historian Theophylact Simocatta relates, Comentiolus could not even find the road.[62] Only after employing the services of an elderly guide did Comentiolus manage to locate the overgrown and dilapidated route. The subsequent passage proved so long and arduous that most of the baggage animals perished, and rather than return directly to Constantinople the exhausted army was required to winter at Philippopolis instead.

Certainly, aspects of Simocatta's story appear to be of questionable historical accuracy, in particular the employment of the well-worn literary trope of the "elderly guide." Yet the thrust of the story is clear; Comentiolus found the passage through the Central Balkan Mountains to be an excruciatingly arduous experience, only accomplished with great hardship and loss of life and material. This stands in direct contrast to the experience of Basil II in the Gates of Trajan, which seemingly proved easily capable of permitting the passage of a relatively large Byzantine army, with attendant baggage and siege train, not to mention the imperial baggage, to Serdica.

Particularly interesting is that the route which Comentiolus likely followed was itself a formerly important Roman road, one which had connected Philippopolis (through the Troyan Pass in the Central Balkan Mountains) with the Danubian legionary barracks located at Oescus. This had been a significant route in the late Roman Empire, linking the agriculturally important Maritsa Valley with the legionary barracks along the Danube to the north; excavations of its surface show that it was exceptionally well made.[63]

For this road to decline in quality so rapidly is therefore startling, and may be accounted for by two factors. The first is that by the late sixth century the roads to the Danube were already long abandoned and therefore heavily deteriorated, likely as a result of the absence of resident populations to keep the route open or carry out necessary repair work.

---

62 Theophylact Simocatta, *The History of Theophylact Simocatta*, trans. Michael and Mary Whitby (Oxford: Clarendon Press, 1986), 214.
63 Mitko Madzharov, *Roman Roads in Bulgaria: Contribution to the Development of Roman Road System in the Provinces of Moesia and Thrace* (Veliko Tarnovo: Faber, 2009), 33–5.

The second is that passes through the Central Balkan Mountains, in particular the Troyan Pass, are far higher than the pass through the Gates of Trajan (approximately 1500 meters above sea level as opposed to 800 meters). This higher altitude exposed the road to greater extremes of weather, and notably the cycle of freezing weather over winter, followed by the spring thaw. The corresponding expansion and contraction of water within the *pavimentum* served to, over time, break the formerly well paved surface to pieces.[64] Without constant supervision and maintenance, such a road would indeed quickly become as untenable as the one Comentiolus followed. In comparison, Basil's outward journey through the Gates of Trajan does not appear to have been impeded at all by a similarly decayed surface, indicating the route was far more successful in enduring the rigors of time and climate.

10 The Central Balkans and the Defense of Thrace

The utility provided by the Via Militaris was also crucial to the defense and administration of the Constantinopolitan hinterland and the strategically vital region of Thrace. The loss of Byzantium's Egyptian provinces in the seventh century had also meant an end to the regular grain shipments to the capital from the Nile Delta. Literary evidence indicates that Constantinople was thereafter predominately supplied by the produce of Thrace which, with its Mediterranean climate, seasonal rainfall and numerous rivers, was well suited to intensive agricultural exploitation.[65]

The Via Militaris consequently played an important role in the transportation of vital food stuffs to the capital, at the very least facilitating its movement to local ports, such as at Selymbria (today Silivri) and Raidestos (Rodosto, today Tekirdağ), where it could be shipped to the capital. Michael Attaleiates relates that in the eleventh century carts were used to bring grain to the *kastron* of Raidestos for sale, which unscrupulous imperial officials attempted to monopolize through the construction of a *phoundax*, a state corn exchange.[66] This example

---

[64] Lynn White, "Technology and Invention in the Middle Ages," *Speculum* 15, no. 2 (1940): 150–1.
[65] John Teall, "The Grain Supply of Byzantine Empire, 330–1025," *Dumbarton Oaks Papers* 13 (1959): 87–139.
[66] Michael Attaleiates, *The History*, trans. Anthony Kaldellis and Dimitris Krallis (Cambridge, MA: Harvard University Press, 2012), 367–9.

suggests a lively overland trade directed towards satisfying the insatiable masses of Constantinople. Indeed, so strong was the influence the capital exerted upon the surrounding regions that Michael Choniates, Bishop of Athens in the mid-twelfth century, complained that all the rivers of goods ran towards the imperial city, as if to the sea.[67]

Accordingly, whilst Byzantium was afforded the possibility of treating enemy encroachment into the periphery of its empire philosophically, the defense of Thrace was fundamental to its well-being. For instance, a Pecheneg raid into Thrace, in the mid-eleventh century, so disrupted the agricultural production of the region that it resulted in food shortages in Constantinople, prompting widespread famine and civil unrest.[68] Food riots in the capital could quickly spread, and often become politically extremely dangerous.

Always sensitive to the mood of the Constantinopolitan populace, the defense of Thrace was naturally a key concern for Byzantine Emperors. Philippopolis, as discussed above, was accordingly repopulated through the forced resettlement of Paulicians from the eighth century onwards. This was far from the only example of this practice in the region, with Byzantium settling large numbers of defeated peoples not only in Thrace and the Maritsa Valley, but further along the approaches to regions, the Nišava and Struma rivers.[69] A fundamental goal of these resettlements was to provide resident garrisons ready to resist, or at least provide ample warning of, incursions into the Empire's heartland. Additionally, they could be tasked with maintaining road surfaces in the immediate vicinity.

Provincial towns subsequently played a vital role as bastions guarding this region. Philippopolis emerges as an important staging post, where imperial forces would congregate to defend against incursions through the vulnerable passes of the Balkan Mountains to the north. For instance, the city played a prominent role in campaigns by Alexius Comnenus in the eleventh century, and the uncovered seals of *horreiarioi*, officials in charge of imperial granaries, indicate the presence of local warehouses that stored grain from nearby imperial estates.[70] Other cities, which also lay along the Via Militaris, assumed similar

---

67 Judith Herrin, *Margins and Metropolis: Authority Across the Byzantine Empire* (Princeton: Princeton University Press, 2013), 24.
68 Michael Attaleiates, *The History*, 379.
69 Paul Stephenson, *Byzantium's Balkan Frontier: A Political Study of the Northern Balkans, 900–1204* (Cambridge: Cambridge University Press, 2000), 90.
70 Angelika Laiou, "Regional Networks in the Balkans in the Middle and Late Byzantine Periods," in *Trade and Markets in Byzantium*, ed. Cécile Morrisson (Washington, DC: Dumbarton Oaks Research Library and Collection, 2012), 129.

roles, such as Druzipara, Selymbria, Bulgarophygon, Arcadiopolis and Tzouroulon (modern Misinli, Silivri, Babaeski, Lüleburgaz, and Çorlu respectively, located in Thracian Turkey) all of which appear to have retained defensive fortifications at least into the twelfth century.

Literary and sigillographic evidence further indicates the Roman post system, the *cursus publicus*, remained intact along this section of the route at least. In the Byzantine era this duty was assumed by the office of the *dromos*, and seals of a "*chartoularios* of the *dromos* of the West," dating to the tenth and eleventh centuries, have been uncovered.[71] The use of post horses is referenced in contemporary Byzantine sources,[72] and in one memorable instance in the late eleventh century the *sebastrocrator* Isaac raced from Constantinople to Philippopolis in "two days and two nights" to defend his son against charges of treason.[73] Such a journey, well over 400 kilometers in length, could only realistically have been possible if fresh horses were readily available along a relatively easy route.

What therefore emerges within this region is a matrix of regional administrative and defensive centers whose importance was derived primarily from their position astride the main overland route to the Byzantine capital. Their subsequent prominence is further emphasized through their enhanced religious authority. Arcadiopolis and Druzipara emerged as autocephalous archiepiscopates, whilst Emperor Manuel II Comnenus raised the city of Selymbria to Metropolitan status in the mid-twelfth century.[74] Additional sources, such as Nicetas Choniates' reference to the "wealthy and illustrious residents" of Arcadiopolis, indicate that this region, at least, belies the general impression of the Byzantine Balkans as a region epitomized by poverty and urban decay.[75]

The available evidence consequently indicates that the Byzantine state relied upon the compulsory labor of populations along the Via Militaris to maintain it in an operable state, with occasional more orchestrated repairs occurring at the request of the Emperor. Traditionally local officials were charged with the main-

---

[71] Nicolas Oikonomides and John Nesbitt, eds., *Catalogue of Byzantine Seals at Dumbarton Oaks and in the Fogg Museum of Art* (Washington, DC: Dumbarton Oaks Research Library and Collection, 1991), 3–4, item 1.5.

[72] Anna Avramea, "Land and Sea Communications, Fourth–Fifteenth Centuries," in *The Economic History of Byzantium: From the Seventh Through to the Fifteenth Century*, ed. Angelika Laiou (Washington, DC: Dumbarton Oaks Research Library and Collection, 2002), 60.

[73] Anna Comnena, *The Alexiad*, 209.

[74] Paul Magdalino, "Byzantine Churches of Selymbria," *Dumbarton Oaks Papers* 32 (1978): 312.

[75] Nicetas Choniates, *O City of Byzantium*, trans. Harry Magoulias (Detroit: Wayne State University Press, 1984), 336.

tenance of infrastructure within their jurisdiction, with emphasis placed on the upkeep of highways and bridges. After Basil's conquest of the Balkans in the early eleventh century we can observe the creation of several new offices with titles such as *doux* or *katepanoi*, offices which undoubtedly were charged with securing imperial authority and ensuring that vital infrastructure was rendered in a good state of repair.[76]

11 The Medieval Via Militaris: One Road or Many?

This evidence still does not, however, give us an accurate picture of the exact quality of the surface at any point along its length, and it would be dangerous to make overly broad assumptions on this point. Certainly, in further afield regions where population density was lower it is not clear how effective these measures were. Indeed, crusader sources describe the road between Naissus and Serdica, for instance, as typically "difficult and uneven," albeit it clearly was far from impassable.[77]

As this was far from the all-weather surface of the Roman era, without its former well paved surface, undoubtedly extremes in weather would have severely impacted the quality of the road. Heavy downpours, as are common in the Maritsa Valley throughout summer, would have quickly turned the surface into a muddy quagmire. During the passage of the second crusade, for instance, a flash flood washed away a large part of the crusaders' baggage.[78] Heavy snows, too, undoubtedly severely prohibited usage of the road. In the late twelfth century Emperor Isaac Angelus was able to lead a force through the Gates of Trajan in the month of December, although the source explicitly states Isaac marched only with "light armed troops."[79] Heavily laden wagons likely would have found passage impossible.

When the road proved particularly difficult to traverse, use could have been made of alternate routes. It is important to note that the Romans did not just build grand highways, but also many lesser secondary routes. Some of these

---

[76] Alexandru Madgearu, *Byzantine Military Organization on the Danube, 10th–12th Centuries* (Leiden: Brill, 2013), 64.
[77] *The Crusade of Frederick Barbarossa: The History of the Expedition of the Emperor Frederick and Related Texts*, trans. Graham. A. Loud (Leeds: Ashgate, 2010), 66–7.
[78] Odo of Deuil, *De profectione Ludovici VII in orientem*, 47.
[79] Nicetas Choniates, *O City of Byzantium*, 219.

may have been utilized when necessary, and Byzantine *taktika* stress the importance of using scouts and guides to locate alternate roads should the main road prove unusable.

What we today think of as the Via Militaris may, in the Byzantine period, more accurately be considered an inter-connected network of roads, each being utilized as and when need arose. Evidence of these alternate routes is even scantier than those pertaining to the main road, but occasional examples occur. Thus, we have the curious incident during the passage of the third crusade when guides led the crusaders by an alternate road (*saxosa et non publica*), prompting the crusaders to angrily demand to be led back to the "main" road (*trita semita seu strata publica*).[80]

A further example is provided on the approach to Constantinople itself. Formerly the road had travelled along the shore of the Sea of Marmara, crossing the lagoon which lay in its path (known to the Byzantines as the Myrmex and in Turkey today as the Küçükçekmece), before entering the city via the Golden Gate. The bridge over the Myrmex, however, fell into disrepair, with the last record of its repair dating to the ninth century.[81] Additionally the Golden Gate, which lays at the far southern end of the Theodosian Walls, was permanently sealed shut in the late twelfth century, and may have been abandoned as early as the eleventh.[82] Thus the approach to the city, rather than following the route of the Roman road, appears in the twelfth century to have followed an alternate route, skirting around the Myrmex and entering the city by a more northerly gate, most likely the Xylokerkos Postern.

12 The Via Militaris and Crusader Logistics

Whilst the picture that therefore emerges of the medieval Via Militaris is undeniably confused, it clearly remained a navigable route throughout this period. This is evidenced by sheer dint of the fact that the crusader hosts, with their enormous material needs, were able to safely take passage along this road until the thirteenth century when technological advances in sea navigation ren-

---

[80] *The Crusade of Frederick Barbarossa*, 59–60.
[81] Constantine Porphyrogenitus, *De administrando imperio*, trans. Romilly J.H. Jenkins (Washington, DC: Dumbarton Oaks Center for Byzantine Studies, 1967), 247.
[82] Thomas Madden, "Triumph Re-imagined: The Golden Gate and Popular Memory in Byzantine and Ottoman Constantinople," in *Shipping, Trade and Crusade in the Medieval Mediterranean: Studies in Honour of John Pryor*, ed. Ruthy Gertwagen and Elizabeth Jeffreys (Farnham: Ashgate, 2012), 318–9.

dered the overland route to the Holy Land obsolete. For those who might view the movement of armies across space, even vast armies such as those represented by the crusades, as a mundane, almost trivial, matter, the significance of this achievement might be lost.

It is important, therefore, to stress that the movement of large groups of people, especially in a pre-modern context, is seldom simple nor straightforward. In particular, the passage of the crusader hosts represents one of the foremost feats of logistical management of the age. One notable example is the contingent of Germans Frederick Barbarossa led on the third crusade. Though some older estimates numbered it anywhere from 100,000 to 250,000 men,[83] modern estimates place the force closer to 12–15,000 men, and whilst this may seem an incredibly small force in comparison, the logistical difficulties attendant in maneuvering even a force of this size through the Balkans were enormous.[84] An army of 15,000, with its necessary mounts, remounts, baggage animals, wagons, and non-combatants would require approximately 32,700 kilograms of provisions per day, and on a road five and a half meters wide would form a marching column approximately 28 kilometers long.[85]

The rates of march subsequently achieved by the crusader hosts are equally impressive. The force led by Peter the Hermit, characterized as a disorderly rabble in contemporary sources, has been calculated as covering, on average, approximately 15 miles (25 kilometers) per day between Naissus and Constantinople.[86] This is an impressively high rate of march for a pre-modern army to maintain, and is mirrored by that achieved by Conrad II along the same route during the second crusade. In comparison, the first crusader force led by Bohemond along the Via Egnatia averaged only eight miles (approximately 13 kilometers) per day.[87]

No neglected, poorly maintained and untrustworthy road could have so satisfactorily accommodated such fundamentally unwieldy hosts. By way of comparison the experiences of the crusaders on the roads of Asia Minor can be con-

---

83 Kenneth Setton, "The Crusades of Frederick Barbarossa and Henry VI," in *A History of the Crusades*, ed. Kenneth Setton, vol. 2, *The Later Crusades 1189–1311* (Madison: University of Wisconsin Press, 1969), 92.
84 Ekkehard Eickhoff, *Friedrich Barbarossa im Orient: Kreuzzug und Tod Friedrichs I* (Tübingen: Wasmuth, 1977), 47.
85 These calculations are largely derived from the equations presented by Haldon, *Warfare, State and Society in the Byzantine World*, 281–93.
86 John Nesbitt, "The Rate of March of Crusading Armies in Europe: A Study and Computation," *Traditio* 19 (1963): 181.
87 Ibid., 176.

sidered, for here the roads were so poor the crusaders bitterly complained of their quality and noted with apprehension that those who wandered from the path were seldom ever found again. Whilst occasional complaints are raised regarding the quality of the Via Militaris, on the whole crusading sources are curiously silent on the topic, suggesting that it proved adequate to their needs. Which, as the above numbers indicate, were in themselves thoroughly remarkable.

Indeed, during the passage of the first crusade the road became symbolically associated with Charlemagne's mythical pilgrimage to Jerusalem, with one source claiming that the crusaders "travelled by the road which Charlemagne, the Heroic King of the Franks, had formerly caused to be built to Constantinople."[88] Whilst the exact interpretation of this passage is open to debate (the crusader chroniclers surely knew Charlemagne had no hand in the road's construction), so fortuitous must the infinitely convenient, vehicular capable, transcontinental road have seemed, it would be no surprise that its origins were potentially couched by the crusaders in mythical, even supernatural, terms.[89]

13 Conclusion

The primary theme of this chapter has been the poverty of definitive proof, both literary and archaeological, relating to the function of Roman roads within the Byzantine Empire. Yet through the collation of disparate evidence pertaining, in particular, to the movement of armies across the Balkans during this period, it has argued that the continued viability of the medieval Via Militaris can be assumed, even if the character of the road cannot be exactly determined at any one point in space or time.

The remarkable longevity of the road was founded on highly practical grounds. The road's original construction owed much to the Roman conquest of Dacia, and the demands created by the consequent need to garrison the Danubian border. It subsequently developed in strategic importance in unison with the rapid growth in size and influence of Constantinople, the new Roman capital. How the road fared during the turbulent period between the seventh and tenth centuries is as yet impossible to determine. Anecdotal evidence suggests

---

88 *The Deeds of the Franks and Other Pilgrims to Jerusalem*, trans. Rosalind Hill (London: Nelson, 1962), 2–3.
89 For further discussion see Anne Latowsky, *Emperor of the World: Charlemagne and the Construction of Imperial Authority, 800–1229* (Ithaca: Cornell University Press, 2013), 216.

traffic along the route, especially consular traffic, almost entirely vanished during a period when the Balkans were rent by near perpetual strife.[90]

Perhaps the Bulgarian Empire, which profited from Byzantine instability to assert itself as a major Balkan power during this period, had expended the resources necessary to maintain those sections of the route which were under its jurisdiction.[91] Perhaps the doughty foundations of what had been the foremost military highway of the Late Roman Empire proved impressively capable of withstanding the considerable rigors of time and decay, such that it remained trafficable without the need for much intervening attention. Whatever the case, into the eleventh century the road re-emerges once more as a viable transcontinental route, conveying an increasing flow of pilgrim traffic and ultimately the vast crusader hordes themselves.

The need of the Byzantine state to maintain military and administrative jurisdiction over the Central Balkans argues for the continuing importance of the Via Militaris into the Middle Ages, especially from the beginning of the eleventh century onwards after Basil II's conquest of the Bulgarian Empire. The strategic importance of the route in projecting Byzantine authority into the Central Balkans, whilst simultaneously securing approaches to Constantinople and the Thracian hinterland, must have been patently obvious. So, whilst Byzantium may indeed have deliberately allowed select roads to decline so as not to allow enemies easy ingress into the heart of the empire, such as those through the Central Balkan Mountains for instance, a functional Via Militaris was of vital strategic importance.

Unquestionably, the measures of road maintenance and repair subsequently enacted by Byzantium compare poorly against those practiced by the Roman Empire at its height, but by the fourth and fifth centuries even Rome could no longer maintain the entirety of its extensive infrastructure network as it once had. Byzantine practice was therefore founded upon the experiences of Late Rome, where important routes were prioritized, whilst others were allowed to naturally decline. The upheavals of the seventh century exacerbated this process, to the extent that the Via Militaris emerges as one of the last remaining viable thoroughfares in the empire.

The exceptionalism of the medieval Via Militaris is therefore inherently derived from the road's formidable foundations and strategic importance. It followed a route through prime agricultural land and resident populations capable

---

90 McCormick, *Origins of European Economy*, 138–50.
91 The Bulgarian Empire was no stranger to large scale construction efforts. See Paolo Squatriti, "Moving Earth and Making Difference," in *Borders, Barriers, and Ethnogenesis: Frontiers in Late Antiquity and the Middle Ages*, ed. Florin Curta (Turnhout: Brepols, 2005), 79–80.

of providing the manpower necessary to maintain the surface. It maintained a course that, by largely avoiding the predominately mountainous terrain of the Balkan interior, allowed it to remain useable by wheeled vehicles. And finally, it ultimately terminated in Constantinople, capital of the Byzantine Empire; the one surviving state on the European continent possessing the administrative traditions and financial means necessary to maintain such an extensive surface in an operable state.

Fig. 1: Remains of the Via Militaris in western Bulgaria, on the outskirts of Slivnitsa. Whilst the remains have not been dated, the width of the surface indicates the formidable proportions of the Via Militaris. Photo by Matthew Larnach, 2014.

Fig. 2: Remains of a premodern road located in the Gates of Trajan; the vital pass which lay between Serdica and Philippopolis, and site of Basil II's famous defeat in 986. Photo by Matthew Larnach, 2014.

Fig. 3: Further road remains in the Gates of Trajan. Photo by Matthew Larnach, 2014.

Fig. 4: A restored fragment of the *Milion*, a fourth century stone monument which marked the starting point of all roads in the Byzantine Empire. Photo by Matthew Larnach, 2014.

Vladimir Aleksić
Continuity of Travel and Transport Infrastructures from Antiquity to the Middle Ages: The Case of Via Militaris in the Morava and Nišava Regions

1 Introduction

This chapter provides an overview of the latest literature and scientific results regarding the re-usage of the ancient road infrastructure of the Via Militaris and the adjacent regions during the Middle Ages. In addition to the road itself, this includes objects such as bridges, resting areas, military camps, etc. Moreover, the chapter examines the various social groups involved in the organisation of transport services as well as the means of transportation for goods and people during peace and wartime. Of more importance than a merely accurate physical description of the route is the long-lasting social, economic and political impact it had on its geographical surroundings.[1] The question of road usage must necessarily be addressed by placing it within a broader framework in order to overcome the shortcomings of available historical data. That larger context includes an analysis of the demographic and economic potential, the settlement configuration, climate change and seasonal weather conditions and many other related topics.[2]

Note: I would like to thank Svetlana Marković and Mimica Petrović Radovanović for proofreading and Tatjana Katić for the help with the Turkish words.

[1] For a similar approach cf. Matthew Larnach, "All Roads Lead to Constantinople: Exploring the Via Militaris in the Medieval Balkans, 600–1204" (PhD diss., University of Sydney, 2016), 17. On the name, Via Militaris, see Larnach, "All Roads Lead to Constantinople," 25–6; Mihailo Popović, *Von Budapest nach Istanbul: Die Via Traiana im Spiegel der Reiseliteratur des 14. bis 16. Jahrhunderts* (Leipzig: Eudora, 2010), 47–52; Aleksandar Uzelac, *Srbi i krstaši (XI–XII vek)* (Belgrade: Utopija, 2018), 12–3.

[2] John Haldon, "Roads and Communications in the Byzantine Empire: Wagons, Horses, and Supplies," in *Logistics of Warfare in the Age of the Crusades: Proceedings of a Workshop Held at the Centre for Medieval Studies, University of Sydney, Australia, 30 September to 4 October 2002*, ed. John H. Pryor (Burlington: Ashgate, 2005): 131–2; John Haldon, "Military Logistics: Problems and Approaches," in *Proceedings of the 21st International Congress of Byzantine Studies, London, 21–26 August*, ed. Elizabeth Jeffreys (Aldershot: Ashgate 2006), 1:55–6; Uzelac, *Srbi*

The question of the continuity of usage of the Roman transport and communication infrastructure deep into the medieval era and beyond will be addressed throughout this chapter. Obviously, the general features of the medieval landscape (such as the location or physical description of roads, their correlation with the different type of settlements, or even the individual military events, the complex social processes etc.) cannot be explained adequately without drawing parallels with the conditions inherited from the previous period. Recently, different authors have been trying to show this in various ways. For example, they strongly support the idea of there having been "persistent urban communities beyond the seventh century" to a more significant extent that has been usually assumed.[3] The concept of a much stronger continuity with the elements of the previous civilization in the aftermath of the Great Migration, which in this part of Europe ended only with the arrival of Bulgarians and Hungarians in the year 680 and 896 respectively, might have had an impact both on a micro and a macro level, such as the rhythm and aspects of everyday life or even the creation of states and ethnic structures.[4]

---

i krstaši, 179–80; Ioannis Telelis, "Weather and Climate as Factors Affecting Land Transport and Communications in Byzantium," in *Proceedings of the 21st International Congress of Byzantine Studies, London, 21–26 August*, ed. Elizabeth Jeffreys (Aldershot: Ashgate, 2006), 1:53. For the climate condition in the Central Balkan Peninsula (first–fifteenth century), see Siniša Mišić, "Dubrave u srednjovekovnoj Srbiji," *Beogradski istorijski glasnik* 3 (2012): 95–6. The situation in the following centuries is explained in: Jelena Mrgić, *Zemlja i ljudi: Iz istorije životne sredine zapadnog Balkana* (Belgrade: Equilibrium, 2013), 49–64.

3 Larnach, "All Roads Lead to Constantinople," 15–6, 85–6, 89–90. For more detailed information on this issue, including the relevant bibliography, see Gilbert Dagron, "The Urban Economy, Seventh–Twelfth Centuries," in *Economic History of Byzantium*, ed. Angeliki Laiou (Washington, DC: Harvard University Press, 2002), 2:400; Dejan Bulić, "The Fortifications of the Late Antiquity and the Early Byzantine Period on the Later Territory of the South-Slavic Principalities, and Their Re-Occupation," in *The World of the Slavs: Studies on the East, West and South Slavs: Civitas, Oppidas, Villas and Archeological Evidence (7th to 11th Centuries AD)*, ed. Srđan Rudić (Belgrade: The Institute of History Belgrade, 2013), 189–223.

4 The creation of the earliest Serbian states in the Adriatic hinterland after their arrival into the new territory required the firm control of the most important lines of communication in that region, see Tibor Živković, "The Urban Landscape of Early Medieval Slavic Principalities in the Territories of the Former Praefectura Illyricum and in the Province of Dalmatia," in *The World of the Slavs: Studies on the East, West and South Slavs: Civitas, Oppidas, Villas and Archeological Evidence (7th to 11th Centuries AD)*, ed. Srđan Rudić (Belgrade: The Institute of History Belgrade, 2013), 34; Jelena Mrgić, "Landscape and Settlements of Southeast Europe: Premodern Bosnia and Serbia," in *Landscape in Southeastern Europe*, ed. Lena Mirošević, Gregory Zaro, Mario Katić, Danijela Birt (Berlin: LIT, 2018), 76.

We are going to deal mostly with the western section of the famous Via Militaris, which starts generally west of the city of Sofia.⁵ This small segment of the complete route may again be divided into two geographical regions, where the city of Niš creates the demarcation point. The east section of the Via Militaris follows the Nišava basin, while the South and Great Morava rivers predominantly determine the northern section. The main focus of the paper is on the medieval period, which in this part of the Central Balkans starts around the middle of the seventh century with the massive Slavic colonization and ends with the final Ottoman conquest in the middle of the fifteenth century. However, the scope of our writing demands in several instances extensive remarks about the situations in the previous and later eras.⁶

The literature dedicated to the complex phenomena of traveling and European travel literature in the Middle Ages and the early modern period offers a valuable framework for understanding the situation in the region of Southeast Europe.⁷ Recently, there have been several important contributions which have revised our general knowledge of the Via Militaris.⁸ This is also true for medieval and early modern travel literature related to South-East Europe. It provides us with extensive experience as to the frequency of the western travelers.⁹ In his book *Von Budapest nach Istanbul: Die Via Traiana im Spiegel der Reiseliteratur des 14. bis 16. Jahrhunderts (From Budapest to Istanbul: Via Traiana as Reflected in Travel Literature, 14th–16th Centuries)*, Mihailo Popović has made an elaborate attempt to reconstruct the Via Militaris, or at least its remains, based on the accounts of western travelers. The presence of these itinerants is essential because

---

5 For the latest methodology applied in the research of Roman roads, see Sara Zanni, ed., *La route antique et medieval: Nouvelles approches, nouveaux outils* (Bordeaux: Ausonius, 2017).
6 Aleksandar Krstić, *Ponišavlje u XV veku* (Belgrade: C-Print, 2001); Marija Koprivica, "Niška oblast od 1428. do polovine XVI veka," *Braničevski glasnik* 5 (2008): 1–133; Larnach, "All Roads Lead to Constantinople," 3, 18–24.
7 Werner Paravicini, *Europäische Reiseberichte des späten Mittelalters: Eine analytische Bibliographie*, 3 vols. (Frankfurt: Lang, 1994–2000).
8 Klaus Belke, "Communications: Roads and Bridges," in *Oxford Handbook of Byzantine Studies*, ed. Elizabeth M. Jeffreys, John Haldon and Robin Cormack (Oxford: Oxford University Press, 2008): 295–309; Larnach, "All Roads Lead to Constantinople."
9 Stéphane Yerasimos, *Les voyageurs dans l'Empire ottoman (XIVe–XVIe siècles): Bibliographie, itinéraires, et inventaire des lieux habité* (Ankara: Imprimérie de la Société turque d'histoire, 1991); Ralf Müller, *Prosopographie der Reisenden und Migranten ins Osmanische Reich (1396–1611): Berichterstatter aus dem Heiligen Römischen Reich, außer burgundische Gebiete und Reichsromania*, 10 vols. (Leipzig: Eudora, 2006). Thanks to ongoing research projects such as "Die Medialität diplomatischer Kommunikation: Habsburgische Gesandte in Konstantinopel in der Mitte des 17. Jahrhunderts," the list of historical sources available is continually expanding, see http://diploko.at/abstract/, last accessed 24 October 2020.

they produced the most relevant reports about many aspects of the economic, social and political environment in this region. Popović's book raises again the question of the multiple factors which contributed to both the stability and the discontinuity of Roman road infrastructure.[10]

After Konstantin Jireček published his famous book on the Via Militaris in 1877, a lot of multidisciplinary efforts by scholars such as Gavro Škrivanić, Olga Zirojević, and Matthew Larnach have become available. Still, unlike in some other cases, the exact determination of the whole route remains elusive, and in some cases not much beyond how it was at the beginning of the research on it two centuries ago.[11] According to my best knowledge, only a few short sections of the road (usually no more than a few meters long, and distinctly separated) have been archaeologically documented until now.[12] The most recent and exciting finds have been made in the Dimitrovgrad region. They are supplemented by several geographically related discoveries on the Bulgarian side of the border. Several fascinating photographs offer a glimpse into the construction techniques and size of the ancient roads and serve at the same time as additional proof that pre-medieval thoroughfares had a long-lasting impact on overall social and political life in this region.[13]

When it comes to the research on the material remains of the Roman infrastructure along the Via Militaris, the situation is even worse. The remains of just a few Roman mansions situated in the central Balkan provinces have been partially studied archaeologically so far. A notable effort has been made to examine the ruins of the post station probably called Idimum near the village of Medveđa. Together with stations at Ad Nonum (Nabrđe), Municipium (Kalište, Malo Crniće), Iovis Pagus (Veliki Popovac), Bau (probably Veliko Laole) and Ad Octa-

---

[10] Popović, *Von Budapest nach Istanbul*. In the case of medieval Belgrade, western travelers left plenty of important information on the various topics, see Jovanka Kalić, "Evropski putopisci o Beogradu," in *Beograd u delima evropskih putopisaca*, ed. Đorđe S. Kostić (Belgrade: Balkanološki institut SANU, 2003): 9–16.

[11] For instance, the section of the road between Singidunum (Belgrade) and Sirmium (Sremska Mitrovica). See Sara Zanni, "La route d'Aquileia à Singidunum: Aspects méthodologiques: Du terrain à la publication et à la mise en valeur," in *La route antique et medieval*, 145–64.

[12] For the remains of the ancient road between the city of Paraćin and the village of Pojate cf. Marija Savić and Nebojša Đokić, "Kontinuitet antičkih komunikacija na tlu rimske provincije Gornja Mezija," *Baština* 41 (2016): 66. The remains of Roman castrum and an "imperial" road were visible near the village of Klenovik near Požarevac a long time ago, cf. Mihailo Miladinović, "Požarevačka Morava," *Srpski etnografski zbornik: Naselja i poreklo stanovništva* 25 (1928): 25.

[13] Miroslav Lazić, "Via militaris: Rimski drum kod Cariброда," *Glasnik Društva konzervatora Srbije* 35 (2011): 69–72; Larnach, "All Roads Lead to Constantinople," 27, 156–170 and figures no. 29–39.

vum (both Dražimirovac and Glogovac), it was one among many places where the passengers could rest up from the journey on the way from Viminacium to Horeum Margum, modern-day Ćuprija.[14] While waiting for the more precise ubication of the Via Militaris, we have to work with the available data, which fortunately provide cumulatively, a good enough data set. The phases of use of the objects in the village of Medveđa and many other details imply that several routes developed on the right bank of the Great Morava valley as a consequence of urban development in the late Roman Empire.[15] However, two of them became the main routes, leaving their strong mark on life in the coming centuries (Fig. 1). The first of these routes went almost parallel with the Great Morava river while at the same time it avoided lower terrain that was subjected to frequent flooding. Starting from the town of Braničevo in the north, this passageway went through the villages of Gornja Živica, Lučica, and Žabari, reaching the contemporary cities of Svilajnac and Paraćin. The second and younger route emerged to shorten the travel time between the Danube region and the municipalities at the south of the province of Moesia Superior. It mostly trailed the river Mlava for approximately the first 100 kilometers of its course. At least two fortifications protected the described route, whose remains are visible in the districts of the villages Veliko Laole, Vezičevo and Zlatovo. The first village in the basin of the Resava River was Rohanda (Roanda). The road continued through the village of Medveđa, where it forked once again. One route ran along the lower part of the Resava River toward Svilajnac where it joined the previously mentioned western branch of Via Militaris. As testified in the fifteenth century written evidence, the second route ran to the south through the village of Moštanica (now the hamlet of the Krušar village) and toward Ravno. In the relative vicinity of the latter, near to the extinct village of Obrasceh, at the site of the contemporary village of Glogovac, there was a ferry over the Great Morava. It led to the medieval route running on the left bank of the river. The existence of an additional path between the Resava valley and Ravno (through the now extinct village of Miroslava located

---

14 Nevertheless, it is not directly relevant for our topic, because it ceased to fulfil its role due to the military destruction in the second half of the fourth century, see Miloje Vasić and Gordana Milošević, *Mansio Idimum: Rimska poštanska i putna stanica kod Medveđe* (Belgrade: Arheološki institut Beograd, Narodni muzej Beograd, 2000); Savić and Đokić, "Kontinuitet antičkih komunikacija,", 64–6. On the excavation of the Bona Mansio near to the city of Vetren in Bulgaria see, https://www.bhfieldschool.org/program/roman-excavations-bona-mansio/, last accessed 23 October 2020. The remains of the station of Meldiis may have been located in the protected area of the Aldomirovsko marsh near to the Bulgarian city of Slivnitza, see Larnach, "All Roads Lead to Constantinople," 165–6.
15 Vasić and Milošević, *Mansio Idimum*, 157–8; the concept of a road network replaced the idea of a single path, see Larnach, "All Roads Lead to Constantinople," 4.

somewhere in the upper stream of the Mirosava river, probably near to the village of Paljane), has been suggested, as well. Furthermore, the villages of Tabanovac, Burovac and Dubnica may have served as a connecting point for an additional diagonal road which connected the village of Veliko Laole and Svilajnac.[16] More to the south, the Via Militaris generally did not diverge so markedly from the main route in the Roman period, leaving in most cases the travelers with just one option. The Mutatio Sarmatorum was presumably situated on the site of the graveyard of the village of Sikirica. The road stations of Praesidium Dasmini (Bračin), Cametae (Ražanj), Presidium Pompei (Rutevac and Ćićina) and Rapiana, (the latter's exact location is still unknown), followed it. Further to the south, Niš was not far away from the last-mentioned road station.[17]

Fig. 1: Map showing the northern section of the Via Militaris. Cartography by Vladimir Aleksić.

---

16 The description intentionally uses the elements of medieval and contemporary topography. Vasić and Milošević, *Mansio Idimum*, 74–9, 129–58; Savić and Đokić, "Kontinuitet antičkih komunikacija," 62–8. For the medieval period cf. Gavro Škrivanić, *Putevi u srednjovekovnoj Srbiji* (Belgrade: Turistička štampa, 1974), 82–94; Ema Miljković and Aleksandar Krstić, *Braničevo u XV veku: Istorijsko-geografska studija* (Požarevac: Narodni muzej Požarevac, 2007), 85, 173, 185, 244–6.
17 Savić and Đokić, "Kontinuitet antičkih komunikacija," 66–7. A detailed road description in the Ponišavlje Region is available in Tatjana Katić's contribution to this volume and in Olga Zirojević, *Carigradski drum od Beograda do Sofije (1459–1683)* (Belgrade: Istorijski muzej Srbije), 1970, 36–40; Krstić, *Ponišavlje*, 96–101.

2 The Via Militaris in Early Medieval/Byzantine Times

The medieval period started in this part of Europe in the middle of the seventh century with the massive colonization of the Slavic tribes and the partial collapse of the Eastern Roman Empire, leaving us with a limited number of written sources through which to investigate topics for the next five centuries. As a consequence, we have to rely on the written knowledge about Via Militaris in western sources. In the middle of the eleventh century, numerous western travelers left their accounts. The first record of a group of courageous pilgrims who dared to take the land route rather than the traditional sea voyage dates from 1026/1027, followed by many others devout Christians. However, only a few decades later, Byzantine-Hungarian hostilities started to pose a new logistical obstacle, making this travel option temporarily much less appealing.[18] A lot of attention in international literature has been given to the Third Crusade, which involved the Emperor Friedrich Barbarossa and many German dignitaries and barons.[19] Reports of this and the previous crusade inform us that the valleys around Niš were fertile and that, as a result of many thriving villages, they provided the numerous travelers with food and fodder in contrast to the regions located to the north of the town.[20]

When thinking of these accounts, the most striking feature, at least for me, is the fact that many frequently quoted descriptions of the Balkan Peninsula are more the outcome of previously created literary templates, which makes it hard or sometimes even impossible to distinguish the real conditions on the terrain from literary imagination.[21] For instance, some of the writers labeled the area of the Great Morava and the northern section of the South Morava as the Bulgarian desert. It kept that designation over the next century, because of its

---

[18] Aleksandar Uzelac, "Zapadnite pătešestvenici v 'Deserta Bulgariae' predi Părvija krăstonosen pohod," *Epohi* 25, no. 1 (2017): 196–9.
[19] Rudolf Hiestand, "Precipua tocius christianismi columpna: Barbarossa und der Kreuzzug," in *Friedrich Barbarossa: Handlungsspielräume und Wirkungsweisen des staufischen Kaisers*, ed. Alfred Haverkamp (Sigmaringen: Thorbecke, 1992), 91–101; Carz Hummel, *Nach Jerusalem! Heinrich der Löwe und Friedrich Barbarossa auf Kreuzfahrt* (Wedemark: Welfenschriften, 2012); Vladimir Aleksić, "Das Treffen von Stefan Nemanja und Friedrich Barbarossa und die Verhältnisse der personalen Bindung in Südost Europa in der zweiten Hälfte des 12. Jahrhunderts," (in preparation).
[20] Uzelac, *Srbi i krstaši*, 52, 57, 66, 108, 127–8, 159–62; Larnach, "All Roads Lead to Constantinople," 145–6, 263–4.
[21] Uzelac, *Srbi i krstaši*, 14, with the most extensive overview of the written sources.

impenetrability due to the dense vegetation and few inhabitants.[22] According to the widespread notion, the Byzantines had transformed the area bordering the northern section of Via Militaris into a vast, scarcely inhabited buffer zone to protect the northern borders of the empire from frequent Hungarian attacks during the eleventh and twelfth centuries.[23] However, as we are going to find out later, basic research has indicated that some development was happening in this area, as well. Furthermore, according to the theory based on the travel descriptions during the first three crusades, the increase in traffic in the eleventh and twelfth centuries had an impact on the road surface, causing its rapid deterioration towards the end of that period.[24] It does not mean that the Byzantine authorities did not pay attention to this strategically important area, but they most probably put their emphasis on the several fortified strongholds that were spaced along the route, and these could help preserve Byzantine power, rather than the quality of the roads.

Those travel reports that are the result of personal perception offer better insight into the features of road infrastructure and its relation to the shifting landscape and settlement network along the road and the changing of political borders. John Kinammos, who was the confidante of the Byzantine Emperor and an educated scholar, wrote about them. Manuel I Komnenos (1143–1180) frequently stayed in the Great Morava river valley to prevent joint Hungarian and Serbian military movements in this part of his empire. John Kinammos, as an eyewitness to the campaign conducted in 1150, confirms once again that Niš was the point of departure for the Byzantine military actions against the rebellions in Serbia. To gather animal fodder, the scouts of the imperial troops advanced to the north, along the Great Morava river. After a skirmish, the overpowered Hungarian soldiers as well as their pursuers faced the challenge of how to cross to the other side. They decided to cross the river south of the city of Paraćin, which stretched along the right bank of the waterway, at the what is today the village of Nevidovo (previously called Gornje Vidovo and Donje Vidovo). The area was called Stri-

---

[22] Francesco Dall'Aglio, "'In ipsa silva longissima Bulgariae': Western Chroniclers of the Crusades and the Bulgarian Forest," *Bulgaria Mediaevalis* 1 (2010): 405–18. See also: Uzelac, *Srbi i krstaši*, 14–6, with an additional attempt to trace the origin of the ethnic component of this name.

[23] Uzelac, "Zapadnite pătešestvenici," 196–202; Boris Stojkovski, "Niš u vizantijsko-ugarskim odnosima u XI i XII veku," *Niš i Vizantija* 7 (2008): 383–94; Larnach, "All Roads Lead to Constantinople," 3–4, 12; Uzelac, *Srbi i krstaši*, 14–5.

[24] Larnach, "All Roads Lead to Constantinople," 144.

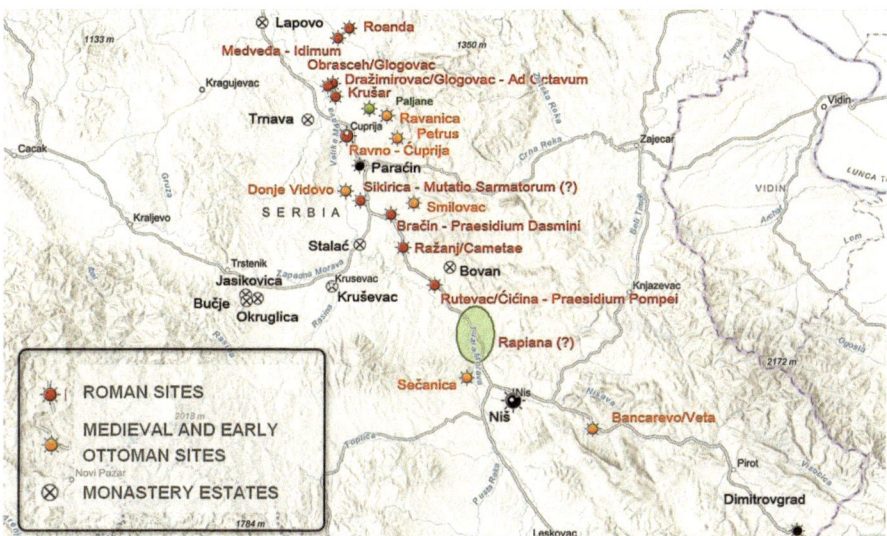

Fig. 2: Map showing the east section and fragment of the northern section of the Via Militaris. Cartography by Vladimir Aleksić.

mon by the Byzantine scholar John Kinammos, and Zastruma in a Serbian fourteenth-century charter.[25]

The fact that several toponyms mentioned here have kept their names until modern day speaks in favor of a gradual stabilization of the demographic structure at that time. A further statement from the well-informed John Kinammos speaks in support of this idea. The region of Smilis, presumably related to the contemporary village of Smilovac, or Smilovci as it was called in the fourteenth century, is located north-east from Stalać, and was well fortified in the middle of the twelfth century.[26] However, what is less clear is the character of the perma-

---

[25] "Jovan Kinam," trans. Jovanka Kalić and Nina Radošević-Maksimović, in *Vizantijski izvori za istoriju naroda Jugoslavije* (Belgrade: Vizantološki institut SANU, 20072), 4:29; Miloš Blagojević, "Sečenica (ΣΕΤΖΕΝΙΤΖΑ) Strimon (ΣΤΡΥΜΩΝ) i Tara (ΤΑΡΑ) u delu Jovana Kinama," *Zbornik radova Vizantološkog instituta* 17 (1976): 67–9; Rade Mihaljčić, "Hrisovulja cara Uroša Manastiru Hilandaru," *Stari srpski arhiv* 4 (2005): 159.

[26] Uzelac, *Srbi i krstaši*, 133; Surprisingly, the above mentioned Roman road stations in the villages of Sikirica, Bračin and Ražanj are only a few hours walk distance from the village of Smilovac, which indicates possible mutual interconnection. This finding is consistent with recent archaeological prospects suggesting the existence of a well-organized defence system in the area where the Great Morava is formed during the period from the tenth to the twelfth century, including the fortification in the village of Smilovci. See, Savić and Đokić, "Kontinuitet antičkih komunikacija," 61–2.

nent logistical support required to provide the crews of the fortresses with supplies and some specialized services, as well with the repeated (re)construction of the city walls and towers and accompanying buildings. In the literature about medieval Serbia, researchers usually associate these tasks with the presence of local peasants and at least a few skilled workers. In the late medieval period, semi-professional road keepers were appointed to watch out over such terrain which offered bandits the greatest opportunity to plunder.[27]

3 Military Camps

As mentioned in the same source, a vast military camp near the village of Sečanica was capable of accommodating a robust imperial army.[28] There are reasons to believe that it was a permanent and gradually upgraded complex, which was used on several occasions during and most probably after Byzantine rule. The location of the site near to Niš where the roads fork in at least five directions was strategically important. Kinammos tells us that the emperor set the camp near Niš precisely between two roads during the 1163 campaign. One of them was suitable for launching an offensive against the Serbs to the west and the other one against the Hungarians to the north. The camp presumably included many facilities designed to raise the combat capability and morale of the soldiers. For instance, the very same Byzantine historian describes the army tents surrounded by newly dug trenches, apparently pretty deep and broad, in which the disobedient Serbian leader called Desa (who ruled briefly in the middle of the twelfth century) was under the permanent custody of the imperial guard. This political incident allegedly caught the attention of the local population, which then started to call the ditches after the name of the person who was detained there, effectively turning it into a small local landmark.[29]

---

27 Srđan Šarkić, "The Legal Status of Villagers in Mediaeval Serbia," *Acta Universitatis Szegediensis: Acta juridica et politica* 75 (2013): 586–7; Aleksandra Fostikov and Vladeta Petrović, "Prilog proučavanju vojne uloge zanatlija u srednjovekovnoj Srbiji," *Beogradski istorijski glasnik* 5 (2014): 63.
28 Blagojević, "Sečenica," 68–70; Vladimir Aleksić, "'Gradski metoh' Niša po turskim izvorima," *Zbornik radova Filozofskog fakulteta Kosovska Mitrovica* 34 (2003): 309, note 61. The local oral traditions recorded recently in the villages Gornji and Donji Komren give similar facts and bring together the name of two villages with the famous Byzantine dynasty of Komnenos. Although the suggested locations are very close to the modern highway and in the vicinity to Sečanica, it might have been influenced by the information coming from recent scientific results.
29 "Jovan Kinam," in *Vizantijski izvori za istoriju naroda Jugoslavije*, 4:62–3.

When thinking of these episodes, it should be pointed out that in the middle of the fourteenth century there was still nothing unusual for the rulers and other high-ranking dignitaries, during summertime, to periodically stay in the camps, which were well-equipped with additional conveniences. In August 1342, negotiations lasting several weeks between the Serbian king Stephan Dušan (1331–1455) and the exiled Byzantine throne candidate John Kantakouzenos (1347–1354) took place under similar conditions, in tents.[30] It is possible that the described facility near Niš was merely a continuation of the practice of marching camps, called *aplêkta* in Greek, which were mentioned as being in Asia Minor along the main military routes from the mid-seventh century on.[31]

Even after the full retreat of the Byzantine Empire from the basin of the Great and South Morava rivers in the middle of the thirteenth century, the camp may still have been in use. In the fourteenth century, the Serbian-Bulgarian border stretched approximately along these two rivers. The Serbs waited for the Bulgarian army in the region of Niš on the eve of the battle of Velbužd on 28 July 1330. The Serbian king Stephan Dečanski (1321–1431) deployed his army in the fertile plains of Dobrič Polje, on the left shore of the South Morava river, opposite to Niš. The previously mentioned village of Sečanica was within the borders of this small geographical region, too.[32] This circumstance raises the question of whether he also used the above-mentioned Byzantine camp.

In addition to that, there were areas in medieval Serbia where trade caravans and even armies frequently stayed to recover their strength. They were called *padalište*, literally meaning the place where travelers "fall down" or "land" after a whole day's journey. According to one opinion, these were areas with covered shelters. In the relative safety of these facilities, the cargo could be unloaded and the animals fed. One such place, named Carevo Padalište, was on the mountain of Kunovica in the vicinity of the villages of Bancarevo and Veta to the east of Niš, and it was related to the early Ottoman period.[33] Later, during the 1521 campaign, Süleyman the Magnificent (r. 1520–1566) established his military camp in the village called Lupic/Lupac near to Niška Banja, whose exact location

---

30 "Jovan Kantakuzin," trans. Franjo Barišić and Božidar Ferjančić, in *Vizantijski izvori za istoriju naroda Jugoslavije* (Belgrade: Vizantološki institut SANU, 1986), 6:386–90.
31 Haldon, "Roads and Communications," 141.
32 Marija Koprivica, "Dobrič Polje u srednjem veku," in *Stefan Nemanja i Toplica (tematski zbornik)*, ed. Dragiša Bojović (Niš: Centar za crkvene studije, 2011): 123, 125.
33 Škrivanić, *Putevi u srednjovekovnoj Srbiji*, 27–8, 91.

remains unknown.³⁴ All of these sites are to be found very close to each other, so that a possible correlation might be found amongst them.

Furthermore, based on what has been said about large scale military camps, it seems that they shared some similar characteristics over several centuries. The resting areas were established at the town's periphery and exactly on or in the close vicinity to the major roads. Taken together, at least two spacious locations on its east and western edges capable of accommodating many troops flanked Niš. From among all the situations when these camps were used, we want to mention a single event which took place in August 1458. After the initial successes of the Serbian Despotate, the supreme commander of the Ottoman troops in Europe, Mahmud Pasha Angelović, established his camp on the field near Niš, but its exact location remains unknown. However, soon the Ottoman army marched against the strategically important Golubac on the Danube. According to the Ottoman historian Tursun Bey, Mahmud Pasha and his troops marched two days and one night to reach their destination at dawn.³⁵

We always have to bear in mind that many factors influenced the time needed to cover the same distance, such as the terrain or the means of transportation.³⁶ When we compare the case of Mahmud Pasha with similar reports from other centuries, it turns out that it is virtually impossible to estimate the average time required to travel this section of the Via Militaris.³⁷ The small data-set, which mostly consists of travel reports, suggests that a gradual improvement took place due to overall social progress in the late Middle Ages compared to earlier centuries. This would have included greater physical security for the traveller, easier provision with food and transport facilities. In other words, negotiating the same distance most likely did not necessarily take less time in the late Middle Ages as compared to the previous eras for the reason that the primary means of transportation remained the same. However, regional and long-

---

34 Aleksić, "'Gradski metoh' Niša," 309, note 60; Zirojević, *Carigradski drum*, 177–80, and 36, where the toponym in question is attributed to the vicinal villages of Gornja and Donja Studena, located more to the west from Veta and Bancarevo. For Lupac, see Koprivica, "Niška oblast," 16, 54.

35 Miljković and Krstić, *Braničevo*, 317–8; Aleksandar Krstić, "Pad Srbije iz ugla osvajača: Ašik-pašazade i Dursun-Beg," in *Pad Srpske Despotovine 1459. godine*, ed. Momčilo Spremić (Belgrade: Srpska akademija nauka i umetnosti, 2011), 312–4. There was a road connecting the medieval towns of Braničevo and Golubac via the contemprary municipality of Veliko Gradište; see Miljković and Krstić, *Braničevo*, 246.

36 Škrivanić, *Putevi u srednjovekovnoj Srbiji*, 40–2.

37 Zirojević, *Carigradski drum*, 35, 37–40; Krstić, *Ponišavlje*, 99; Larnach, "All Roads Lead to Constantinople," 26–7, 31, 48, 72–3, 87, 127–8, 135, 138–41, 144, 146, 173, 177–8, 182, 225, 253, 263–73, 279–83; Uzelac, *Srbi i krstaši*, 28, 52, 56, 74, 62, 65–6, 93, 108, 10, 112–3, 115–7, 126, 153.

distance travel activity became more popular and significantly less stressful, increasingly involving more people belonging to quite varied social groups or professions.

4 The Via Militaris in the Late Middle Ages

Impressed by the informative eleventh- and twelfth-century descriptions of the desolate landscape in the region of the Great Morava river, many scholars concluded that almost nothing changed until the end of the medieval era with regard to the demographic situation. As indicated previously, the number of permanent settlements probably was increasing near the city of Paraćin already by the middle of the twelfth century. To label the unfavorable demographic situation in the same region, a mid-fourteenth-century Serbian charter used the term Petruška pustinja, i.e., the Desert of Petrus, which was the name of the local fortress. A closer examination of this charter and other domestic medieval documents indicates, however, that a continuous flow of "internal colonization" entirely transformed the demographic, social and economic characteristics in this section of the Serbian realm. Where the unpleasant marshlands and impenetrable forests previously were the primary feature of the landscape, a network of rural settlements slowly emerged. In many cases, these settlements so developed and increased in size that the boundaries of villages were physically touching each other. In this way, the village communities left only a limited space for the relicts of the past landscape, namely, the oak tree groves or the wetlands near the rivers or low-land lakes.[38] The former were frequently left undisrupted, because they were valuable for cattle breeding and, even more importantly, the pigs were fed with acorns. So, they were the source of income for their owners, who predominantly belonged to privileged social groups.[39] Due to the advancing reforestation which took place during the Little Ice Age (ca. 1550–1850), we are

---

[38] Rade Mihaljčić, "Selišta: Prilog istoriji naselja u srednjovekovnoj srpskoj državi," in *Prošlost i narodno sećanje*, ed. Mile S. Bavrlić (Belgrade: Gutenbergova galaksija, 1995), 131–91; Rade Mihaljčić, "Hrisovulja cara Uroša Manastiru Hilandaru," *Stari srpski arhiv* 4 (2004): 151–60; Siniša Mišić, "Zaselci u srednjovekovnoj Srbiji," *Beogradski istorijski glasnik* 4 (2013): 47–8. The assumption of an undeveloped Balkan unfortunately is still represented in the esteemed recent thesis by Larnach, "All Roads Lead to Constantinople," 13. An overview of the demographic and environmental situation is available in Aleksandar Krstić, "Podunavlje i Posavina Srbije u poznom srednjem veku: Istorijsko-geografski aspekti istraživanja," in *Istorija i geografija: Usreti i prožimanja, tematski zbornik radova*, ed. Sofija Božić (Belgrade: Geografski institut Jovan Cvijić SANU, INIS, Institut za slavistiku RAN, 2014), 23–39; Mrgić, Landscape and Settlements, 69–87.
[39] Mišić, "Dubrave u srednjovekovnoj Srbiji," 95–103; Miljković and Krstić, *Braničevo*, 158, 235.

familiar with several vivid descriptions from the modern era of seemingly endless oak forests in the historical region of Šumadija.⁴⁰ The last preserve of these consists of approximately three-hundred-year-old trees surviving in the secluded protected marshy area of 19 hectares (47 acres) close to the mouth of the Great Morava river into the Danube near the villages of Šalinac and Kulič.⁴¹

Furthermore, during the late Middle Ages and early Ottoman era, some of the villages acquired some proto-urban features transforming them into settlements classified in modern scholarship as unprotected market towns. According to a recent theory, such settlements on average clustered between 20 and 35 villages, having approximately 2000 to 4000 inhabitants and covered an area whose borders were no more than one to four hours of walking distance and separated by no more than 18 kilometers. This remarkable change is partially a result of the influence of the northern segments of Via Militaris. Most likely this resulted in the relatedness of these towns, Lučica, Starci and Orašje, in that all of them are located on the road, as well as with many others in the historical region of Braničevo.⁴² As suggested in this chapter on several occasions, the stabilization of the demographic situation in this region was a foundation for many positive processes such as the sustainability of state organization and the progressive administrative division, which generally favored any rudimentary attempts to logistically organize and support travel and transport activities.

Due to the language barrier, non-Serbian speaking authors usually neglect the information related to the Via Militaris preserved in local charters. For example, the grant issued by Duke Lazar (r. 1378–1389) to the Monastery of Ravanica indicates that at least two sections of the ancient road still served its original purpose. They formed the limits of the villages Gornja Živica (today Živica near the city of Požarevac) and the Dubnica, located to the north-east to the city of Svilajnac. The road was called Veliki put, i.e. Major Road, which means

---

40 Larnach, "All Roads Lead to Constantinople," 143–4; Mrgić, *Zemlja i ljudi*, 53–4.
41 Cf. https://en.wikipedia.org/wiki/%C5%A0alinac_Grove, last accessed 4 June 2019.
42 Miljković and Krstić, *Braničevo*, 86–88; Aleksandar Krstić, "Srednjovekovni trgovi i osmanski pazari u Braničevu: Kontinuitet i promene," in *Moravska Srbija: Istorija, kultura, umetnost*, ed. Siniša Mišić (Kruševac: Istorijski arhiv Kruševac, Odeljenje za istoriju Filozofskog fakulteta u Beogradu, 2007), 95–113, especially 108. Regarding the size of the urban settlements and geographical limits of trade activities (local, regional and interregional) in the Middle Ages, see Dagron, "The Urban Economy," 2:394–495; Cécile Morrisson, "Introduction," in *Trade and Markets in Byzantium*, ed. ead. (Washington, DC: Harvard University Press, 2002), 4–5.

that it was not a simple caravan or more common local road, which themselves also left their mark in historical topography.[43]

Recently, the shifting character of the road network in the historical and geographical region of Šumadija in the fifteenth century, which borders to the west on the Great Morava river, has become more apparent. Traveling was to some extent dependent on economic changes, such as the increase of mining and trade activity as well as growing urbanization. The latter included the creation of the new Serbian capital towns in Belgrade and Smederevo in 1404 and 1430 respectively, which motivated numerous merchants from Serbia and abroad to permanently or temporarily settle down there. Additionally, the creation of new road options in the described geographical area was triggered by the steady Ottoman territorial advance. Travelers in general were looking for roads which kept them out of the Ottoman realm as much as possible. The most remarkable change happened due to a partial abandoning of the ancient road that mostly stretched along the right bank of the Great and South Morava rivers. Although it was still used both for military and civilian purposes, as the book *De itineribus in Turciam libellus* attributed to Martin Segon testifies, new itineraries gradually emerged on the left bank of the Great Morava river. Their usage was first recorded in the book of Bertrandon de la Brocquière which describes his trip through several Ottoman provinces in 1433. The connecting points of the route chosen by him were the towns of Kruševac and Stalać, followed by the court complex of the Serbian Despot called Nekudim near contemporary Smederevska Palanka. From here, he reached Belgrade after a day and a half long trip. The road forked in Smederevska Palanka: to Belgrade or Smederevo or to the Hungarian city of Kovin, depending on the desired destination. The first of two options included the passage through the village of Grocka. It was on this new road that the majority of the military and civil transport took place in the early Ottoman period. Those voyagers who wanted to go to Belgrade crossed over the river Morava near the city of Paraćin. The traveler heading to the north would encounter the villages of Kolare and Batočina before reaching the small town of Smederevska Palanka. It was established by the Ottomans to additionally protect the travelers and initially was called Hasan Pasha Palanka (Fig. 1). Generally speaking, the new route was shorter and therefore preferable to the traditional roads located

---

43 Siniša Mišić and Aleksandar Uzelac, "Putevi i trgovina," in *Šumadija u 15. veku: Kolektivna monografija*, ed. Siniša Mišić and Marija Koprivica (Belgrade, 2018), 278; Miljković and Krstić, *Braničevo*, 132–3, 158, 246, 249.

on the right bank of the Great Morava, as described in the previous sections. However, the latter still served their purpose, but with lower intensity.[44]

One of the critical and yet only partially answered questions is what and if any additional support the travelers could expect during the journey. To make travel more comfortable and safer, the most significant monasteries in late medieval Serbia usually had facilities along the roads which connected the different parts of their big estates. This may have been the case with the monastery of Saint Panteleimon from Mount Athos, as seen in the grant at the end of the fourteenth century. The monks had possessions of different types close to the juncture of the three Moravas (Fig. 2). These were as follows: a church in a village of Bučje accompanied by three nearby villages, Jasikovica, Okruglica, and Trnava (the latter near the contemporary town of Jagodina); the market town of Hlapova Poljana, which is now the center of the municipality of Lapovo; individual serfs inhabited the fortified cities of Bolvan, near to the contemporary villages of Bovan, Kruševac, and Stalać. The structure and geographical positions of the benefices were presumably deliberately chosen, considering that some of them were only a one-day walking distance from each other. Therefore, they may have created a network of mutually connected nodes providing for travelers related to the monastery, both the monks as well as their servants, offering various accommodation options.[45]

There was nothing uncommon about this, as many legal documents in medieval Serbia authorized a similar practice. The dependent inhabitants of each village all over the country were required to jointly provide accommodation and one meal during a short stay of the ruler's dignitaries and helpers of different ranks. For instance, kennel men, falconers, and swineherds, messengers or even eminent diplomats could stay in any given village when they were performing their public tasks. The same rule applied to their horses, which had to be fed with oats and other fodder on the same occasion. These two liabilities were called *obrok* (literally meal) and *pozob* (from *zob* = oat) respectively. Presumably,

---

[44] Zirojević, *Carigradski drum*, 20–35; Škrivanić, *Putevi u srednjovekovnoj Srbiji*, 92–3; Mišić and Uzelac, "Putevi i trgovina," 278–88. The communication on the west-east axis located near the village of Dubnica may have served as a connection between two parallel branches of Via Militaris, see Miljković and Krstić, *Braničevo*, 246. It has been suggested that one more river crossing functioned near to the village of Žabare in the late Middle Ages. See, Savić and Đokić, "Kontinuitet antičkih komunikacija," 55–6.

[45] Nebojša Đokić, "Neka zapažanja o likovima na živopisu Veluće," in *Vlast i moć: Vlastela Moravske Srbije od 1365. do 1402. godine*, ed. Siniša Mišić (Kruševac: Narodna biblioteka Kruševac, Centar za istorijsku geografiju i istorijsku demografiju Filozofskog fakulteta Univerziteta u Beogradu, 2014), 374. Furthermore, the charter implies the increase of the intensity of the travel activities between the two remote regions, i.e. northern Greece and central Serbia.

it was much harder for the serfs to accomplish work duty (burden) called *ponos*, i.e., providing the rulers and his court entourage with a transport service when they were crossing through the country.⁴⁶

Riding animals were an essential part of the equation when it comes to the travel of high-ranking notables of the most important monasteries. Therefore, professional shepherds, frequently chosen from among the dependent Vlach population, were responsible for the full-blooded horses of the rulers, the highest nobility, and the most significant imperial monasteries going back to the beginning of the thirteenth century. The training of these saddle horses and war horses lasted for three years, from the age of two until five, and it was primarily skilled horse keepers who conducted it.⁴⁷ Also a few members of a dependent agricultural population called *sokalnik* escorted esteemed monks while traveling across the land. One can imagine them helping their master to mount or dismount on the riding animals or taking care of the luggage. To secure the caravan members, a few members of lesser nobility (*vlasteličić* and *pronijar*) rode with them as well, accompanied by some number of Vlach soldiers.⁴⁸

The transport system had further extensions within the same social and economic environment. The so-called Poor Vlachs were breeders of smaller but very robust horses for transport purposes. We should differentiate between underprivileged members of this social group, who were more numerous than the wealthier Vlachs, the latter being allowed to carry arms and enjoy more privileges.⁴⁹ Being the owners of abundant flocks of small cattle and herds of cows, they seasonally migrated from their lowland settlements to the proximate high mountain pastures, which was not possible without horses capable of carrying heavy weights. Therefore, the low-ranking Vlachs were ideal for providing both their secular and ecclesiastical lords with different types of transport services as a part of their work duty. This practice firmly linked all kinds of different commer-

---

46 Marko Šuica, "Ponos," in *Leksikon srpskog srednjeg veka*, ed. Sima Ćirković and Rade Mihaljčić (Belgrade: Knowledge, 1999), 552; Šarkić, "The Legal Status," 585–6.
47 Siniša Mišić, "Konjusi: Prilog socijalnoj strukturi srpskog srednjovekovnog društva," *Beogradski istorijski glasnik* 6 (2015): 91–7. Vlachs had a distinctive social and tax status in medieval Serbia and Southeast Europe. The members of this social group practiced nomadic and semi-nomadic pastoral life, although in a process of sedentarization many Vlach communities settled down permanently in the late Middle Ages. Consequently, the ethnic differences between the Vlach, deriving from the Romanized native population, and Slavic inhabitants were significantly diminishing at that time. See, D. Dinić-Knežević, "Vlasi," in *Leksikon srpskog srednjeg veka*, 86–7.
48 Vladimir Aleksić, "Medieval Vlach Soldiers and the Beginnings of Ottoman Voynuks," *Beogradski istorijski glasnik* 2 (2011): 105–28.
49 Škrivanić, *Putevi u srednjovekovnoj Srbiji*, 30–1.

cial and administrative centres at distant locations within the realm of Serbia. Although there are no direct written references to similar activities along the Via Militaris, one may easily imagine a similar situation there, too.[50]

Let us now turn to improvements in travel methods caused by some gradual technical development in the late Middle Age. There is direct and indirect (but compelling) information on the frequent use of horse and ox wagons both by the local population as well as by foreigners when visiting this part of the world (for the most different of reasons).[51] Transport by wagon was of great importance, especially when the transportation of heavy loads could not be hauled effectively by horses, mules, donkeys or even camels.[52] The resident population presumably used just the local road sections.[53] In contrast, the eleventh and twelfth-century crusaders and the fifteenth-century western Christian armies had to carry with them numerous carriages along the whole route. Unsurprisingly, the common complaint found frequently in the texts describing these journeys was that these were not the most suitable means of transportation.[54] The Hungarians, allied with the neighboring military powers, undertook campaigns against the Ottoman Turks in 1443–1444 and 1448. In both cases, application of the *tabor* tactic, which included the use of thousands of battle carriages as well as regular wagons, would not have even been conceived in the first place without a clear awareness that the road network in Southeast Europe was appropriate for that kind of endeavor.[55] The most famous march into the heart of the

---

[50] Ibid., 25–6.
[51] Zirojević, *Carigradski drum*, 56–65; Škrivanić, *Putevi u srednjovekovnoj Srbiji*, 16–7, 30–5; Larnach, "All Roads Lead to Constantinople," 274, 290.
[52] The issue of human interaction with animals for transport recently has attracted more attention, cf. Esad Kurtović, "Magarci u dubrovačkom zaleđu," *Inicijal: Časopis za srednjovekovne studije* 1 (2013): 137–58; Esad Kurtović, *Konj u srednjovjekovnoj Bosni* (Sarajevo: CIP, 2014); Aleksandar Uzelac, "Kamile u srpskim srednjovekovnim zemljama," *Inicijal: Časopis za srednjovekovne studije* 3 (2015): 23–34.
[53] As witnessed by Brocquière on the mountain located to the east to Niš in 1433, see Popović, *Von Budapest nach Istanbul*, 130–1.
[54] Haldon, "Roads and Communications," 140–1; Elena Koytcheva, "Logistical Problems for the Movement of the Early Crusades through the Balkans: Transport and Road System," in *Proceedings of the 21st International Congress of Byzantine Studies, London, 21–26 August*, ed. Elizabeth Jeffreys (Aldershot: Ashgate, 2006), 1:54; Elena Koytcheva, "Logistics of the Early Crusades in the Balkans on Via Militaris," in *Die Vielschichtigkeit der Straße: Kontinuität und Wandel im Mittelalter und der frühen Neuzeit*, ed. Kornelia Holzner Tobisch, Thomas Kühtreiber and Gertrud Blaschitz (Vienna: Verlag der Österreichischen Akademie der Wissenschaften, 2012): 209–32; Larnach, "All Roads Lead to Constantinople," 3, 77–8, 273–7.
[55] John Jefferson, *The Holy Wars of King Wladislas and Sultan Murad: The Ottoman-Christian Conflicts from 1438–1444* (Leiden: Brill, 2012), 206–9.

Ottoman Empire happened in 1443/1444. The crusaders used the Via Militaris to penetrate deep into Ottoman territory. The valleys and gorges along this narrow stretch of land were again the place of clashes between the armies of most different origins from Europe and Asia. With the rapid advance of military techniques and especially with the vast production of small firearms, new strategies developed. This time, the crusaders were hoping that battle wagons could bring them an advantage against agile, light Ottoman cavalry and the disciplined janissaries. Based on the experiences acquired during the Hussite wars waged in the contemporary Czech Republic just a few years earlier, the Christian ground troops were equipped with the special carriages that could quickly transform into an open field bastion, the so-called *wagenburg,* or temporary night camp providing shelter and security from sudden enemy attacks. Small guns and crossbows were responsible for the additional protection of its crew.[56]

5 River-Crossing

Travelers for the most part could cross rivers effortlessly during the late Middle Ages. Yet the historical data do not always clearly depict this. After the troops of Friedrich Barbarossa had crossed the Great Morava river, a military camp was erected in the fields surrounding the city of Braničevo. This is where the river flows into the Danube and where the examined section of Via Militaris started. The fact that the Hungarian military leader John Hunyadi's army used the ferries over the Danube near the city of Kovin in 1448 indicates that the vessels of this kind had notable transport capacities. After having crossed the big river, he positioned his troops near the market town of Subotica, again in the Braničevo District.[57] Other historical sources, for example, Bertrandon de la Brocquière in 1433, Serbian medieval charters and early Ottoman *defter*s mention many ferries along this route.[58] They were the obvious choice when it came to crossing untamed rivers, which spilt over their swampy shores and flooded nearby flat terrain and sometimes even changed their bed for many hundreds of meters from their previous position. In this respect, it seems that the Vojinovića Bridge in the modern city of Vučitrn, which is an early fifteenth-century structure, did not serve its pur-

---

56 Ibid., 213–5.
57 Uzelac, *Srbi i krstaši*, 155.
58 The term *brod* means equally the river section convenient for crossing to the other bank as well as the floating structures capable of transporting people and goods without getting them wet in exchange for a reasonable fee, see Siniša Mišić, "Brod," in *Leksikon srpskog srednjeg veka*, 64–5. For the ubication of some of them see Miljković and Krstić, *Braničevo*, 243–4.

pose for a long time, because the river Sitnica changed its course leaving the bridge "shipwrecked" in the middle of dry land.[59]

Nonetheless, it should be pointed out that several physical remains of medieval bridges or many written pieces of evidence contradict the general assumption that the Serbian medieval authorities were not capable or willing to invest a significant amount of money and resources into the costly buildings that would make it possible to cross the expanse of water easily.[60]

Bridges can also serve as a case to test the thesis of there being a continuity in transport and communication infrastructure from the Roman to medieval times. Regarding the Via Militaris, the case study of ancient Horeum Margum, which is the medieval city of Ravno, i.e., the contemporary town or Ćuprija, is instructive. It seems that the bridge within its urban core survived for many centuries after the collapse of the Roman Empire. There are no direct references to this object in the medieval period, except perhaps a vague account in a book from John Mandeville. The compilation made by this unknown author, most probably between 1365 and September 1371, contains a fantastic, and more importantly, imaginary description of a world trip that never took place. Although the section devoted to the central Balkans is usually attributed to the eleventh-century manuscript of Albert of Aix-la-Chapelle, it is most likely that Mandeville also used some other sources. That is the reason why it appears that the report attributed to John Mandeville offers a better insight into the transport situation between Belgrade and Niš in the eleventh and twelfth century. Namely, it states that Belgrade was the entering point into the land of the Bulgarians, where a stone bridge ran over the river Marrok. Following the path, the traveler would later encounter the Land of Pechenegs, and the city of Serdica in Greece. In one version of the book, the latter has been replaced with the toponym of Nye, which some researchers identify as Niš.[61] The metrical version of Mandeville's book contains an account of the city of Belgrade in the fifteenth century, and it is slightly discordant with other redactions of the same book, because it names the mysterious river Marraone.[62] The idea that the bridge mentioned in Mandeville's book was the stone bridge over the Nišava river, which is a right tributary to the Southern Morava, and in front of the fortress of Niš, sounds

---

59 Siniša Mišić, "Mostovi," in *Leksikon srpskog srednjeg veka*, 419.
60 Škrivanić, *Putevi u srednjovekovnoj Srbiji*, 21–3, 18–9.
61 Aleksandar Uzelac, "Od Engleske do Konstantinopolja u Knjizi čudesa sveta Jovana Mandevila," in *Moravska Srbija: Istorija, kultura, umetnost*, ed. Siniša Mišić (Kruševac: Istorijski arhiv Kruševac, Odeljenje za istoriju Filozofskog fakulteta Beograd, 2007), 197–211, escpecially 202–6.
62 Aleksandar Uzelac and Bojana Radovanović, "Jedan opis Beograda i jugoistočne Evrope u engleskoj književnosti XV veka," *Beogradski istorijski glasnik* 3 (2012): 259–62.

rather reliable. However, the famous book of geography written by the twelfth-century Arab scholar Idrisi also testifies to the existence of a bridge over the Morava, without specifying its precise location.[63] In the eleventh century, to increase defensive capacities, the government of Constantinople settled groups of Pechenegs, a semi-nomadic Turkic people, in flat and less inhabited regions of the Balkan peninsula, including the basins along the whole Via Militaris. However, Mandeville's book places the geographical location of this ethnic group (*terre de* Pincemarcz, the *lande* of Pyncerasse) in the urban areas of Belgrade and Niš.[64] Having this in mind as well as the revised corpus of available data on this topic, I would propose a new reading that the described bridge may have actually been in Ravno, which is the contemporary town of Ćuprija.[65]

One may presume that two bridges significantly contributed to the cities of Niš and Ravno in their transition period during the early Middle Ages, as testified to by many other constructions across the former Roman world.[66] It is possible that they were the foundation of urban expansion of the two settlements around the tenth and eleventh centuries. At the same time, the local community as well as the authorities—be they Bulgarian, Byzantine, Serbian, or Ottoman—must have carefully maintained these bridges on which they were so dependent through the centuries.[67] However, in contrast to the city of Niš, it seems that the urban structure of Ravno decayed after the establishment of the Serbian-Hungarian borderline only a few kilometers to the north, when the basin of the Great Morava river was divided by two regional powers who replaced the By-

---

63 Aleksić, "'Gradski metoh' Niša," 311–2; Uzelac, "Od Engleske do Konstantinopolja," 202–6.
64 Aleksandar Uzelac, "Čuvaj se Belijalovih sinova i otrovnih strela! Pomoravlje u drugoj polovini XII veka," in *Stefan Nemanja i Toplica (tematski zbornik)*, ed. Dragiša Bojović (Niš: Centar za crkvene studije, 2011), 97–107; Miloš Antonović, "Etnička kretanja u Pomoravlju u XI i XII veku," in *Moravska Srbija: Istorija, kultura, umetnost*, ed. Siniša Mišić (Kruševac: Istorijski arhiv Kruševac, Odeljenje za istoriju Filozofskog fakulteta u Beogradu, 2007), 73–84; Uzelac, *Srbi i krstaši*, 93, 136–40.
65 It has been suggested that the stone bridge described in Mandeville's book was located near to the contemporary town of Požarevac, which is now the most significant urban settlement in the Braničevo region, see, Larnach, "All Roads Lead to Constantinople," 133. However, Požarevac does not have an urban history in the Middle Ages, see, Miljković and Krstić, *Braničevo*, 50–1, 125.
66 Haldon, "Roads and Communications," 138–9.
67 Aleksić, "'Gradski metoh' Niša," 312, note 79. The stone bridge over the Nišava witnessed heavy fighting between the residents of Niš and the crusaders in 1093, see Uzelac, *Srbi i krstaši*, 57–60. Within the contemporary city core, the remains of three Roman bridges spanning the Gabrovačka Reka River on the road heading to Sofia have been determined, see, Zirojević, *Carigradski drum*, 36; also cf. Dragana Amedoski and Jovana Šaljić, "Most na Nišavi u osmansko doba," *Niški zbornik* 16–17 (2008): 140–145.

zantine authority at the beginning of the thirteenth century. Because of the frequent hostilities and the political instability in the Great Morava valley, travel and trade activities related to Ravno significantly diminished after the first half of the thirteenth century.[68] Consequently, the town gradually lost its urban appearances and the Ottoman document from 1476–1478 categorized it only as a village with a ferry. The local bridge was again rebuilt sometime before 1658.[69] Several documents dating from the early modern period and contemporary archaeological surveys record the remains of the Roman bridge in Ćuprija and its precise location.[70] It must have been maintained and repeatedly renovated since it is hard to believe that if it had been at some point a thoroughly derelict structure, it would have been so well preserved through the centuries, while exposed to the elements and erosive river currents.

Furthermore, it has become clear that it was the obligation of the local authorities in the middle and late Byzantine period to maintain the local infrastructure, including the fortifications, bridges and the strategically most important roads.[71] Written reports made by early modern travelers on relatively well-preserved remnants of the old road infrastructure are most frequent in the vicinity of the cities along the south segment of the investigated route. The possibly stronger effect of the soil erosion or the massive accumulation of the river's sand deposits to the north is not the sole reason for this situation. It is possible that the majority of travelers frequently diverted from the ancient roads. Therefore, they would become aware of its ruins only in the vicinity of the old Roman cities which had endured more or less uninterrupted until the modern era, where they just could not be avoided. A case in point is the journey of Antun Vrančić.[72]

---

[68] Aleksandar Uzelac, "Ravno," in *Leksikon gradova i trgova srpskih srednjovekovnih srpskih zemalja*, ed. Siniša Mišić (Belgrade: Zavod za udžbenike, 2010), 235.

[69] Zirojević, *Carigradski drum*, 27.

[70] Škrivanić, *Putevi u srednjovekovnoj Srbiji*, 84. Also cf. the oral presentation delivered by Dorotée Poirier from the Montaigne University of Bordeaux during the third session of the Student Seminar Stojan Novaković at the University of Niš.

[71] Haldon, "Roads and Communications," 136–8; Larnach, "All Roads Lead to Constantinople," 86–90. About the predominantly military character of the Byzantine dignitaries nominally in charge of roads and travelers, see Bojana Krsmanović, "O vojnim ovlašćenjima logoteta droma," *Zbornik radova Vizantološkog instituta* 53 (2016): 47–62. A short overview of the Byzantine road management before 1204 is also available in Larnach, "All Roads Lead to Constantinople," 77–90, 273.

[72] Vasić and Milošević, *Mansio Idimum*, 78, with previous literature. Consult also map no. 4: "Belege für die Via Traiana in Ungarn und Serbien," in Popović, *Von Budapest nach Istanbul*, 18 and 176–8.

An additional reason why the Roman road infrastructure was more visible in and around long-lasting towns might be that it was more or less continuously in use, as attested by several written accounts and by the eleventh to thirteenth-century archaeological finds near the city of Dimitrovgrad. Namely, the metallic objects (arrow tips, horseshoes etc.) that can be dated to the Middle Ages have been found stacked between the massive stones of the Roman road before all of them were covered by layers of black soil.[73] For our topic, it is even more critical that over many centuries the remains of the Roman road infrastructure were repeatedly being repaired. The relatively high population density in and around cities offered more resources and reasons for, at least provisional, maintenance than was the case in rural parts of the central Balkans.[74]

6 Exchange of Goods

According to scarce written and only partially examined archaeological evidence, the trading activity along the Via Militaris reached its peak in the early Middle Ages during the reign of Manuel I Komnenos in the second half of twelfth century. In this period, the central Balkan area was the most connected region to the distant production and trade centers on the shores of the Aegean and the Black Sea as a consequence of the political unity brought about by the supremacy of the emperors of Constantinople. Expensive imported objects were part of the consumption by the wealthy inhabitants of urban communities located along the Via Militaris (such as Niš and Braničevo) to a much higher degree than in the isolated geographical regions without permanent Byzantine military outposts. This situation testifies to the processes of the slow transformation of military strongholds into real cities with advanced stages of social stratification.[75]

---

[73] Lazić, "Via militaris: Rimski drum kod Caribroda," 71; Miroslav Lazić and Milorad Miljković, "Selište kod Dimitrovgrada: Neolitsko naselje i rimski put," in *Arheološka istraživanja na putu E80*, ed. Ivana Prodanović Ranković (Belgrade: Republički zavod za zaštitu spomenika kulture Beograd, 2017), 538–9, 542–3.
[74] As testified to in late antiquity in the vicinity of Constantinople, see Haldon, "Roads and Communications," 137.
[75] Vesna Bikić, "Trgovinski promet na centralnom Balkanu (XI–XIII vek): Između neophodnog i luksuznog," in *Vizantijsko nasleđe i srpska umetnost: Procesi vizantinizacije i srpska arheologija*, ed. Vesna Bikić (Belgrade: Nacionalni komitet za Vizantijske studije, Službeni Glasnik, Vizantološki institut SANU, 2016), 1:125–31; Larnach, "All Roads Lead to Constantinople," 146. The Byzantine luxury goods prevailed in Hungary, too, see Gordana Milošević Jevtić, "The Suburb of the Town of Braničevo: A Model of a 12th Century Settlement," in *Byzantine Heritage and Serbian Art: Processes of Byzantinisation and Serbian Archaeology*, ed. Vesna Bikić (Belgrade: Nacionalni

However, the borders established after the collapse of the Pax Byzantina at the beginning of the thirteenth century were also not entirely impenetrable for merchants, especially when two neighboring regions were forced to cooperate. For example, from the end of fourteenth century, a part of the fortress of Bovan may have been a storage site for Hungarian stone salt imported through the city of Kovin (Hung. Kewe).[76] Located on the Danube's left bank opposite to the medieval towns of Morava and Braničevo, Kovin perfectly met the conditions for trade activities with the regions to the south. Its inhabitants possessed numerous privileges dating from the fourteenth and fifteenth centuries, which allowed them easy travel and trade in Hungary.[77] The fact that the population of Kovin was mostly of Serbian ethnic origin may indicate that their business activities prospered due to the repeated contacts with their relatives and business partners of the same ethnic background on the other side of the river. The city of Braničevo was also famous for its wealth over a number of centuries, or at least that is how several narrative historical sources describe it. Unfortunately, detailed insight into the type of goods traded and the scale of the exchange remains obscure due to the lack of diplomatic and archival testimonies. The received idea that the town was decaying in the late Middle Ages does not correlate with the economic growth of Kovin nor with the depiction of Braničevo in the Ottoman sources. The elaborate trade activity in Braničevo diminished only after the final Ottoman conquest in 1458.[78] Other cities in the region such as Belgrade and Smederevo were only commercially important during the time when they were the principal seats of the Serbian rulers in the first half of fifteenth century. This illustrates how unstable and fluid the trade conditions were.[79]

Regardless of which commercial center on the shores of the Sava and Danube ephemerally flourished during the fourteenth and fifteenth centuries, their success was not based on trade within a limited geographical range or exclusively with one political unit. The activities of both local and foreign entrepreneurs operating in these centers, including the city of Sremska Mitrovica situated on the Sava river, were part of a bigger business scheme. Namely, the significant

---

komitet za Vizantijske studije, Službeni Glasnik, Vizantološki institut SANU, 2016), 1:117–23; Dejana Vasin, "Pogranični srpski i ugarski gradovi na Savi i Dunavu u srednjem veku" (PhD diss., University of Novi Sad, 2017), 134–5.
76 Siniša Mišić, "Bovan u srednjem veku," *Časopis Karadžić* 1 (2009): 16. The fortress of Bovan was a part of a road grid too, see Škrivanić, *Putevi u srednjovekovnoj Srbiji*, 84.
77 Vasin, *Pogranični srpski i ugarski gradovi*, 170–9.
78 Miljković and Krstić, *Braničevo*, 75–7; Vasin, *Pogranični srpski i ugarski gradovi*, 203–4. For the description of the events which took in 1458, see Krstić, "Pad Srbije," 317–8.
79 Vasin, *Pogranični srpski i ugarski gradovi*, 178–202.

expansion of the metallurgy of all precious metals in several mining districts in various regions of medieval Serbia (Novo Brdo and Janjevo in Kosovo, Koporić in the Kopaonik Mountains and Srebrenica, Zajača and Krupanj in the Rudnik Mountains) required the creation of new points for export. The cities in the vicinity of the north branch of the Via Militaris such as Belgrade and Smederevo were to some extent the meeting points dedicated to the domestic and international exchange of silver and gold. The extensions of this elaborate network occasionally spread beyond the shores of the Danube to the most prominent mining communities and market towns regardless of their geographical position, so, even to the most southern regions of Serbia.[80] As a consequence of increased mining activity, one may presume there was a partial re-birth of long distance trade along some sections of the Via Militaris. The volume of this activity was not massive since the Adriatic coastal communities were the common mediators in this matter. Besides, the non-local merchants indeed avoided the geographical area under discussion for the reason that many military operations that took place there. However, the very fact that trade activity most probably existed is relevant to our topic. It has been recorded both in written as well as in visual historical sources. For instance, an engraving shows a Ragusan merchant caravan near to the city of Niš sometime between the fifteenth and sixteenth century.[81]

The high demand in the Kingdom of Hungary for luxury goods from Asia and Italy was partially satisfied thanks to trade activity attributed to the merchants of Ragusa.[82] Furthermore, the noticeable presence of merchants who were direct subjects of the Ottoman sultans in the north of Serbia, which had been an Ottoman vassal since 1389/1390, has attracted only limited attention from scholars. The undisputed authority of their supreme lord protected the Muslim traders in semi-subjugated Serbia. One may imagine that in comparison with the domestic competition, they had direct access to the highly sought-after Asian products readily available in some of the provinces of their motherland such as Thrace or some of the Black Sea and Aegean coastal towns. Once they brought them to North Serbia, they exchanged them mostly for the locally produced precious metals. Because of the high value and low weight of the exchanged objects, they

---

80 Ibid., 142–52. For example, the relative safety offered by the recently established city of Smederevo attracted numerous merchants from Dubrovnik previously settled in Novo Brdo, Prishtina and Trepča, especially during the 1454 Ottoman campaign, see Ibid., 196.
81 Andrija Veselinović, *Država srpskih despota* (Belgrade: Zavod za udžbenike i nastavna sredstva, 1995), with no pagination and without the source indication.
82 For instance, one such trade route was established for 1390, see Dejana Vasin, *Pogranični srpski i ugarski gradovi*, 195.

could be quickly shipped to remote destinations.[83] This situation indicates that there possibly may have been early attempts to use Serbia to gradually reopen long-distance trade routes between Central Europe and Asia. A similar strategy has been recently attributed to Sigismund of Luxemburg (r. 1387–1437) in the second decade of the fifteenth century with the difference that he intended to attach the Kingdom of Hungary to the Levantine business circles via Transylvania and the Lower Danube region.[84]

The issue of a free exchange of goods was of great importance for other rulers, too. During peace negotiation in 1449, the Serbian Despot Đurađ Branković (r. 1427–1456) unsuccessfully proposed the idea of assigning five specially designated towns along the middle Danube on the Hungarian side of the border for unobstructed commerce between the subjects of the sultan and local Christian rulers.[85] Unquestionably, this measure would have mostly affected local trade. Even so, one should not exclude the possibility that spices or luxury cloth and handicrafts from exotic countries had already sporadically found their buyers in the south of Hungary thanks to middlemen who came to North Serbia through the Via Militaris. Even though the first exchange of this type must have been sporadic and of low intensity, it increased massively in the following centuries.

7 Conclusion

The most obvious finding to emerge from this chapter is that the investigated geographical area went through a dynamic development during the Middle Ages. Although the social and economic improvements were not always linear and faced many challenges, the general setting changed gradually in favor of satisfactory travel conditions. This result may be explained by the fact that local authorities, regardless of their origin—Byzantine, Bulgarian, Serbian, Ottoman—in-

---

83 Vasin, *Pogranični srpski i ugarski gradovi*, 167–8. Since Ottoman merchants were present in the vassal kingdom of Bosnia at the beginning of the fifteenth century, there is no reason to believe that it was not the case with Serbia, too. Cf. Sima Ćirković, *Istorija srednjovekovne bosanske države* (Belgrade: Srpska književna zadruga, 1964), 207.
84 Zsigmond Pál Pach,"Die Verkehrsroute des Levantehandels nach Siebenbürgen in der Zeit Sigismunds," in *Sigismund von Luxemburg: Kaiser und König in Mitteleuropa 1387–1437*, ed. Josef Macek, Ernő Marosi and Ferdinand Seibt (Warendorf: Fahlbusch, 1994): 192–9. It is not unusual to find written testimonies about the import of the luxury goods originating from the Levantine workshops, see Vasin, *Pogranični srpski i ugarski gradovi*, 164, note 614, 165, 175.
85 Vasin, *Pogranični srpski i ugarski gradovi*, 176–7.

vested a significant amount of time and resources in improving road infrastructure.

The findings of this investigation complement those of earlier studies, which suggest that the remains of the Roman road infrastructure in many ways still affected the conditions in the Middle Ages and at the beginning of the Ottoman rule. For instance, this is clearly visible in the re-using of road infrastructure or in the distribution of settlements such as fortifications, villages and market towns. Especially the position of market towns in the historic region of Brančevo correlated with the Roman route. On a general level, the Roman road prefigured the space in which some military or political events took place.

This study has raised important questions about the nature of the changing political, social, economic, and demographic factors which contributed to the intensity of travel activity. For instance, under the stable political conditions during the middle Byzantine period (beginning of the eleventh until the end of the twelfth century) the long-distance trade with the Levantine and Black See regions increased. The massive presence of western pilgrims during this era may be partially explained by the same factor. Contrary to the common concept based on the data extracted from the western written historical sources, it seems that the Byzantine local authorities were involved in construction projects with the aim of improving the defense capability of the strategically located Via Militaris.

Our results add to the rapidly expanding field of research aimed at documenting how the remnants of Roman and early Byzantine technological achievements or human activities shaped everyday life in the Middle Ages. This research could be further improved by archaeological excavations and digital geospatial analysis.

Tatjana Katić
Transforming the Landscape of the Constantinople Road in the Fifteenth and Sixteenth Centuries (Section Niš–Dragoman)

1 Introduction

The shortest land route linking the Bosphorus with Central Europe, the famous *Heerstrasse* of Konstantin Jireček, has been one of the most important communication links through the Balkan peninsula throughout history.[1] During the Roman Empire it was one of the many *viae militares* built, overseen and secured by the Roman army. The Byzantines regarded it as one of the high-ranking roads of their empire.[2] It gained particular significance at the time of the Ottomans who used it during their campaigns in Europe. The route that led from Constantinople to Buda, passing through the valleys of the rivers Maritsa, Nišava, Morava and Danube, was designated in Ottoman sources as an "imperial road" (*şah rah*), and as a "public road" (*tarîk-i âm*). The Balkan peoples called it Trajan's road, since they gave that Roman emperor's name to all paved roads; but it was also variously called the Imperial, Big and Stambol road.[3] This road of many

---

[1] This paper arose out of the research project "From Universal Empires to Nation States: Social and political changes in Serbia and the Balkans" (no. 177030) funded by the Ministry of Education, Science, and Technological Development of the Republic of Serbia.
[2] Klaus Belke, "Roads and Travel in Macedonia and Thrace in the Middle and Late Byzantine Period," in *Travel in the Byzantine World: Papers from the Thirty-Fourth Spring symposium of Byzantine Studies, Birmingham, April 2000*, ed. Ruth Macrides (Aldershot: Ashgate, 2002), 74, 81–3. The Via Egnatia, another important Balkan route, was designated as an "imperial road" (*hodos basileos*) during Byzantine time, whereas there is no such information for the Via Militaris i.e. the Constantinople road. Nevertheless, even though no data exist to confirm its high rank, it appears that it was regarded as of primary importance and maintained much better than the Via Egnatia. For more details, see Matthew Larnach, "All Roads Lead to Constantinople: Exploring the Via Militaris in the Medieval Balkans, 600–1204" (PhD diss., University of Sydney, 2016), 84–6.
[3] Ottoman and European voyagers of the sixteenth and seventeenth centuries also used other names, depending on direction of their travel: Istanbul road, Belgrade road, Buda road. Olga Zirojević, *Carigradski drum od Beograda do Sofije (1459–1683)* (Belgrade: Istorijski muzej Srbije, 1970), 21; Mihailo St. Popović, *Od Budima do Konstantinopolja: Via Traiana u svetlu putopisne literature u periodu od 14. do 16. veka* (Novi Sad: Akademska Knjiga, 2017), 43–6.

https://doi.org/10.1515/9783110618563-005

names led the South Slavs for centuries to the centre of power and the seat of the universal empire. Whether it was named Constantinople, Kostantiniye or Istanbul, for the South Slavs it was always the City of Caesar or Tsargrad, Tsarigrad. Thus, the road itself was widely known as the Tsarigrad road.

Being one of the major long-distance trade routes in the Ottoman Empire and the main military road in the European part of the empire from the fifteenth century onwards, the Constantinople (Tsarigrad) road was regularly maintained and secured by the Ottoman authorities. All the state's measures taken to ensure the good functioning of the road had an impact on its appearance as well as on its immediate natural environment. In addition to that, they also had far-reaching consequences for the local settlements and their populations, a topic which, hitherto, has not been dealt with in detail. The goal of this chapter is to determine how the Ottoman governance of the road influenced the cultural and demographic landscape. Through an examination of the Ottoman cadastral surveys, the registers of outgoing orders from the Ottoman Finance Department, travelogues and other available sources, it is possible to explain the development of the road infrastructure and the security system, as well as their effects on the local population, its social status, and mobility.

In the present study, attention will be given to the section of the road that follows the middle course of the river Nišava. It has been chosen as an example of how the Ottomans addressed the challenges of travel through a diverse landscape. Furthermore, this part of the Tsarigrad road passed through a specific ethno-cultural region, distinguished by its unique Torlakian dialect. The difference between the Torlakians and their neighbours is quite discernible in the sixteenth-century Ottoman sources, which open up an opportunity to detect ethnic changes in the settlements along the road.

2 Geographical Setting and Physical Appearance of the Road

The source of the river Nišava is in the Balkan Mountains, facing the Kom Peak on the east, near the village of Gintsi in today's Bulgaria. It flows south and then, near Godeč village, it changes its direction flowing west. Near the village of Kalotina it met the Constantinople road coming from the southeast i.e. from the direction of Dragoman. Beginning at Kalotina, almost to the entrance to the Sićevo gorge, the Nišava River and the Constantinople road ran side by side, with the road crossing back and forth over the river at several points. First, after leaving the Dragoman pass, a narrow valley of the Nišava tributary Eževica, the road stayed on the left side of the Nišava and followed the route of the contemporary railway and the E80 road. It has been assumed up to now that the old and the new routes were congruent almost to the town of Pirot.[4] However, the Ottoman road, as well as the Roman *via militaris*, crossed the river approximately six kilometers before Tsaribrod (today's Dimitrovgrad), near the village of Bačevo, and, paralleling the river's right side for more than ten kilometers, re-crossed it before the village of Gojin Dol.[5] From Gojin Dol to Pirot both went through an open plain, about 27 kilometers long, continuing to follow the modern routes. Near Pirot it divided into two routes, both leading to the valley of Bela Palanka. One immediately turned west, bypassing a marshy land southwest of Pirot, then traversed Mount Belava and reached the valley of Bela Palanka; the other passed through Pirot, crossed the Nišava and followed the right side of the river to the village of Sinjac, where it re-crossed the river and then turned west in order to arrive at Bela Palanka.[6]

Coming out from the valley of Bela Palanka, the Constantinople road did not enter the Sićevo gorge. Instead, it entered the mountains again, forking into three separate routes. The middle and the lower routes passed by the Suva Planina mountain, while the upper one traversed Mount Kunovica. The middle way was made by the Ottomans probably in the second half of the fifteenth century. It was a caravan road and more frequented than the two others during the Ottoman times.[7] The upper way, the old Roman *via militaris*, was used mainly by the Ottoman army, while the lower way, dated from the Middle Ages, was used by numerous Western travelers and envoys in the sixteenth century.[8] All three branches of the road merged back into one in the vicinity of the village of Banja (Niška Banja) and continued to Niš (see Fig. 2).

Different landforms, such as gorges, valleys, open plains, mountains and plateaus in the given area had an influence on the course of the road. The river Nišava had the same impact, as it frequently overflowed and changed its

---

4 Zirojević, *Carigradski drum*, 39.
5 A well-preserved fragment of the Via Militaris was excavated in 2010 between Bačevo and Dimitrovgrad, at the site Selište (K'ndina bara). Also, previous archaeological excavations have revealed traces of the Via Militaris i.e. the Tsarigrad road, almost all the way from today's state border to the remnants of the Gojin Dol fortress on the right side of the Nišava. For more details see Miroslav Lazić and Milorad Miljković, "Via militaris: Rimski drum kod Caribroda," *Glasnik Društva konzervatora Srbije* 35 (2011): 69–72. Furthermore, Ottoman sources confirm the existence of bridges at the villages of Bačevo and Gojin Dol. Prime Minister's Ottoman Archive, Istanbul, Başbakanlık Osmanlı Arşivi (hereafter BOA), Tapu defteri (hereafter TD), 492: 407–8.
6 Zirojević, *Carigradski drum*, 38.
7 The modern highway also follows this route.
8 Zirojević, *Carigradski drum*, 35–6.

riverbed. In the most pleasant part of the route, going through the plain of Pirot, from the confluence of the river Jerma with the Nišava to Pirot (13 km), one can discern the existence of four to six ancient Nišava riverbeds, whose freshness and level of preservation grow as we approach the current course. The traces of a bridge over one of the old riverbeds and the remnants of a fort nearby show that the Roman *via militaris* pursued a fluvial terrace to avoid the alluvial plain through which the Nišava meanders, at times changing its stream during periods of high water and floods.[9]

The Ottoman road followed the same route i. e. the edge of the alluvial plain that extends in width from a few hundred to 2500 meters wide towards the village of Krupac. Frequent inundations of the Nišava, which started at Krupac where the river channel is shallow,[10] endangered the road and the very town of Pirot. In the 1560s, after a couple of severe floods happened not only during winter, but in late fall and early spring as well, the local notables from Pirot sent a petition to Istanbul asking for help. According to their report, floods caused great damage to the town, especially to the Sultan Mehmed mosque, the oldest mosque in Pirot, filling it with flood water and rendering it unusable for prayers and gatherings of believers. For this reason, the Ottoman authorities made a decision to establish regular maintenance of this part of the Nišava by appointing forty people from the village of Krupac to remove logs, stumps and shrubbery from the river channel on a regular basis. In return they were exempted from extraordinary taxes and customary levies (*avarız-ı divaniye ve tekâlif-i örfiye*).[11]

Aside from the flood control, the Ottomans took care to provide safe and comfortable river crossings. Perhaps already in the second half of the fifteenth century, a small stone three-arched bridge, still standing today, was built over the Bistrica Creek, near the Pirot fort. In the same period, a bridge was erected over the river Nišava in the town of Pirot itself. Both bridges were constructed and maintained through pious endowments from the members of the local elite.[12]

---

[9] Jovan Ćirić, "Promene u prirodnoj sredini pirotskog polja i Via Militaris," *Glasnik Srpskog geografskog društva* 54 (1974): 113 – 7.

[10] There are seven karst springs and a swamp near the village of Krupac, sometimes called Krupac Lake. For more details see Jovan Ćirić and Vitomir Živković, *Krupac: Geografija, istorija, društveni život, narodnooslobodilački rat* (Pirot: Muzej Ponišavlja, 1974), 14 – 33.

[11] A decision on the special status of 40 out of 60 taxpayers, residents of the Krupac village, was recorded in cadastral survey compiled in 1570, BOA, TD 492: 374.

[12] The bridge near the Pirot fort was erected by a certain Asil Bey, who also had a masjid built in the town. This person, founder of one of the Pirot *mahalle*s, might be identical with Aslibegi who held the aforementioned village of Krupac as a *timar* in 1452/53. See Halil İnalcık, Evgeni Radushev and Uğur Altuğ, *1445 Tarihli Paşa Livâsı İcmâl Defteri* (Ankara: Türk Tarih Kurumu,

Wooden bridges over the Nišava existed in the town of Niš[13] and in the vicinity of Tsaribrod (Dimitrovgrad)—an older bridge was near the village of Gojin Dol, and a newer one near the village of Bačevo. It is not known when the bridge at Gojin Dol was built. The earliest information mentions dates from the middle of the sixteenth century, but it is probably older than that, since the place was a river crossing in ancient times as well.[14] The bridge near Bačevo most probably was not built prior to 1566. For decades there was a ford or a stepping-stone bridge that met the needs of travelers in the summer months, but not in winter and early spring, when it was almost impossible to cross it with some level of convenience. Consequently, between 1566 and 1570, the villagers of Bačevo were ordered to build a sturdy timber bridge. They were also tasked with guarding and repairing it whenever necessary. As a reward for the service of being bridge-keepers, they all were exempted from extraordinary taxes and customary levies.[15]

Between Tsaribrod and Pirot, the road crossed the river Jerma over a bridge near the village of Sukovo, but the available sources provide no details about it.[16]

The largest part of the Constantinople road on the section Niš–Dragoman was paved with cobbles or broken stone. Western travelers recorded that this was the case with three-fourths of the mountain section between Niš and Pirot.[17] From Pirot to Dragoman, the road was cobbled from the beginning to

---

2013), 32, 306, here transliterated as Kıdviçe instead of Krupçe. The second bridge, on which a toll was levied, was the endowment from Halil Bey *kilercibaşı* (warden of the servants who prepared and served the sultan's meal). The same benefactor erected in Pirot one masjid, hamam and caravanserai. The first so far available data on these bridges originate from the Ottoman census of 1525, but they were most likely constructed much earlier. BOA, TD 130: 620–1.

13 It was replaced by a stone bridge in 1619. The bridge, erected by Mehmed Pasha governor of Buda *eyalet* (province), was 65 meters long. It had two lanes for wagon traffic and pedestrian paths on both sides. More details on the Niš bridge through centuries are found in Dušanka Bojanić, "Niš do Velikog rata 1683," in *Istorija Niša*, ed. Danica Milić (Niš: Gradina, 1983), 1:116–7; Dragana Amedoski and Jovana Šaljić, "Most na Nišavi u osmansko doba," *Niški zbornik* 16–17 (2008): 145–51.

14 On the hilltop above the Nišava, the ruins of the Early Byzantine fortress called Gojindolsko kale still stand. The fortress guarded an ancient road junction located below the hill, fragments of which were excavated recently. For more details see Miroslav Lazić, "Rimski put Via militaris i Malo kale kod Dimitrovgrada kao primer devastacije istraženih arheoloških nalazišta na koridoru E-80," *Glasnik Srpskog arheološkog društva* 30 (2014): 340–3. For Gojin Dol bridge in the sixteenth century and its significance for the growth of the village see Tatjana Katić and Srđan Katić, "Gojin Dol, naselje i stanovništvo u 16. veku," *Pirotski zbornik* 40 (2015): 126–9.

15 BOA, TD 492: 407–8.

16 Zirojević, *Carigradski drum*, 39.

17 Ibid., 42.

the end; the traces of old Via Militaris were still visible on both sides of the Ottoman road in the second half of the sixteenth century and later.[18] This clearly suggests that the new surface was applied directly to the old Roman road-bed.[19] Recent excavations have revealed the fragments of the road at K'ndina bara, one kilometer east from today's Dimitrovgrad, and near the village of Bačevo.[20] Several kilometers to the south-east of these findings, in Bulgaria, on the northern bank of the Nišava and in the suburb of Kalotina, there are exposed fragments of the same route. Further remains, approximately four kilometers long, are detectable between Kalotina and Dragoman, passing through the Dragoman pass.[21] The surface of the aforementioned sections is made of small rough stones of irregular size, loosely fitted to the bed, which made it easy to maintain; any potholes that emerged could be simply filled with gravel or broken stone. Whereas the surface, most likely of the Ottoman origin, consisted of rough uneven stones, the curbs were made of regular-sized paving stones.[22]

The preserved fragments of the route are seven and a half to eight meters wide. Needless to say, the Constantinople road was not this wide throughout its entire length, but it was fully suitable for large volumes of wheeled traffic. It was the main trade route in the European part of the Ottoman Empire over which tens of thousands of ox or water buffalo carts and wagons passed each year.[23] Nevertheless, in some parts, the road was not wide enough to allow four-wheeled vehicles to pass each other. Western travelers particularly emphasized that the parts in the mountainous areas and dense forests were difficult to travel on, namely the sections of Dragoman–Kalotina and Pirot–Niš.[24] Otto-

---

18 Constantin Jireček, *Die Heerstrasse von Belgrad nach Constantinopel und die Balkanpässe: Eine historisch-geographische Studie* (Prague: Tempsky, 1877), 24.
19 For more on rebuilding techniques through the Middle Ages and the Ottoman time see Larnach, "All Roads Lead to Constantinople," 255–6.
20 Lazić and Miljković, "Via militaris," 70.
21 Larnach, "All Roads Lead to Constantinople," 158–9.
22 Ibid., 159. Another way of marking road edge lines were channels dug by the side of the road. This technique was applied by Ottomans solely before military campaigns. The channels were dug wherever the road passed through arable fields, orchards and vineyards in order to prevent soldiers from unintentionally damaging the crops, especially during night marches; the culverts served as a guide through fields in places where there were no embankments. Being shallow, these channels filled up rapidly and were dug out again prior to the next campaign. BOA, Mühimme defteri (hereafter MD), 5: 283, order 1761.
23 Western and Ottoman travellers report on hundreds of wagons loaded with wood, rice, wine, salt, lead, carpets, textiles and other commodities from the Balkans, Anatolia, Persia or Egypt, passing along the road every day. Zirojević, *Carigradski drum*, 57–9.
24 Sergije Dimitrijević, *Dubrovački karavani u južnoj Srbiji u XVII veku* (Belgrade: SANU, 1958), 70, 116, 118.

man campaign diaries of the sixteenth and seventeenth centuries are full of accounts about the difficulties that the army was faced with the steep and (here and there) unpaved mountain road between Pirot and Niš. For example, in the autumn of 1690, after a heavy rainfall, it took artillery wagons being drawn by water buffalo more than fifteen hours to pass the distance between Pirot and Bela Palanka, while the expected time was seven hours. Mud and steep terrain slowed down the movement of cattle, while the poor road surface caused damage to the wagons and extended delays. Evidently this part of the road was so narrow that the whole line of artillery wagons had to wait for the broken ones to be repaired.[25]

Much of the given route was forested and no part of it would have been navigable without regular maintenance. Whereas the most extensive road works were conducted by the specialized units of the Ottoman army in the course of a military campaign, small-scale works such as cutting trees and shrubberies and repairing road surface were carried out by the local population, especially by those who were assigned to guard mountain passes (*derbenci*s or *derbentçi*s).[26] It is not known how often maintenance work was performed, but its scope had to have increased in the sixteenth century when the volume of road traffic, and consequently the number of road guardians increased, too. All of this affected the natural landscape in terms of a gradual deforestation, but influenced the cultural landscape as well in terms of road infrastructure development.

3 Travelers' Rest Stops: Dervish Lodges, Caravanserais and Menzils

After passing through different states and empires for several hundred years, the fifteenth century saw the largest portion of the Constantinople road in one polity—the Ottoman Empire. Having been initially defined only as a route for conquest, it quickly became the vital artery for dissemination of a new state ideology, culture and religion throughout the Balkans. Along this one and other major Balkan communication routes, Ottoman warriors (*akıncı*s), *gazi* dervishes, and incomers from Anatolia settled in urban centers or deserted places;

---

[25] Tatjana Katić, *Tursko osvajanje Srbije 1690. godine* (Belgrade: Srpski Genealoški Centar i Centar za osmanističke studije, 2012), 47.
[26] Zirojević, *Carigradski drum*, 45; Cengiz Orhonlu, *Osmanlı İmparatorluğunda Derbend Teşkilâtı* (Istanbul: Eren, 1990), 70–1.

this was one of the methods for marking the newly conquered territories as Ottoman.[27] Another method was founding institutions whose purpose was to bind the conquerors and the vanquished, that is, the ruler and his subjects. Among them, the vital role was filled by the *zâviyes-imârets* or dervish lodge-soup kitchens, which provided free meals to everyone in need—travelers, dervishes, the poor and the wealthy—and as well as there were caravanserais, which offered lodgings.[28]

These facilities, whose services were available for use to everyone regardless of their religious affiliation, were the main features of Ottoman roads. They were built in cities, at crossroads and along roads, usually at a distance of one-day's walk. Probably the first dervish lodge on the section we are concerned with was built in Pirot (which the Ottomans called Şehirköy) in 1385.[29] It belonged to itinerant "heterodox" dervishes called *abdals*, namely to Kara Abdal, one of the most prominent *abdals* of the fourteenth century.[30] His dwelling place (*mesvâ*) was erected in the immediate vicinity of Pirot, on *mezraa* (field) Postanje, which was granted by Sultan Murad I (r. 1362–1389) for that very purpose.[31]

In Niš, conquered in 1386,[32] Sultan Murat I, in all likelihood, enabled opening of a *zâviye*, just like in Pirot. Unfortunately, sources offer no information on

---

27 Although there are no preserved censuses from the earliest decades of Ottoman rule in Pirot and Niš, it is indicative that in the 1520s there were nine *akıncıs* among 165 registered Muslims in Pirot and eight *akıncıs* among 145 Muslims in Niš. BOA, TD 130: 112–4; Bojanić, "Niš do Velikog rata 1683," 163.
28 For more details on their significance for establishing the Ottoman rule in the Balkans and the difference between *imârets* in the western and eastern part of the empire, see Heath Lowry, "The 'Soup Muslims' of the Ottoman Balkans: Was there a 'Western' and 'Eastern' Ottoman Empire?," *Osmanlı Araştırmaları* 36 (2010): 97–133.
29 On the Ottoman conquest of Şehirköy see, Mehmed Neşri, *Kitâb-ı Cihan-Nümâ*, ed. F. Reşit Unat and M. Köymen (Ankara: Türk Tarih Kurumu, 1987), 1:261–3.
30 He is mentioned in *Abdal Musa Menâkıbnâme* as one of those participating in the miracles of this *veli*. See, Musa Seyirci, *Abdal Musa Sultan* (Istanbul: Der, 1992), 119. There were Kara Abdal's dervish lodges in the *kazâ* of Uşak, in Ayıntab, Aksaray, and possibly in other Anatolian places. See Mehtap Özdeğer, *15.–16. Yüzyıl Arşiv Kaynaklarına Göre Uşak Kazasının Sosyal ve Ekonomik Tarihi* (Istanbul: Filiz, 2001), 375; Leslie Peirce, *Morality Tales: Law and Gender in the Ottoman Court of Aintab* (Berkeley: University of California Press, 2003), 62; Doğan Yörük, *XVI. Yüzyılda Aksaray Sancağı, 1500–1584* (Konya: Tablet, 2005), 268. In the Balkans, besides Pirot, its existence is testified to in Dimetoka: Ourania Bessi, "The Topographic Reconstruction of Ottoman Dimetoka: Issues of Periodization and Morphological Development," in *Frontiers of the Ottoman Imagination: Studies in Honour of Rhoads Murphey*, ed. Marios Hadjianastasis (Leiden: Brill, 2015), 50–1.
31 BOA, TD 130: 620.
32 Marko Šuica, "Pripovesti o srpsko-turskim okršajima i 'strah od Turaka' 1386. godine," *Istorijski časopis* 53 (2006): 112.

the dervish convent from the time, most likely because the city was severely devastated during the battles of the early fifteenth century and in 1443 and 1454.[33] The oldest preserved census, from 1498, registers two *zâviye*s in Niš. One *zâviye*, probably the older one, was in the vicinity of a large bridge over the Nišava in *mahalle* Vrhmost (Köprübaşı).[34] The other one was founded by Ali Beg Mihaloglu a famous raider (*akıncı*) commander, when he was *sancakbeği* of Smederevo.[35] Mihaloglu's *zâviye* in Niš had at least three separate structures: a dervish lodge, an *imâret* and a public well.[36] According to the description by a Prussian doctor and pharmacist, Reinold Lubenau, who stayed there in 1587,

> [i]n this imaret, everyone is given a meal, be they Turks, Jews, Christians, anyone a piece of mutton, a round loaf of bread, a bowl of pottage, actually rice cooked in the mutton soup, and the horses are fed forage. But one must not give tips for this, as they won't accept it, and will perceive taking the money as a serious sin.[37]

Sources do not record the name of the person who ran Ali Beg's *zâviye*. It can be assumed that it was Mihalzâde Hızır Dede, who had a *türbe* in Niš.[38] So far what is known is that Ali Beg's father, brother and son had the same name,[39] along with another close ancestor who fought alongside Sultan Murat I.[40] Maybe the *türbe*, *zâviye* and *imâret* were built to honor this or some other ancestor who

---

33 Bojanić, "Niš do Velikog rata 1683," 115–6.
34 Milan Vasić, Olga Zirojević and Aleksandar Stojanovski, "Popis niškog kadiluka iz 1498. godine," *Spomenik SANU* 131 (1992): 100. According to the seventeenth-century Ottoman traveler Evliyâ Çelebi, the most reputable dervish lodge in Niš was this one, called Köprübaşı, and in his time it belonged already to the Bektashi Order. *Evliyâ Çelebi Seyahatnâmesi*, ed. Yücel Dağlı, Seyit Ali Kahraman and Ibrahim Sezgin (Istanbul: Yapı Kredi, 2001), 5:188.
35 Vasić, Zirojević and Stojanovski, "Popis niškog kadiluka," 146. Ali Beg was the Smederevo *sancakbeği* (govenor) six times, from 1463 to 1499.
36 The *zâviye* was supported by the income from the mills on the Nišava and one rice field, as well as from the hamams that Ali Beg built in the fortresses Resava and Hram. For more details see Bojanić, "Niš do Velikog rata 1683," 119, 122.
37 Toma Popović, "Niš u delima putopisaca XVI–XVII veka," in *Istorija Niša*, ed. Danica Milić (Niš: Gradina, 1983), 1:188.
38 *Evliyâ Çelebi Seyahatnâmesi*, 5:189.
39 Ayşe Kayapınar, "The Gazi Mihaloğulları Waqfs in Northern Bulgaria (15th–16th Centuries)," in *Proceedings of the Second International Symposium on Islamic Civilisation in the Balkans, Tirana, Albania, 4–7 December 2003*, ed. Ali Çaksu (Istanbul: IRCICA, 2006), 172.
40 This Hızır Dede built a mosque in the city of Kırkkilise in 1383/4. See Mariya Kiprovska, "Shaping the Ottoman Borderland: The Architectural Patronage of the Frontier Lords from the Mihaloğlu Family," in *Bordering Early Modern Europe*, ed. Maria Baramova, Grigor Boykov and Ivan Parvev (Wiesbaden: Harrassowitz, 2015), 195.

lost his life while conquering the city.⁴¹ Likewise, it is possible that one of Ali Beg's family members decided to lead a dervish lifestyle and to run the lodge and *imâret*. Also, the name Mihalzâde might be just a reflection of an oral tradition about the patronage of the Mihaloglu family over the dervish complex, and not an indicator of a blood relation. What is much more certain is that the *zâviye* was meant for the brotherhood of the itinerant dervishes, *abdal*s, or *baba'i*s as they were also referred to. According to the biography of Otman Baba, the most venerated fifteenth century *abdal* leader in the Balkans, Ali Beg Mihaloglu was a faithful follower of his teachings, considering him a saint and his spiritual leader. Ali Beg and other family members were patrons of *baba'i* lodges and *türbe*s in Anatolia and the Balkans.⁴² Therefore, it can with some confidence be assumed that the dervish hospice in Niš, whether headed by a person related to the dynasty of Mihaloglu or not, was intended for the *baba'i* brotherhood. This conclusion is also supported by the fact that at the beginning of the sixteenth century there was another *baba'i* convent in Niš, founded by Mustafa Baba;⁴³ there were also two mausoleums, one was Sefer Baba's and the other Koyun Baba's.⁴⁴

In the second quarter of the sixteenth century, a Bektashi *tekke* was built in Niš, run by a respectable woman Zahide Baci.⁴⁵ Another *tekke*, of Haydar *kethüda*, was opened in 1590/91.⁴⁶ Niš was among the major hubs on the Constantinople road, so it is no surprise that there were a number of *zâviye*s built in the first two centuries of Ottoman rule.⁴⁷ However, as the volume of traffic expanded

---

41 For one example of the transformation of the cult of the *gazi* warrior from the Mihaloglu family to a cult of a saint, see Mariya Kiprovska, "Legend and Historicity: The Binbir Oklu Ahmed Baba Tekkesi and Its Founder," in *Monuments, Patrons, Contexts: Papers on Ottoman Europe Presented to Machiel Kiel*, ed. Maximilian Hartmuth and Ayşe Dilsiz (Leiden: Nederlands Instituut voor het Nabije Oosten, 2010), 29–45.
42 For more details on the Mihaloglu family's patronage on *baba'i* hospices and on the political context of this powerful dynasty of *akıncı* commanders and the heterodox dervish brotherhood, see Mariya Kiprovska, "The Mihaloğlu Family: Gazi Warriors and Patrons of Dervish Hospices," *Osmanlı Araştırmaları* 32 (2008): 193–222.
43 Bojanić, "Niš do Velikog rata 1683," 126.
44 *Evliyâ Çelebi Seyahatnâmesi*, 5:189.
45 Evliyâ Çelebi speaks about her as a person people knew little about in this time. Therefore, the founding of her *tekke* is set after 1522/23, the time when the last available census of waqfs in Niš was conducted, in which she is not mentioned. BOA, TD 135: 126–7.
46 The time of the construction is estimated based on the numeric value of letters in a chronogram on Haydar *kethüda*'s fountain. Hazim Šabanović, *Evlija Čelebi Putopis, odlomci o jugoslovenskim zemljama* (Sarajevo: Veselin Masleša, 1979), 63.
47 Meanwhile the number of dervish lodges in Pirot increased too, the most reputable being Gazi Ahmed Baba Sultan's *tekke*. See *Evliyâ Çelebi Seyahatnâmesi*, 5:188.

in the early sixteenth century due to peace and trade agreements between the Ottoman Empire and the Kingdom of Hungary, these facilities became insufficient. The increasing scope of caravan traffic created a need for more specialized buildings—caravanserais, which could accommodate high numbers of beasts of burden and travelers.[48]

Caravanserais were mostly free lodgings, with large inner yards for merchandise and animals; travelers prepared food themselves and slept in common rooms. In the seventeenth century the name *han* began being used for these types of lodges on the Tsarigrad road. Unlike in caravanserais, *han*s offered better service for which there was a charge: they offered food and lodgings in private rooms.[49] As services of caravanserais became more similar to those of *han*s, these two terms started being used interchangeably, as synonyms.

Till the end of the fifteenth century, the first caravanserais were built in Niš and Pirot. The one in Niš was the endowment of Hacı Durmuş,[50] while the one in Pirot was the endowment of Halil Beg *kilercibaşı*.[51] Like all other buildings of this type, it had a place for draft and pack animals in the inner court. Yet, the peculiarity of the Pirot caravanserai was that it also had a special stable for camels, outside the complex.

Niš, having been a larger and more important urban center, got yet another caravanserai in the 1550s from an unknown endower, and it was reported by contemporaries as one of the most beautiful on the Tsarigrad road. According to Hans Dernschwam, who described it in 1553 as unfinished, parts of old Roman structures built in the ground floor greatly contributed to its beauty.[52] In the decades to come, more caravanserais and *han*s were built in Niš and Pirot, mostly in their *çarşı*s.[53]

In 1598/99, due to persistent attacks by haiduks from Wallachia and Transylvania during the Long Turkish War (1593–1606), the Ottoman government or-

---

48 An agreement between Matthias Corvinus and Bayezid II guaranteed free and safe trade on the territory of both countries, which resulted in an increase in the exchange of many products at the beginning of the sixteenth century; Turkish carpets among other wares. Nazan Ölçer, "The Role of Turkish Carpets in Ottoman Art," in *Ottoman Civilization*, ed. Halil İnalcık, Günsel Renda (Ankara: Ministry of Culture, 2002), 2:794.
49 Other than in *han*s/caravanserais, travelers could buy food in towns and along the road from villagers who offered their produce. It is noted that there were improvised wattle shelters for food sale in the vicinity of Bela Palanka, near the villages of Klisurica and Novo Selo; near Tsaribrod a villager built a small shed and sold wine there. Zirojević, *Carigradski drum*, 55.
50 For Hacı Durmuş and his waqf see Bojanić, "Niš do Velikog rata 1683," 124–6.
51 See footnote 12.
52 Popović, "Niš u delima putopisaca," 182.
53 The exact number is, unfortunately, unknown. *Evliyâ Çelebi Seyahatnâmesi*, 5:188–9.

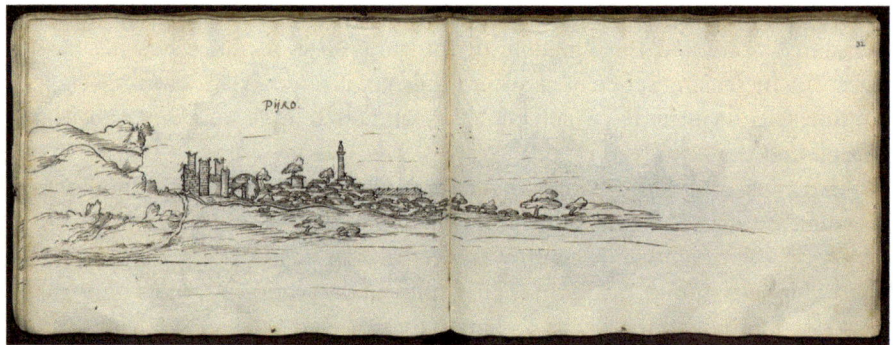

Fig. 1: Pirot from the Leiden Sketchbook (1587). The Pirot caravanserai is depicted here as an elongated building to the right of the mosque. Image courtesy of Leiden University Library, shelf mark VLO 50.

dered the construction of a wooden stockade and a *han* in Izvor (today's Bela Palanka).[54] As they were not made of durable materials, they deteriorated after a few decades. In their stead Musa Pasha, a governor of Buda, built new, stone structures in 1638/39. The settlement itself was named after him, Musa Pasha's Palanka, later known as Bela Palanka. The *han*, the endowment of Musa Pasha, differed from most others by having separate rooms for harems of high dignitaries, and was painted on the inside by a Buda artist.[55] In the seventeenth century there was another *han* on this section of the road, located in Dragoman.[56]

The post stations (*menzils*) were an integral part of the road infrastructure too. These shabby structures, where state couriers changed horses, consisted of a stable and a wattle and daub hut for people who took care of animals. More often than not there was a tavern too. The *menzils* existed on all major roads, connecting administrative and trade centres of the Ottoman Empire. On the given route they were established during the fifteenth century in Niš, Jelašnica, Gradašnica and Big Tsaribrod. In Niš and Jelašnica, forty Christian families provided two horses for state officials and maintained the post station (according to the census from 1498).[57] In Gradašnica and Big Tsaribrod all of the inhab-

---

54 Života Jocić, *Belopalanačka naselja u pisanim izvorima do 1877 godine* (Bela Palanka: Narodna biblioteka Vuk Karadžić and Niš: Imprimé, 2014), 27–9.
55 Katić, *Tursko osvajanje Srbije*, 48.
56 *Evliyâ Çelebi Seyahatnâmesi*, 5:187.
57 Vasić, Zirojević and Stojanovski, "Popis niškog kadiluka," 101, 123.

itants were assigned as *ulakçıs*—that is, the ones who provided *menzil* horses.⁵⁸ In return for their service, they were freed from extraordinary taxes and customary levies, and paid an extremely small amount of fees on agricultural products. Thanks to the tax exemptions related to the *ulakçı* status, these settlements experienced steady population growth.

4 Guarding the Road

Densely forested and less inhabited mountain routes, which provided ample opportunities for brigands to assault, were always the most dangerous to travel. Every state developed its own security system against road robberies, whether it was *straža* in the Serbian medieval state,⁵⁹ *vigla* in Byzantium⁶⁰ or *derbend* in the Ottoman Empire. *Derbend* is a compound word of Persian origin meaning mountain pass or guardhouse at a pass (*der*, pass; *bend*, to hold). It denotes also a guard post by a river or seaside, or on an island.

Much research on the *derbend* institution in the Ottoman Anatolia and in the Balkans has been done so far.⁶¹ Olga Zirojević has determined that at the height of the development of *derbend* organization in the 1560s, there were 11 *derbend*s on the section Niš–Dragoman: Kunovica, Draškova Kutina, Lower Topolnica, Upper Glogovica, Vrgudinac, Klisurica, Telovac, Ponor, and Sinjac, on the route Niš–Pirot, and further to the southeast, Kalotina and Dragoman.⁶² She also gives the approximate foundation dates and the number of taxpayers in every village according to the sixteenth-century Ottoman surveys. However, by analyzing in depth these as well as other sources, we may assert that one of

---

58 BOA, TD 130: 117, 414.
59 Aleksandar Stojanovski, *Dervendžistvoto vo Makedonija* (Skopje: Institut za nacionalna istorija, 1974), 46–9.
60 On the institution of *vigla* and its continuity in the Ottoman Empire, see Ayşe Kayapınar and Levent Kayapınar, "Application of derbend Organization in the Balkans: An Example of Continuity of Balkan Institutions in the Ottoman System," in *State and Society in the Balkans Before and After Establishment of Ottoman Rule*, ed. Srđan Rudić and Selim Aslantaş (Belgrade: The Institute of History, Yunus Emre Enstitüsü Turkish Cultural Centre Belgrade, 2017), 205–22.
61 Bistra Cvetkova, "K voprosu o položenii derventdžijskogo naselenija v bolgarskih zemljah v period tureckogo gospodstva," *Učenie zapiski Instituta slavjanovedenija* 20 (1960): 196–220; Orhonlu, *Derbend Teşkilâtı*; Stojanovski, *Dervendžistvoto vo Makedonija*; Zirojević, *Carigradski drum*, 96–108.
62 Zirojević, *Carigradski drum*, 108.

the aforesaid villages did not exist on the given route[63] and, additionally, that her data on taxpayers are not always reliable.[64] Furthermore, we have ascertained that there were actually 15 guard stations, 13 of *derbenci*s (keepers of mountain pass) and two of *köprücü*s (bridge-keepers).

Derbend organisation in the Balkans was probably established soon after the Ottoman conquest.[65] According to the first available data from the fifteenth century, along the Niš–Dragoman route there were only four *derbend*s at the beginning: Kunovica situated between Niš and Bela Palanka,[66] Klisurica and Telovac (Tiholovac/Tihelovac in Ottoman sources) between Bela Palanka and Pirot,[67] and Şehirköy i. e. Pirot itself. Şehirköy *derbend* is introduced only in a brief note from January 1454 as the place where a timariot (fief-holder) lost his life.[68] Its *derbend* status is not corroborated by other sources (maybe because it was abolished in the next decades when Pirot became a larger settlement and the administrative center of the Şehirköy *kaza*).

In the opening decades of the sixteenth century, the volume of traffic on the Constantinople road increased as well as the number of *derbend*s. A survey from 1525 shows that six new *derbend*s were established in the meanwhile: Ravni Do, Draguša, Vrgudinac, Balvan, Ponor, and Sinjac.[69] In the next twenty years certain changes occurred; the *derbend* status of Ravni Do and Balvan were abolished while the same status was given to the adjacent villages of [Lower] Topolnica and Bogorodica.[70] A new guard station was founded in the villages of Lower and Upper Studena.[71] Also, the Dragoman pass was secured by the *derbend*s

---

63 Upper Glogovica (today's Glogovica) is situated south of Trn in Bulgaria. It is incorrect to identify this village with Glogovac, northwest of Bela Palanka, because it was founded in the 1580s under the name of Treštavica. *Jocić, Belopalanačka naselja*, 74–6.
64 The number of taxpayers from 1570 (BOA, TD 492) is doubled by Zirojević in a way that the total number of taxpayers is quoted as the number of *derbenci*s while individual data on households, bachelors and widows are quoted as the number of the non-*derbenci* residents of the same village.
65 Cvetkova, "K voprosu o položenii derventdžijskogo naselenija," 203; Stojanovski, *Dervendžistvoto vo Makedonija*, 40–1.
66 Vasić, Zirojević and Stojanovski, "Popis niškog kadiluka," 106.
67 BOA, TD 82: 5, 61.
68 İnalcık, Radushev and Altuğ, *1445 Tarihli Paşa Livâsı*, 138.
69 BOA, TD 130: 175, 335, 372, 418, 425, 444. Ravni Do, Draguša and Balvan are not mentioned by Zirojević.
70 BOA, TD 236: 357, 378, 395, 412. Bogorodica was also an unknown *derbend* village until now. It does not exist today; it was situated between the Topolnička and Nišava Rivers, in the vicinity of the villages Vrgudinac and Novo Selo.
71 Lower Studena and Upper Studena were not registered as *derbend* in 1516 (BOA, TD 1007: 487, 525) as well as in 1564 (Österreichische Nationalbibliothek, Vienna (hereafter ÖNB), Cod.

of Kalotina and Dragoman.[72] Additionally, the river crossing at Gojin Dol was strengthened. The villagers gained the status of *köprücü*s, which meant that they were responsible for overseeing the bridge and the part of the road.[73]

By the 1570s another *derbend* was established, Draškova Kutina,[74] as well as another guard post by the river, Bačevo (*köprücü*s).[75] Eventually, the Niš–Dragoman route of almost one hundred kilometers in total length was protected with fifteen guard stations. Ottoman surveys conducted around 1585 show that the number of stations in the mountains and by the river had not changed (Tab. 1).[76]

The safety of travelers did not depend just upon *derbenci* and *köprücü* villages. Niš (in addition to Pirot) was the seat of an officer called *subaşı*. He and his military escort were responsible for maintaining public order and security in the town and its surroundings. Furthermore, many other villages along the road were inhabited by *voynuk*s i.e. "soldiers" who may also have performed guard duties.[77] *Voynuk*s were Christians in the military service of the Ottoman Empire in the fifteenth and in the first half of the sixteenth centuries; they served as armored horsemen. Later, many of them lost their military status and became tax-paying subjects (*reaya*). The others performed auxiliary, semi-military duties; a number of Bulgarian *voynuk*s took care of the Sultan's horses and served in the

---

Mixt. 632: 203a–b, 216b). That is why the villagers submitted a petition in 1566 claiming they had been *derbenci*s guarding the mountain pass Sveti Jovan since the days of yore (*kadîmden*). However, because they were not listed as such in the census, apparently by scribal mistake, tax collectors asked of them the taxes they were exempted from (BOA, Mâliye defteri (hereafter MAD), 2775: 845). Assuming that expression *kadîmden* designates a time period of more than twenty years ago, we have set the founding date of this *derbend* in the third or fourth decade of the sixteenth century.

72 Kalotina is noted as *derbend* in the census from 1544, while Dragoman is registered as an ordinary village. BOA, TD 236: 270, 439. That Dragoman became *derbend* shortly before 1544 is testified to by a large influx of new settlers, recorded by the same census, which always indicates that something in the status of the settlement had been changed. Moreover, there was a petition submitted in 1566 by the residents of Dragoman who asked of authorities to recognize their *derbend* status gained since the previous census i.e. in 1544. BOA, MAD 2775: 1683.

73 Katić and Katić, "Gojin Dol," 126–7.

74 Draškova Kutina (today's Taskovići) belonged to the Niš *kazâ*. It was not *derbend* in 1516 (BOA, TD 1007: 431) and in 1564 (ÖNB Cod. Mixt 632: 183b) which means it became a guard station later, before the census in 1585 (Tapu ve Kadastro Genel Müdürlüğü Kuyûd-ı Kadîme Arşivi, Ankara (hereafter TKGM), Tapu Tahrir defteri (hereafter TTD), 166: 293).

75 BOA, TD 492: 407–8.

76 For Draškova Kutina, Kunovica and Studena see TKGM, TTD 166: 293, 307, 333; for all others TKGM, TTD 61: 129b, 137a, 141b, 179b, 183a, 185b, 203b, 206b, 217b, 226a, 230b, 222a.

77 *Voynuk*s were noted in the villages of Mokra, Suhodol, Sredorek (today's Barje Čiflik), Držina, Prisjan and Smrdan (today's Petrovac) as well as in *derbend* villages of Klisurica and Ponor and in the villages of *köprücü*s, Gojin Dol and Bačevo. BOA, TD 130: 266, 274, 275, 284; TD 236: 418.

Tab. 1: *Derbenci* and *köprücü* (*) villages along the Niš–Dragoman route.

in the 15th c.	by 1525	by 1544	by 1570	by 1585
Kunovica	Kunovica	Kunovica	Kunovica	Kunovica
Klisurica	Klisurica	Klisurica	Klisurica	Klisurica
Telovac	Telovac	Telovac	Telovac	Telovac
Pirot	Ravni Do	→ Topolnica	L. Topolnica	L. Topolnica
	Draguša	Draguša	Draguša	Draguša
	Vrgudinac	Vrgudinac	Vrgudinac	Vrgudinac
	Balvan	→ Bogorodica	Bogorodica	Bogorodica
	Ponor	Ponor	Ponor	Ponor
	Sinjac	Sinjac	Sinjac	Sinjac
		L./U. Studena	L./U. Studena	L./U. Studena
		Kalotina	Kalotina	Kalotina
		Dragoman	Dragoman	Dragoman
		Gojin Dol*	Gojin Dol*	Gojin Dol*
			Draškova Kutina	Draškova Kutina
			Bačevo*	Bačevo*

Imperial stables. *Voynuk*s on the territory of present-day Serbia served as a local rural police force. They protected mines, mints and roads and escorted shipments of money, ore and other valuable goods.[78] Although, there is not yet explicit confirmation that the *voynuk*s along this section of the Tsarigrad road performed the same duties, it is reasonable to assume that this was the case.[79]

Road guardians were equipped with firearms and organized in units of 30 men called "drums."[80] They patrolled over a portion of road assigned to them, while a number of guards observed the surroundings from a wooden watchtower or a hut on a hilltop.[81] More often than not a mountain tavern served as

---

[78] Stojanovski, *Dervendžistvoto vo Makedonija*, 59; Srđan Katić, "Rudnik pod osmanskom vlašću u XV i XVI veku," *Istorijski časopis* 55 (2007): 143.
[79] In the *voynuk* village of Prisjan there is a place called Kale, with the remains of ditches, and, in the vicinity, at a place called An (*han*), there are traces of a Turkish inn. Also, the toponym Anište in the *voynuk* village of Sredorek, indicates the existence of another inn. Jovan Ćirić and Novica Živković, "Legende i predanja o selima pirotskog kraja," *Pirotski zbornik* 19–20 (1994): 130, 133. Knowing that in many cases road guardians used an inn as a guard post (Orhonlu, *Derbend Teşkilâtı*, 29–32), the aforementioned data appear to support our assumption that the voynuks too held some sort of guard stations.
[80] Stojanovski, *Dervendžistvoto vo Makedonija*, 80–2.
[81] Sentries at Gojin Dol used the Early Byzantine fortress (Gojindolsko kale) above the Nišava for that purpose. For more details see Katić and Katić, "Gojin Dol," 128–9.

derbenci station.⁸² By beating a drum, *derbenci*s gave the sign that passage was safe. Thus, the sound of drums became a part of the road environment as is confirmed by many contemporary travelogue writers⁸³ and local tradition.⁸⁴

*Derbenci*s were exempted from extraordinary taxes and customary levies, and, in most cases, from the tithe on agricultural products, except one bushel of wheat and one bushel of barley per household; additionally, they paid only 10, 12 or 15 *akçe*s of personal tax (*ispençe*) instead of 25 *akçe*s.⁸⁵ These tax exemptions contributed to the rejuvenation of less inhabited or abandoned settlements and that is why the Ottomans utilized them as a method for colonizing deserted places. However, this well-known strategy did not have a long-term effect and did not enable a continuing growth in population. It did boost the settlement of villages with guard duties, but only at the time of the announcement of their special status. As we can see in Tab. 2, the last four villages acquired guard duty prior to the census from 1545 and 1570 respectively (the entries marked with asterisks) which was reflected immediately in the number of their inhabitants. The first six villages had a special status already in 1525, but since data from the earlier period are not available, one cannot determine whether the number of taxpaying subjects changed significantly after gaining this status or not.

---

82 Orhonlu, *Derbend Teşkilâtı*, 29–32. We have noticed that some of the *derbend* villages paid a high amount of tax for the wine they sold (*bâc-ı hamr*), which exceeded many times the yearly production from local vineyards and/or the average wine consumption of their inhabitants. For example, Bogorodica village, consisting of 24 households, paid 300 *akçe*s while Draguša of 30 households paid only 74 *akçe*s. BOA, TD 236: 354–5, 412. The extremely high amounts of wine tax were paid by other *derbend*s in the Balkans; Banjska in Kosovo with only 11 *derbenci* households paid 200 *akçe*s. Tatjana Katić, *Opširni popis Prizrenskog canžaka iz 1571. godine* (Belgrade: Istorijski institut, 2010), 255. That means that large quantities of wine were sold on the spot. This is a direct evidence of the existence of inn or tavern at the guard station
83 Stojanovski, *Dervendžistvoto vo Makedonija*, 72–80.
84 According to a folk tale, related to the dispute between the villages of Prisjan and Držina over territory, the range of the sound of a beaten drum marked the range of the village territory. For more details see Ćirić and Živković, "Legende i predanja," 130.
85 The amount of *ispençe* depended on the importance of the *derbend*. Hence 10 *akçe*s were paid in *derbend*s notorious for banditry: Klisurica, Vrgudinac, Balvan-Bogorodica, Telovac and Lower Topolnica, while 25 *akçe*s were paid in Dragoman.

Tab. 2: Number of taxpayers in the villages of *derbenci*s and *köprücü*s according to sixteenth-century Ottoman censuses. Only settlements with complete data from all of the four censuses are included. Underlined numbers indicate non-*derbend* status while the entries marked with asterisk show the first census in which the taxpayers are listed as *derbenci*s.

	1525	1545	1570	1585
d. Klisurica	68	81	130	129
d. Telovac	28	28	54	45
d. Draguša	49	55	24	26
d. Ponor	13	24	28	39
d. Sinjac	88	72	71	86
d. Vrgudinac	7	24	12	22
d. Kalotina	42	*81	81	79
d. Dragoman	19	*37	38	60
k. Gojin dol	23	*43	41	38
k. Bačevo	49	14	*46	50

Tax exemptions, public service and the right to bear arms induced a large influx of new settlers. The population of Kalotina, Dragoman, and Gojin Dol was increased twofold and in Bačevo threefold. In Dragoman, 23 out of 37 taxpayers were registered as newcomers (in South Slavic *preselac*).[86] In the next decades only Dragoman and Bačevo continued to grow while Kalotina and Gojin Dol stagnated or slowly decreased. The demographic fluctuation is visible in other *derbend* villages too. In some of them the population diminished significantly in spite of all privileges (see Draguša and Vrgudinac). Therefore, it can be concluded that gaining *derbend* status was a major impetus to intensive settlement, but only in the beginning. The rapid rise did not last long because Ottoman authorities usually restricted the number of derbencis to 30 or 60 men per village, except in the most endangered places.

The other villages, with no special duties, were also subject to demographic fluctuation throughout the sixteenth century, no matter whether they were situated close to the road or far from it. According to a widely held opinion, the vicinity of a highway is alleged to have had a negative impact on nearby settlements due to the frequent transits of the Ottoman troops through the area. Consequently, the depopulation of the villages has been considered to be the main feature of the history of the Constantinople road in Ottoman times. However, the present study, while preliminary and limited to the sixteenth century, does not support the aforementioned opinion. After all, the town of Pirot was spreading out in the direction of the road. Before the census of 1525, a town quar-

---

86 BOA, TD 236: 439.

ter was founded in the immediate vicinity of the road, and, accordingly, it was named *Mahalle-i şehrek üstü*, which means "Mahalle by the Imperial road."[87]

Derbend organization undoubtedly influenced the small-scale internal migrations. Anthroponomastic analyses of 95 villages in the area between Bela Palanka and Dragoman, entirely inhabited by Christians in the sixteenth century, provide compelling facts about the origins of *derbenci*s and *köprücü*s. The area, known by the name Torlak, represents a part of a wider ethno-cultural region in the central Balkans, and a transitional area where the Serbian and Bulgarian ethnicities are blended. It is characterized by a particular dialect, whose oldest and most significant feature, the transition of Proto-Slavic *тj, *дj into Ч (Č), Џ (Dž), instead of Ћ (Ć) Ђ (Đ), is reflected in the formation of anthroponyms. Consequently, the typical names of Torlakians are: Čora, Džurko, Džurdža instead of Ćora, Đurko, Đurđe. This anthroponymic feature is quite discernible in the Ottoman censuses from the sixteenth century, as well. It indicates that the names starting with non-Torlakian Ð were noted exclusively in the villages that enjoyed a special status. Also, in the same villages the names starting with Rad- and Vuk- (Rade, Radič, Radoj, Radivoj, Vuk, Vukašin) were registered far more frequently than in other villages. These two roots are extremely productive, and were, judging by the Ottoman censuses, used for the most part in the area west and southwest of Torlak, among mountain transhumant herders with Vlach status. This led us to conclude that the *derbenci*s were mostly of Vlach origin, i.e. they originated from the mountain region in southwest Serbia known as *Istari Eflak* or Stari Vlah (Old Vlach, not to be confused with Walachia in today's Romania).[88]

Besides the hitherto discussed impact of tax exemptions and other benefits on internal migrations, it is necessary to address another question: whether the fact of being a part of the state security system influenced the identity and self-confidence of the *derbenci*s, bridge-keepers or *voynuk*s? The reply is definitely yes. All of the aforementioned categories were proud of their privileges and defended them whenever they were violated. Usually it happened when local tax collectors tried to extort levies from which they were free. In such cases they

---

[87] BOA, TD 130: 114. The word *şehrek* is distorted form of *şehreh, şahrah*, which means emperor/sultan (*şah*) road (*rah*).

[88] For more details on this onomastic research see Vladimir Polomac, Tatjana Katić and Srđan Katić, "Antroponimija Gornjeg i Srednjeg Ponišavlja u XVI veku, prema defteru Sofijskog sandžaka iz 1571. godine," *Zbornik Matice srpske za filologiju i lingvistiku* 61, no. 2 (2018): 21–41.

sent their representatives to Istanbul to seek justice.[89] In each of these cases, the central authority sided with the petitioners and confirmed their special rights and immunity. *Derbenci*s, *voynuk*s, and others did not hesitate to oppose the Ottoman state itself when it tried to restrict their number or even to abolish their status. In these situations, they abandoned their villages, temporarily or forever. At the end of the sixteenth century, when a wooden stronghold was built in Izvor (Bela Palanka), a number of janissaries were appointed to serve there and to guard the surroundings. As a consequence, the *derbend* status of nearby villages was abolished, which provoked great discontent among former *derbenci*s. Even twenty years later, they tried to avoid paying taxes by fleeing from their villages every time tax collectors came. The same holds true for those who lost *voynuk* status. According to Peter Mundy, an English merchant and traveler who passed through Bela Palanka in 1620, the nearby village of Klisurica was at that time empty for this very reason.[90]

Compared with the non-privileged tax-paying subjects, *derbenci*s, *voynuk*s, and other similar groups were always more ready to act in their own interests, to protect their rights, and even to resist the state when necessary. Their identity and self-perception were shaped by several factors. They were in service to the mighty Ottoman Empire. They were by the nature of their profession entitled to possess arms and ride horses. They paid significantly lower taxes; consequently, many of them were richer than an average peasant. Bearing all this in mind, it is reasonable to conclude that they must have considered themselves superior to others. Memories fade away over time, but in some communities there still exists a vague notion of a former social status. An ethnographic research carried out after the Second World War brought to light the so-called "Voynuk graveyard" in Lower Koritnica, in which only three families from this village were buried, while the other families were buried in another cemetery. The members of these three families knew that their forefathers came from Klisurica, formerly the biggest *derbend* and *voynuk* village on this section of the Tsarigrad road. Moreover, they emphasized that their ancestors were of "noble" origin and especially esteemed because they rode horses.[91] Although the peasants with semi-military duties were far from noblesse, these rather embellished and distorted memories testify to how deep the impact of the discussed

---

89 Petitions were submitted by the guardians from Dragoman, Vrgudinac, Studena and Gojin Dol, all from the second half of the sixteenth century. BOA, MAD 7534: 87, 91; MAD 2775: 845, 1643.
90 Jocić, *Belopalanačka naselja*, 29.
91 Ibid., 114–5.

Ottoman institutions was on the stratification of the rural society and in the shaping of identities.

5 Conclusion

The Constantinople road, the most important overland route in the European part of the Ottoman Empire, was significant in multiple ways, not only for the state, but also for the population of the areas it passed through. In the period of Ottoman expansion both in the Balkans and further, towards central Europe, it played a dominant role as a military road and the main artery for spreading the new state ideology. The first decades of Ottoman rule were, therefore, marked by a settling of *akıncıs* warriors and dervishes, as well as by the building of dervish lodges and *imârets* along this and other major routes. At the same time, the Ottomans replaced the medieval system of *straža* with *derbends*. In the mid-fifteenth century there were only four *derbends* between Niš and Dragoman, but as time passed and the trade volume increased, the number of guard posts rose to fifteen, and the number of facilities for travelers grew at the same time.

A large number of *derbends* were conditioned by the extraordinarily demanding mountain sections that the road passed through. The physical characteristics of the terrain also forced the Ottomans to apply measures such as: regulating the course of the Nišava River, building and maintaining bridges, deforestation, and so forth, which lead to a gradual transformation in the cultural landscape. On the other hand, the *derbend* system with its tax exemptions and other special rights influenced the demographic landscape. Villages which were declared *derbends* gained a significant number of newcomers quite quickly. They, for the most part, were not native Torlakians, but rather settlers from the areas west of the Velika Morava River, who belonged to mountain transhumant herders of Vlach origin and/or with Vlach status. They were the most mobile part of the Balkan population, who were traditionally recruited for military or semi-military duties in the Serbian medieval state, as well as in the Ottoman Empire. The *derbend* organization thus influenced the social mobility and ethnic picture of the area.

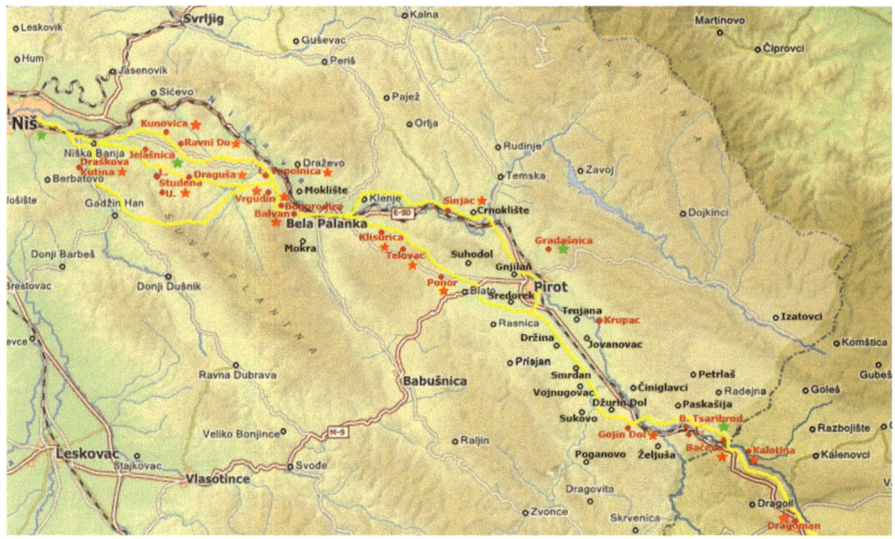

Fig. 2: Map of the Constantinople road (section Niš–Dragoman). Villages with special status are marked by red color. Cartography by Tatjana Katić.

Florian Riedler
The Istanbul–Belgrade Route in the Ottoman Empire: Continuity and Discontinuity of an Imperial Mobility Space

1 Introduction

In recent years, the modernization of transport infrastructure in Bulgaria and Serbia has literally brought to light the long history of one of the most important overland routes in the Balkans, which connects Istanbul to Belgrade from whence it continues to Budapest and Vienna.[1] When a modern highway as part of the European Traffic Corridors 4 and 10 was being constructed, the remains of the Roman roads which ran along this route were unearthed. In some places, archaeologists were able to preserve the finds, while in others the remains were destroyed, because they stood in the way of the modern infrastructure development.[2]

In the same wave of recent infrastructural modernization, in the heart of the Bulgarian capital Sofia, the remains of the Roman city of Serdica were dug up while constructing a new line of the underground. One of the most impressive archaeological discoveries was Serdica's central street axis (*decumanus maximus*), which represents the inner-city part of the overland route on which the Roman city was founded in the first century AD and which is identical with the above-mentioned highway. Rather than seeing these Roman remains as a nuisance to the speedy completion of the work, Bulgarian politicians have opted for their preservation. Since 2016, the finds have been put on display under a glass cupola adjacent to the new station, aptly named Serdica.[3]

We can get a sense for the rationale for these sophisticated and costly preservation measures from information panels, tourist brochures and other publications: Serdica connects modern Bulgaria to European history by evoking an era

---

[1] An earlier version of this paper was published as "'Orta Kol' als osmanischer Mobilitätsraum: Eine transregionale Perspektive auf die Geschichte Südosteuropas," in *Jenseits etablierter Meta-Geographien: Der Nahe Osten und Nordafrika in transregionaler Perspektive*, ed. Steffen Wippel and Andrea Fischer-Tahir (Baden-Baden: Nomos, 2018).
[2] See http://www.worldbank.org/en/news/feature/2014/05/07/breaking-through-to-future-discovering-past-serbia and https://archaeologynewsnetwork.blogspot.com/2010/06/roman-road-unearthed-in-bulgaria.html#VVRcqGA51qB1uo2e.97, both last accessed 2 November 2019.
[3] See the blog archaeologyinbulgaria.com for more information on this project.

https://doi.org/10.1515/9783110618563-006

when borders between the Balkans and the rest of Europe were absent. In the Roman Empire, Sofia was no less peripheral than today's European metropolises such as London or Paris. In the attempt by Bulgarian politicians to use Roman history for identity politics, Roman roads are also a frequent point of reference. In the Serdica display (as well as at other sites, e. g. in Serbia) these roads belong to the archaeological objects that lay visitors can decipher most easily. They can experience them directly by walking over the historical pavement, which often is very well preserved. Displayed on a map, Roman roads very evidently demonstrate the connectivity of the Roman Empire beyond modern-day borders. As Via Militaris or Via Diagonalis (both have become brand names), archaeologists, tourist managers and local politicians frequently invoke the continuity of the ancient route from Byzantium to Singidunum, present day Belgrade.[4]

At first sight, the continuity from Roman road to European transport corridor is truly fascinating. However, one is left with an uneasy feeling regarding the instrumentalization of history by tourism managers and politicians. By directly connecting Antiquity with the present day, several centuries of the route's history are being dropped from the picture entirely. Following the general approach of this volume to balance out the fixation on Antiquity, this chapter will focus on the Ottoman period of the Istanbul–Belgrade road connection. I will give an overview of the historical developments by reviewing three aspects of the route: firstly, its material side such as the road itself and other infrastructures that supported mobility; secondly, its social manifestation based on the interaction of mobile actors such as travelers and transporters, but also those who lived alongside the route (although they stayed put, they were part of the mobility network); and thirdly, the symbolic aspect of the route e. g. as part of representations or mental maps. These aspects in combination constituted a dynamic mobility space, whose expansion and contraction and technological and social transformations this chapter will map.

Together with differentiating the route's constitutive aspects, I also seek to complicate the very simple narrative of continuity when it comes to the history of the route. A meaningful understanding of continuity always has to include discontinuity, phases when the route was not working properly, because the road was cut, and travelers had to use alternate routes to reach their destinations. Thus, by looking at the route's different aspects as outlined above, the following two sections will juxtapose the story of continuity and mobility to that of discontinuity and immobility.

---

[4] Sonya Alexieva, "Via Diagonalis: The Message of Cultural Tourism," in *Cultural Corridor Via Diagonalis: Cultural Tourism without Boundaries* (Sofia: Geja Libris, 2013).

2 The Imperial Road

The river valleys of Maritsa, Nišava and Morava, the basin of Sofia as well the mountain passes at Dragoman and Ihtiman provide the geographical basis of the route, which crosses South-East Europe from the south-east to the north-west. Due to its accessibility, it must have been used for human migration and traffic long before the Romans turned it into a series of interconnecting roads in the first century AD. With its integration into a network of roads, halting places, and exchange stations for horses, for the first time the route became part of an infrastructure of power sustaining an empire.[5] Roman roads count as the archetype of pre-modern infrastructure and still today spark the imagination each time remains of one of them are discovered. Ironically, Via Militaris, the name today used as the most common shorthand for the route as a Roman road, is a modern invention that is derived from a class of roads, which, in the context of the Roman Empire, had a special status. In contrast to other Roman roads, e.g. Via Egnatia connecting Byzantium with the Adriatic or several roads in Italy, most probably the Istanbul–Belgrade route had no proper name. In each regional context it was named after the places it was heading towards.[6]

This was also one of the naming practices for the route in Ottoman times, when it was called Istanbul Road in the different languages of the empire.[7] Another related practice was to connect its name to political authority: The road was frequently called the Royal Road, i.e., Basilike Hodos and Via Regia by the Byzantines as well as Şahrah and Tarik-i Sultani by the Ottomans.[8] These names indicated that the route was in its essence an infrastructure of power. Sometimes the road was also attributed to particular rulers. In the early modern period, it was known as Via Traiana after the Roman Emperor who was not only seen as the ideal ruler, but in fact initiated many infrastructure projects in the Balkans.[9] A very similar way of thinking might explain why the chroniclers of

---

[5] Gavro Škrivanić, "Roman Roads and Settlements in the Balkans," in *An Historical Geography of the Balkans*, ed. Francis W. Carter (London: Academic Press, 1977).
[6] Michael Rathmann, "Viae publicae," in *Brill's New Pauly*, ed. Hubert Cancik and Helmuth Schneider, first published online 2006, consulted online on 24 October 2020.
[7] Olga Zirojević, "Zur historischen Topographie der Heerstraße nach Konstantinopel zur Zeit der osmanischen Herrschaft," *Études Balkaniques* 23, no. 1–2 (1987): 84.
[8] Also cf. Tatjana Katić's chapter in this volume.
[9] Mihailo Popović, *Von Budapest nach Istanbul: Die Via Traiana im Spiegel der Reiseliteratur des 14. bis 16. Jahrhunderts* (Leipzig: Eudora, 2006), 47–52.

the crusades, who also used the route on their way to the Holy Land, called it Charlemagne's road.¹⁰

Because it was so central to their domination of the Balkans, the Ottomans invested in the route's material infrastructure when it came under their control beginning in the fourteenth century. This concerned not just the road surface, but also the construction of many big and small wooden or stone bridges. Some of the most impressive examples are in use even today in and around Edirne, the largest Ottoman city in the Balkans, which acted as a capital before the conquest of Constantinople.¹¹ Caravanserais and khans are another part of infrastructure that did not concern the road's material face as such, but provided services such as shelter and food to travelers. Additionally, for protection against bandits at critical spots such as mountain passes and river crossings, the route was fitted with watchtowers, small forts or fortified khans. A corps of watchmen (*derbentçi*) was not only charged with watching the route, but its tasks also comprised repair and maintenance of the roads, bridges and khans.¹² In many cases khans also functioned as official halting places, *menzil* in Ottoman, that were the backbone of a communication system by providing post riders (*ulak*) and traveling officials with fresh horses. Also, the Ottoman army frequently used the route for its campaigns into Central Europe. For military purposes there existed a separate chain of grain and fresh-water depots and halting places. The army also had its own corps that was responsible for cleaning and repairing the roads that formed part of its marching routes.¹³

Officially, the distance of ca 960 km from Istanbul to Belgrade was counted as 170 hours.¹⁴ A chain of post riders could cover the distance in five days to deliver an urgent message. A normal caravan would take 20 to 30 days.¹⁵ Even for

---

10 Matthew Larnach, "All Roads Lead to Constantinople: Exploring the Via Militaris in the Medieval Balkans, 600–1204" (PhD diss., University of Sydney, 2016), 26.
11 Florian Riedler, "Building Modern Infrastructures on Ancient Routes: Road and Rail Development in Nineteenth-Century Edirne," in *The Heritage of Edirne in Ottoman and Turkish Times: Continuities, Disruptions and Reconnections*, ed. Birgit Krawietz and Florian Riedler (Berlin: De Gruyter, 2019), 439.
12 Cengiz Orhonlu, *Osmanlı İmparatorluğunda Derbend Teşkilâtı* (Istanbul: Eren, 1990), 70–3; also cf. Yusuf Halaçoğlu, "Derbend," in *Türkiye Diyanet Vakfı İslâm Ansiklopedisi*, 9:162–4.
13 Yusuf Halaçoğlu, *Osmanlılarda Ulaşım ve Haberleşme (Menziller)* (Istanbul: İlgi Kültür Sanat Yayıncılık, 2014), 17–50; Ümit Ekin, "Klasik Dönemde Osmanlı İmparatorluğu'nda Karayolu Ulaşımını ve Nakliyatı Etkileyen Faktörler (1500–1800)," *Belleten* 81, no. 291 (2017): 392–3.
14 Halaçoğlu, *Osmanlılarda Ulaşım ve Haberleşme*, 110.
15 Constantin Jireček, *Die Heerstrasse von Belgrad nach Constantinopel und die Balkanpässe: Eine historisch-geographische Studie* (Prague: Tempsky, 1877), 9.

larger retinues such as the Austrian embassies of the seventeenth and eighteenth centuries, which could be composed of up to 170 wagons, it took roughly a month;[16] for the Ottoman army, a travel time of about seventy days was normal.[17]

Fitted with this infrastructure, the route played an important role in protecting the sultan's power over the provinces by enabling the circulation of officials and soldiers. This military and administrative function is also evoked by the name Middle Branch, *orta kol* in Ottoman Turkish, which denotes a corridor that was defined by the route and the districts within its reach. Erroneously, today this name is often understood as the Ottoman name for the road itself. From an Ottoman imperial viewpoint *orta kol* was just one of three corridors radiating out from Istanbul into Ottoman Europe. The Left Branch (*sol kol*), connecting the capital with the Morea via Salonica, was in large parts identical with the route of the Via Egnatia of Antiquity, but did not continue to the Adriatic. The Right Branch (*sağ kol*) ran north along the coast of the Black Sea towards southern Ukraine and the Crimea. On the Anatolian side there existed a corresponding system of corridors that used the same names. In modern research this has prompted the idea to perceive the Istanbul–Belgrade route as part of one Great Diagonal Route that traversed the whole of the empire from Belgrade to Damascus.[18] In Anatolia, this central route was constituted by a the Anatolian Right Corridor that ran from Istanbul via Konya and Adana into Syria. The main importance of this second half was as the pilgrims' route on which every year the official Imperial caravan proceeded towards Mecca.

From their reliance on such overland routes for their expansion as well as their generating revenue by levelling tolls, the Ottoman as well as other empires have been called dromocracies (from Greek *dromos* = pathway, corridor).[19] As compared to the Roman Empire, in Byzantine and Ottoman times the Istanbul–Belgrade route was even more defined, given the fact that the capital was at one end point of the route and, at least in certain periods, Belgrade constituted its other terminus.

---

16 Karl Teply, ed., *Kaiserliche Gesandtschaften ans Goldene Horn* (Stuttgart: Steingrüben, 1968), 130–2.
17 Rhoads Murphey, *Ottoman Warfare, 1500–1700* (London: UCL Press, 1999), 65–7.
18 Robin Wimmel, "Edirne as a Stopover Destination: The Ekmekçioğlu Caravanserai and the Ottoman Road Network," in *The Heritage of Edirne in Ottoman and Turkish Times*, ed. Birgit Krawietz and Florian Riedler (Berlin: De Gruyter, 2020), 154–7.
19 Jacques Ancel, *Peuples et nations des Balkans: Géographie politique*, new ed. (Paris: CTHS, 1995), 101.

3 The Route on the Ottoman Mental Map

The central role that the route had for the Ottoman state also created a symbolic level, not only in the naming practices referred to above, but also in architecture, arts and science where the route was represented as state space *par excellence*. The caravanserais built along the major routes are a pertinent example: While many of them were functional buildings, it was especially those endowed by the Ottoman sultans or other high-ranking members of the elite that were intentionally designed to represent the power and munificence of the ruler and state. In the sixteenth century, the Ottoman Imperial Architect Sinan (d. 1588) developed a special type of double-wing caravanserai of which many examples were built through the early seventeenth century to serve as halting places in Ottoman Europe. One of the most impressive examples, was the caravanserai in Harmanli in present-day Bulgaria, which is today no longer extant. A similar building is the still standing early seventeenth-century Ekmekçioğlu Ahmed Pasha Caravanserai in Edirne.[20]

Another example of the symbolic significance of the route is the way it makes an appearance in the work of Matrakçi Nasuh (d. 1564), a military commander, translator and chronicler, who composed a series of works on the famous Ottoman sultans and their conquests. By defining the Ottoman dynasty's place in history and the borders of the Ottoman empire in geography, he was part of a larger venture by a group of sixteenth-century geographers who shaped the Ottoman imperial vision during the reign of Sultan Süleyman I.[21] One of Matrakçi Nasuh's richly illustrated campaign itineraries, the *History of the Conquest of Siklós, Esztergom and Székesfehérvar/Tarih-i Feth-i Şikloş ve Ustûrgûn ve Ustûnibelgrâd* (950/1543), which depicts Sultan Süleyman I's war in Hungary, deals in particular with the route from Istanbul to Belgrade and beyond. The work stands out because of its miniatures, a series of city views and depictions of smaller halting places, which together with the textual description form one continuous map of *orta kol*. The work can, in fact, count as a sophisticated form of a *menzilname*, a list of halting places, as it was usually compiled before each campaign to indi-

---

[20] Wimmel, "Edirne as a Stopover Destination."
[21] Kathryn Ebel, "City Views, Imperial Visions: Cartography and the Visual Culture of Urban Space in the Ottoman Empire, 1453–1603" (PhD diss., University of Texas, 2002), 52–5; Pınar Emiralioğlu, *Geographical Knowledge and Imperial Culture in the Early Modern Ottoman Empire* (Farnham: Ashgate, 2014), 13–55.

cate for the Ottoman army where what kind of supplies could be found.²² Its author, Matrakçi Nasuh, continued in the tradition of the famous Ottoman admiral Piri Reis who had been one of the first to include city views in his maritime atlases. In contrast to Piri Reis, Matrakçi's works with some exceptions follow land routes and, in this way, can be judged as an attempt to take stock of territories just conquered. At the same time, they also defined the limits of the empire by visualizing border cities (e.g. in Hungary) as fortresses with thick walls.

Matrakçi's work also discloses how the Ottoman elite of officials for whom it was composed understood Ottoman territory and power: as a succession of cities that were sequenced on a route. This understanding was the consequence of these officials' careers, which led them to circulate along the empire's roads when on campaign or on the way to their various posts in the provinces. Interestingly, the road itself was not depicted in the miniatures, but other infrastructures such as bridges and khans are present throughout. It is the sequential nature of cities that marks the route as an imperial space.²³

A third example as to the ability of the route to define mental maps is the way it figures as an organizing principle in Ottoman geographical writing. A case in point is the work *Cihannüma/View of the World*, a compilation of contemporary geographical knowledge by the famous Ottoman encyclopedist Katib Çelebi (1609–57), composed and continuously revised in the second quarter of the seventeenth century.²⁴ In the eighteenth century, one version was among the first printed Ottoman books. In the manuscript version of the book, in the chapter which describes the Rumelian clime (*iklim-i Rum*) comprising Anatolia and the Balkans, Katip Çelebi uses the three administrative corridors to structure his account. After describing the three Ottoman capitals, Istanbul, Bursa and Edirne, the description follows *sağ kol* until Silistre and from there moves up the Danube to Vidin. He starts anew with the description of *orta kol* until Sofia and then continues with *sol kol* until Salonica before redirecting to Üsküp (Skopje). At the end he adds outlying provinces such as Morea, the Adriatic coast and Hungary. This intuitive way of mapping the Ottoman Empire remained standard until the eight-

---

22 Hüseyin G. Yurdaydın, "Matrakçi Nasuh'a Göre İstanbul–Budapeşte Arası Menzillleri," in *VIII. Türk Tarih Kongresi, 11–15 Ekim 1976, Ankara: Kongreye Sunulan Bildiriler*, vol. 2 (Ankara: Türk Tarih Kurumu, 1976).
23 Ebel, "City Views, Imperial Visions," 170–211.
24 Gottfried Hagen, *Ein osmanischer Geograph bei der Arbeit: Entstehung und Gedankenwelt von Kātib Čelebis Ǧihānnümā* (Berlin: Schwarz, 2003).

eenth century as seen, for example, in the work of the geographer İbrahim Hamdi (who relied heavily on Katib Çelebi).²⁵

While the *Cihannüma*'s eighteenth-century printed version used maps copied from European atlases, in the original manuscript version, the author inserted many sketch maps in the tradition of strip or portolan maps. These are often arranged along the flow of a river similar to other and more elaborate Ottoman river maps, e.g. of the Euphrates or the Nile. This evidence provoked Gottfried Hagen, the expert on Ottoman geography, to make the following evaluation:

> In a way, it is quite possible that entire mental maps of the Ottoman Empire were more structured by means of axes of movement than conceived as two-dimensional expanses. The axes here might for instance be provided by the main roads radiating from Istanbul to the European provinces, known as sağ kol, orta kol, and sol kol, in reflection of the perspective from Istanbul.²⁶

Fitted with overlapping infrastructures for travelers, merchants, officials and most importantly the Ottoman army, the Istanbul–Belgrade road clearly continued the earlier functions it had in Roman and Byzantine times. As one of the backbones of the Ottoman state in the Balkans, the route was inscribed in the mental maps of the contemporaries and, together with similar axes of traffic, structured the perception of Ottoman territory. Arguably, still today the route is integrating larger political entities such as the European Union, which is the main investor in the recent modernization of the route. The result is the impression of a continuity that stretches from Antiquity to the present. However, in order to set this narrative of continuity into perspective, it is also important to take the aspect of discontinuity into account. The next section will examine those instances when the route did not function or was overshadowed by other routes.

4 Discontinuities: Weather, Disease, Bandits and Borders

In Ottoman times as well, the route's long continuity as an imperial infrastructure was punctured by intermittent phases of discontinuity. Most mundanely,

---

25 Cengiz Orhonlu, "18. Yüzyılda Osmanlılarda Coğrafya ve Bartınlı İbrahim Hamdi'nin Atlas'ı," *Tarih Dergisi* 14, no. 19 (1964): 115–39.
26 Gottfried Hagen, "Kātip Çelebi's Maps and the Visualization of Space in Ottoman Culture," *Osmanlı Araştırmaları* 40 (2012): 283–93.

bad weather such as heavy rain or snow routinely turned Ottoman roads (like all early modern roads) into swamps and sometimes destroyed important bridges. As a consequence, transportation became slower, more costly and, in the worst case, the route was entirely impassable for days or weeks.²⁷

Another important factor, which had a short-term negative impact on mobility, was the outbreak of diseases, notably wide-spread and recurrent epidemics such as the plague. As Nükhet Varlik has shown in her study on the plague in the sixteenth-century Ottoman Empire, the epidemic thrived on Ottoman imperial expansion and on the circulation of goods and people inside the empire. Plague networks ran parallel to and became an inherent (albeit unintended) part of other mobility networks. In the late fifteenth century, the plague travelled from the Adriatic coast (Venice, Ragusa/Dubrovnik) towards Istanbul using the main trade routes which partly coincided with the Istanbul–Belgrade route.²⁸ The rapid growth of Ottoman cities along the route, most notably Edirne, made them easy targets for the epidemic. In the early sixteenth century, during the campaigns of Süleyman I, the plague frequently travelled with the Ottoman army in the opposite direction from Istanbul, the hub of Ottoman plague networks, to Hungary. And later as well, the route remained a frequent vector of plague epidemics decimating the populations of cities and villages on the way. Because inhabitants often fled the plague to the countryside, the service infrastructure for traveling was also affected.²⁹

When officials died and soldiers fled, epidemics became entwined with the security situation as a medium to long-term problem for mobility. Highway robbery and banditry were constant threats to travelers and merchants using Ottoman roads. There are numerous examples of bandits cutting important trade routes including the pilgrim route, sometimes for several years.³⁰ Normally, these disruptions were kept in check by security personnel such as the *derbentçi*s; but in periods when the central authority was weak, these institutions themselves could come to a point of disintegration. This happened during the widespread disturbances in Anatolia at the end of the sixteenth and beginning of the seventeenth centuries. In the Balkans, banditry was on the rise since the late seventeenth century. As a consequence, many *derbend* villages (particularly in Alba-

---

27 Ekin, "Karayolu Ulaşımını," 402–5.
28 Nükhet Varlik, *Plague and Empire in the Early Modern Mediterranean World: The Ottoman Experience, 1347–1600* (Cambridge: Cambridge University Press, 2015), 139–40.
29 Ibid., 171–81.
30 Ekin, "Karayolu Ulaşımını," 394–402.

nia, Macedonia and Epirus) were given up; in some cases, highway watchmen were accused of conspiring with local bandits.³¹

In the Balkans, banditry peaked in the last quarter of the eighteenth and first quarter of the nineteenth century. Large companies of armed bandits composed of Muslims as well as Christians, many of them discharged soldiers, plundered villages and cities in the entire Balkan region, sometimes cooperating with local warlords and officials.³² The direct impact on communication and traffic on the Istanbul–Belgrade route has yet to be examined in detail. However, an economic historian has directly linked the rising overland transport costs in the Balkans from the late seventeenth to the first quarter of the nineteenth century with banditry.³³ The security situation probably also prevented road maintenance or new investment in the infrastructure, which was particularly important in times of technological innovations, which had started to transform transport and communication in the eighteenth century.

As a final cause of friction on the route, we must discuss territorial borders. With the conquest of Belgrade in 1521, for the first time the route from Istanbul was entirely under Ottoman control. By the middle of the sixteenth century, Ottoman control was extended into Hungary. In 1699, as a result of the wars after the unsuccessful second siege of Vienna, Belgrade became the Ottoman border city once again. At the Habsburg-Ottoman border, Habsburg quarantine stations at Semlin (Zemun) and Pančova located west and north of Belgrade were an obstacle to free movement: to prevent pestilence from spreading from the Ottoman Empire to the Habsburg Monarchy, all travelers were examined, all goods were unpacked, aired and cleaned, and everyone and everything had to wait until it was clear that they were not infected. For a short period between 1718 and 1739, the border even moved further south to the north of Niš and there was a quarantine at Paraćin.³⁴

When the Ottoman Empire adopted the quarantine system in the 1830s, in plague years it created internal quarantines, e.g., between Niš and Pirot and in Sofia, to prevent the epidemic from spreading along the route. Similarly, in

---

31 Orhonlu, *Derbend Teşkilâtı*, 122–5.
32 Tolga U. Esmer, "Economies of Violence: Banditry and Governance in the Ottoman Empire Around 1800," *Past and Present* 224, no. 1 (2014): 163–99.
33 Ljuben Berov, "Transport Costs and Their Role in Trade in the Balkan Lands in the 16th–19th Centuries," *Bulgarian Historical Review* 3, no. 4 (1975): 81–2.
34 Erna Lesky, "Die österreichische Pestfront an der k.k. Militärgrenze," *Saeculum* 8 (1957): 82–106; Miloš Đorđević, "Sanitary Policy of Habsburg Monarchy and Organization of Paraćin Quarantine in 18th Century," *Acta Historiae Medicinae, Stomatologiae, Pharmaciae, Medicinae Veterinariae* 35, no. 1 (2016): 29–38.

later years, the spread of cholera was also prevented with local and temporary quarantines. In 1873, all travelers to Istanbul were stopped in Plovdiv and even letters were fumigated to stop the cholera from reaching the Ottoman capital.[35]

At the same time, the inter-imperial border also stimulated traffic. The commercial provisions of the 1718 Habsburg-Ottoman peace treaty of Passarowitz (today Požarevac in Serbia) regulated the economic relations between the two empires. Although the treaty gave Habsburg merchants the right of free navigation on the Danube up to Ruse, this passage was seldom or only somewhat used. The Danube was difficult to navigate, because of shallows and rapids such as the ones at the Iron Gate. Until the regulation of the river in the nineteenth century, most trade between Central Europe and Istanbul passed along the land route from Belgrade.[36]

At the beginning of the nineteenth century, the Serbian Uprising (1804–17) added another layer of borders to the region, which affected any circulation on the route through the rebels' territory. Already during the uprising, the Serbian and the Ottoman side negotiated an agreement to keep the route open and install a customs regime.[37] After the Serbs had won autonomy in 1817, this customs agreement was continued and merchants going from the Habsburg Monarchy to Istanbul had to acquire passports from the Serbian authorities. Beginning in 1836 there was a quarantine station at Aleksinac, at the southern border of the Serbian Principality. Additionally, a wooden gate in a palisade fence marked the border between the Serbian Principality and the Ottoman Empire.[38]

The Russian-Ottoman war of 1878 again re-ordered the political map of Ottoman Europe and resulted in an autonomous Bulgaria and an autonomous province called Eastern Rumelia, whose capitals Sofia and Plovdiv were important stations on the route. Both remained part of the empire, but they had a different

---

35 Christian Promitzer, "Grenzen der Bewegungsfreiheit: Die Diskussion um Quarantänen am Beispiel des Osmanischen Reichs und Bulgariens vom Beginn des 19. Jahrhunderts bis zu den Balkankriegen (1912/13)," in: *Zonen der Begrenzung: Aspekte kultureller und räumlicher Grenzen in der Moderne*, ed. Gerald Lamprecht, Ursula Mindler and Heidrun Zettelbauer (Bielefeld: Transcript, 2012), 37, 41.
36 Numan Elibol and Abdullah Mesud Küçükkaly, "Implementation of the Commercial Treaty of Passarowitz and the Austrian Merchants, 1720–1750," in *The Peace of Passarowitz, 1718*, ed. Charles W. Ingrao, Nikola Samardžić and Jovan Pesalj (West Lafayette: Purdue University Press, 2011), 159–78.
37 Stojan Novaković, *Die Wiedergeburt des serbischen Staates (1804–1813)* (Sarajevo: B.-h. Institut für Balkanforschung, 1912), 72.
38 Felix Kanitz, *Das Königreich Serbien und das Serbenvolk von der Römerzeit bis zur Gegenwart* (Leipzig: Meyer, 1909), 2:125, 134.

customs status and therefore there were controls at their borders. The time until the First World War was characterized by two trends, one of blockage and one of modernization of the route. The more the Ottomans were forced to retreat from the Balkans, the more the imperial logic of the route vanished. It was only partly substituted for by an imperialist logic to connect Europe with the Middle East as was visible in the development of the railroad. The next section will review briefly the bifurcated history of the route in the nineteenth and early twentieth centuries until the end of the Ottoman period.

5 Nineteenth-century Acceleration and Friction

In the nineteenth century, the policy of the Ottoman government to modernize the country and strengthen the power of the central administration also abolished many of the hindrances that slowed down circulation on the route. Most importantly, the government brought the widespread banditry under control, which had characterized the Balkans at the beginning of the century. Moreover, a reform program proclaimed in 1839 known as the Tanzimat, directly addressed the modernization of transport infrastructure. In 1847, the government issued a concrete plan to renew the most important roads in order to encourage trade and raise the welfare of the country. The connections of port cities such as Izmir or Samsun to their hinterlands were at the top of the agenda; but also the route from Istanbul to Niš at the border with the Serbian Principality was mentioned in the plan. In a first step, the Ottoman government hired an engineer from the Austrian Empire to assess the costs of upgrading to a macadamized highway the approximately 200-kilometre-long road from the Ottoman capital to Edirne. In the end, the costs proved too high, so that the old imperial route was only modernized slowly and in a piecemeal fashion.[39]

The fact that the route remained in poor condition between Istanbul and Edirne is a graphic illustration of the limitations of the Ottoman reform effort. Instead of taking the direct land route, travelers between the two cities went from Istanbul by steamer to the port of Tekirdağ on the Marmara Sea from whence they continued on a new road towards Edirne located 130 kilometers to the north-west. The advantages of steam shipping became apparent soon after it was introduced in the 1830s; this can also be seen on a larger scale regarding two sea routes which began to compete with the direct land route through the Balkans. The first was the steamboat line of the Donaudampfschiffahrtsgesell-

---

[39] Riedler, "Building Modern Infrastructures," 447–9.

schaft from Vienna down the Danube to its mouth where passengers would transfer to sea-going ships to Istanbul. In the 1867, when Sultan Abdülaziz visited Europe to open the Ottoman pavilion at the World's Fair, he took this route on his way back home via Vienna and Budapest. The second was the route Trieste–Istanbul, which was served by the steamers of the Austrian Lloyd. These alternatives were used for mail and goods as well, until the direct rail connection between Vienna and Istanbul was established in 1888.[40]

Rather than in one go as had been envisaged in the 1840s, the Istanbul–Belgrade road was modernized in bits and pieces over the following decades. At the beginning of the 1850s it could still not be travelled by carriage along its entire course, as the Austrian geologist Ami Boué remarked in an essay on the transport situation in the Balkans. The two mountain passes near Ihtiman between Sofia and Tatarpazarcık (Pazardzhik) as well as a difficult passage between Hasköy (Haskovo) and Harmanli, also in today's Bulgaria, were so steep that they could only be travelled on horseback.[41]

The modernization of transport infrastructure received an important impulse in 1861 when Ahmed Şefik Midhat Pasha (1822–84), a career official in the Tanzimat bureaucracy, was appointed governor of the province of Niš. In this position, Midhat acquired his reputation as an expert in provincial administration with a stress on local economic and infrastructure development. As an immediate measure, he reorganized road construction, which was one of the main demands of the local population. This reorganization concerned technical aspects, but most importantly it included the organization of the essential peasant labor. As a result, within two years the road between Niš and Sofia was turned into a macadamized highway; especially the mountain passes between Niš and Pirot as well as at Dragoman were given priority, so that they were easier for modern coaches to use.[42]

Because one of the main goals of road construction was to revitalize the local economy, other roads were also built, such as the connection south toward

---

40 Alexander Vezenkov, "Entangled Geographies of the Balkans: The Boundaries of the Region and the Limits of the Discipline," in *Entangled Histories of the Balkans*, vol. 4, *Concepts, Approaches, and (Self-) Representations*, ed. Roumen Daskalov, Dina Mishkova and Tchavdar Marinov (Leiden: Brill, 2017), 215–23.
41 Ami Boué, *Sur l'établissement de bonnes routes et surtout de chemins de fer dans la Turquie d'Europe* (Vienna: Braumüller, 1852), 4.
42 Nejat Göyünç, "Midhat Paşa'nın Niş Valiliği Hakkında Notlar ve Belgeler," *Tarih Enstitüsü Dergisi* 12 (1982): 289, 313. The local consequences of this modernisation program will be discussed in Nenad Stefanov's contribution "Tsaribrod, a Dot On the Line: A Microhistorical Approach to Societal Change Along the Route in the Nineteenth and Twentieth Century" in this volume.

Kumanovo in Macedonia and north toward Vidin on the Danube. As Midhat's biographer Ali Haydar claims, for the local population these new routes proved most important for exporting local products such as wine to neighboring regions. Also trade with Europe was strengthened, because with the new roads between Niš and the Danube, Serbian territory could be bypassed to avoid duties and long delays at the quarantine stations.[43]

Another important project initiated by Midhat was the founding of a coach company that operated on his new roads. In the memorandum explaining his initiative, he remarked that in order to use the road network to its full capacity, vehicles were needed that were quicker than the ox carts of the local villagers. A company to be founded by a group of shareholders of rich traders, local notables and government officials was to buy coaches and organize a regular connection for passengers and goods between Niš and Plovdiv. According to this plan, after a while this line could even replace the official post service and take over the *menzil* stations along the way at a lower cost than that payed currently by the Imperial Treasury.[44]

According to the newspaper of the province, this company operated very successfully and in 1865 it had a rolling stock of 46 coaches and 129 horses. That same year, it started a regular service to Edirne, which was possible because road construction had also picked up in this province.[45] Subsequently, the Niš coach company was merged with a similar venture founded in Rusçuk (Ruse), the capital of the Danube Province, to which Midhat had been appointed governor in 1864.[46]

After Ottoman Europe had thus been catapulted into the age of stagecoaches, the next technological step, the introduction of the railway, followed almost immediately. In the Ottoman Empire, the first railroads were inland extensions of steamer lines, which linked port cities with the hinterland. In Izmir, on the initiative of the local merchants, two railway lines were completed in 1857 and 1865. The first two railway lines in Ottoman Europe, which opened in 1860 and 1866, followed a similar logic in providing a shortcut for traffic from the Danube to the Black Sea. At the same time, the Ottoman government also planned a more comprehensive railway network for Ottoman Europe. However,

---

43 Ali Haydar Midhat, *Midhat Paşa'nın Hatıraları*, ed. Osman Selim Kocahanoğlu (Istanbul: Temel, 1997), 1:33; Göyünç, "Midhat Paşa'nın Niş Valiliği," 313–5.
44 Prime Minister's Ottoman Archive, Istanbul (Başbakanlık Osmanlı Arşivi), İ.MVL 498–22521/ 001, 19 Cemaziyelevvel 1280/1 November 1863.
45 *Tuna* 6, 23 Zilkade 1281/19 April 1865; *Tuna* 8, 7 Zilhicce 1281/3 May 1865.
46 Milen V. Petrov, "Tanzimat for the Countryside: Midhat Paşa and the Vilayet of Danube, 1864–1868" (PhD diss., Princeton University, 2006), 114–6.

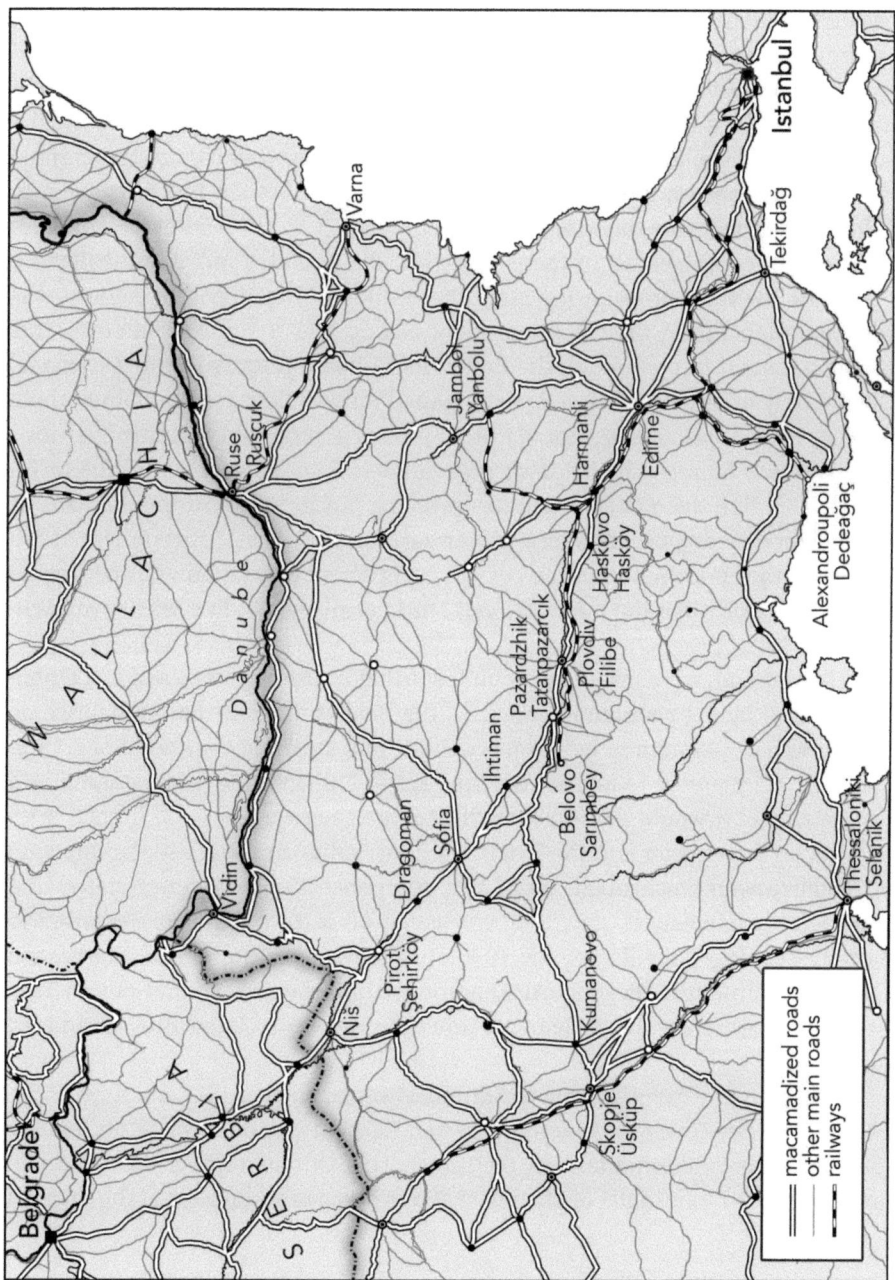

Fig. 1: The Istanbul–Belgrade route in the 1870s Ottoman transport network. Redrawn by Florian Riedler from H. Kiepert, "General-Karte der europäischen Türkei," four sheets, 1:1,000,000, new edition (Berlin: Reimer, 1871) with added railway lines opened until 1874.

because of the lack of know-how and capital, it was highly dependent on investors from Europe. Until such a network was commenced in the 1870s, many unrealized plans give insight into the way different actors tried to use this new technology. In 1856, a British consortium won a concession for a line connecting the Danube via Edirne to the Aegean, but never built it. Another concession granted in 1860 envisioned a line from Istanbul to Niš with a branch line from Sofia to Salonica, but this was likewise not realized. In 1863, a new and even more ambitious plan combined all of these lines, but this too also proved unrealistic.[47]

While for the European investors the economic function of a railway was very important, the Ottoman government clearly had a strategic interest. This is why the main route through the Balkans still had a priority for the Ottomans. But not only international developers planned railway lines for Ottoman Europe. In 1866, Hurşid Pasha, governor of Edirne province, proposed building a narrow-gauge railway financed by Ottoman shareholders from Plovdiv via Edirne to Tekirdağ. This line was not so much for travelers, but to transport the products of the province to the port at the Sea of Marmara. The provincial government of Edirne had other priorities than the central government in Istanbul, but because it won no support, like the other projects, the narrow-gauge line was never realized.[48]

The railroad, which was finally built starting in 1870 (under the name Oriental Railway) by a consortium headed by the Belgian investor Baron Maurice de Hirsch, was a compromise between economic and strategic considerations. Originally, it was planned to reconstruct the central Balkan route from Istanbul into Bosnia, where it would link up with the Austrian network. Several branch lines to ports on the Aegean and the Black Sea, into Serbia and south in the direction of Salonica were envisioned, too. Later, the concession was renegotiated and considerably downsized, now only consisting of: a trunk line from Istanbul to Sarımbey (Belovo), a village some 30 kilometers west of Tatarpazarcık; a branch line from Edirne to Dedeağaç (Alexandroupoli) on the Aegean and one to Yanbolu (Yambol) in central Bulgaria. From Salonica an isolated line terminated in Kosovo.[49]

The main line from Istanbul to Sarımbey was opened in 1873, but any further extensions were forestalled by the Ottoman-Russian war of 1877–78. In the war the railroad proved important for the transport of Ottoman troops and to evacuate hundreds of thousands of Muslim civilians fleeing the advance of the Russian

---

47 Vahdettin Engin, *Rumeli Demiryolları* (Istanbul: Eren, 1993), 31–60.
48 Riedler, "Building Modern Infrastructures," 455–9.
49 Engin, *Rumeli Demiryolları*, 49–100.

army.⁵⁰ But because of the Ottoman defeat and the creation of an autonomous Bulgaria, most of the route ceased to be under direct Ottoman control. It was not until 1888 that the rail link along the Istanbul–Belgrade route was completed and from 1889 on the Orient Express mainly used this route, covering the way from Budapest to Istanbul in 35 hours.

In summary, in the first half of the nineteenth century, the modernization of the Istanbul–Belgrade road could be implemented only slowly by the Ottoman government. Only the second half of the century saw the construction of a modern, i. e., a macadamized road, the introduction of modern vehicles, and an organization for public transport along the route. By the 1870s, parts of the route were even fitted with a railway, which accelerated traffic and promised to give it the edge over alternative routes. Perhaps Konstantin Jireček was inspired by this foreseeable revitalization when he researched and wrote *Die Heerstraße* during the 1870s. However, the technological re-invention of the route, which the Ottomans could only implement with European capital and knowhow, also changed its function and meaning. This was already indicated by its name, Oriental Railway, which only makes sense when looking from Europe; from an Ottoman imperial perspective it should rather be the Occidental or Rumelian Railway. The subsequent political changes, the fact that after 1878 only a fraction of the route was under direct Ottoman control, finally pushed the European imperialist dimension of the railway to the foreground. It no longer had any integrating function for the Ottoman Empire, but primarily served as an intercontinental connection between Europe and the Middle East. As such it was owned and operated by Deutsche Bank, before it was nationalized by the Bulgarian and Turkish governments. On a regional level, the newly established Balkan national states such as Serbia, Bulgaria and later Turkey, had different agendas for the integration of their territories, and consequently the route played no or at least only a subordinate role.⁵¹

6 Conclusion

It was the aim of this chapter to show how the Istanbul–Belgrade route was constituted in Ottoman times by a combination of three dimensions. The first two of them, the infrastructural and social dimension, established what in the sociolog-

---

50 Ibid., 178–81.
51 Cf. Dobrinka Parusheva's contribution as well as Nenad Stefanov's "Tsaribrod, a Dot On the Line," both in this volume.

ical perspective of the actor-network theory (ANT) has been called a heterogeneous network. John Law has used this term to describe the *Carreira da India*, the sixteenth and seventeenth-century sea route from Lisbon to Calicut on the west coast of India. This sea route was constituted by elements from several spheres such as the social, the political, the technological as well as the natural: "Of course kings and merchants appear in the story. But so too do sailors and astronomers, navigators and soldiers of fortune, astrolabes and astronomical tables, vessels and ports of call, and last but not least, the winds and currents that lay between Lisbon and Calicut."[52] In a like manner, we can say that the Istanbul–Belgrade mobility network was constituted by various and changing combinations of Ottoman pavement, bridges and caravanserais, rails and locomotives, but also by marching armies and sultans, traveling European diplomats, merchants, transport workers and villagers living and working along the road side.

Moreover, the chapter has added the symbolical dimension of the road, which has no place in ANT. Because of its central importance as an axis to project power on the Ottoman territories, the route was endowed with a special symbolic value. It was a way to structure Ottoman mental maps and was thought of as the spine defining a corridor (*kol*) of domination running through the Ottoman territories.

Because the mobility networks on the Istanbul–Belgrade route were sponsored by the Ottoman central government, the decline of its power negatively affected the route. Different sorts of frictions such as epidemics, banditry and borders (since the beginning of the nineteenth century) slowed down the flows of traffic. For international trade from Central Europe it remained the most direct communication line with Istanbul in the eighteenth century, but was increasingly substituted for by other routes in the nineteenth. Only with the construction of the railway line was this function as a long-distance line of communication re-established.

---

[52] John Law, "On the Methods of Long-Distance Control: Vessels, Navigation and the Portuguese Route to India," *The Sociological Review* 32, no. 1 (1984): 235.

Dobrinka Parusheva
Cities along the Route: Plovdiv Becoming "Modern" at the End of the Nineteenth Century

1 Introduction

The importance of communication networks in the modern period in Europe and for the process of becoming modern is paramount. Already in the 1970s, Eugen Weber described the pivotal role of roads in French nation-building, supporting his argument with empirical data.[1] Yet, as Erik van der Vleuten and Arne Kaijser pointed out in a bibliographical study about a decade ago, in contrast with the asserted importance of communication networks, most narratives on European history generally do not systematically include the building of infrastructure.[2] Since then, a few large scale projects have contributed to the field and a number of books has been published which discuss the importance of (transnational) infrastructures for the shaping of Europe.[3] For the Balkans, despite the fact that the approaches have varied, the scholarly interest has been focused, in general, either on the institutions involved in the construction of lines of communication (states, companies, financial bodies, etc.) or on some prominent figures (experts like engineers, bankers or company owners). Topics like governmental projects and discussions about them at diverse public levels, the ways of financing rail construction and the like, dominate the discussion of the modernization of infra-

---

[1] Eugen Weber, *Peasants into Frenchmen: The Modernization of Rural France* (Stanford: Stanford University Press, 1976).
[2] The authors pay particular attention to the transnational infrastructure building. Cf. Erik van der Vleuten and Arne Kaijser, "Networking Europe," *History and Technology* 21, no. 1 (2005), 21–48. A year later, in 2006, van der Vleuten and Kaijser edited the volume *Networking Europe: Transnational Infrastructures and the Shaping of Europe, 1850–2000* (Sagamore Beach: Science History Publications, 2006).
[3] For example, two of the sub-projects of the ESF funded EUROCORES program "Inventing Europe: Technology and the Making of Europe, 1850 to the Present" dealt with infrastructures: "Europe Goes Critical: the Emergence and Governance of Critical Transnational European Structures (EUROCRIT)" and "The Development of European Waterways, Road and Rail Infrastructures: A GIS for the History of European Integration, 1825–2005 (WATER, ROAD AND RAIL)," see http://archives.esf.org/fileadmin/Public_documents/Publications/InventingEurope_01.pdf, last accessed 24 October 2020.

https://doi.org/10.1515/9783110618563-007

structure in the region.⁴ At the same time, other "lines" have not attracted sufficient scholarly attention and need further elaboration: for example, the attitude of other social actors, like people in their role as users, who were experiencing all the changes accompanying the introduction of the technological novelties (and not only the ones related to transportation infrastructure).

Research on people's attitude and their everyday life practices of accommodation would undoubtedly enrich the overall picture of the Balkan people moving into a modern mode.⁵ Yet, since the road, and the Istanbul–Belgrade route in particular, is the main character of this volume, I will discuss here the role of communication in the development of one of the cities along this road, Plovdiv (Philippopolis in Greek, Filibe in Turkish). The last decades of the nineteenth century (1870s to 1890s) will be the focus of attention, for one important reason: in 1870 the company named Oriental Railway (owned by Baron Maurice de Hirsch) started the construction of the Istanbul–Belovo railway line, which was officially opened in 1873. This year marked the appearance of Plovdiv on the European railway map and it is of interest to see if this new development was actually an advantage, or if it turned into a challenge for the city and its population in the decades that followed. In addition, another factor played a crucial role too: Plovdiv was the capital of the Ottoman province Eastern Rumelia for seven years from 1878 to 1885, at which point Eastern Rumelia became part of Bulgaria. Here borders, as a supporting character, come into the picture.

---

4 In his newest book, the Bulgarian historian Alexandăr Kostov, a renowned specialist in the field, presents a wide regional reading of the development of transport and communications during the crucial start-up period for the introduction of new technologies in the Balkans from the end of the eighteenth century until the First World War, i.e. over the entire long nineteenth century. In addition, he offers us a successful attempt, albeit in a nutshell, for a selective overview of the development of historiography on the issues discussed for the entire Balkan region and for the whole period under consideration. Cf. Aleksandăr Kostov, *Transport i komunikacii na Balkanite (1800–1914)* (Sofia: Universitetsko izdatelstvo Sv. Kliment Ohridski, 2017). For new approaches, e.g. introducing the use of the HGIS, see Kaloyan Stanev, Eduard Josep Alvarez-Palau and Jordi Martí-Henneberg, "Railway Development and the Economic and Political Integration of the Balkans, c. 1850–2000," *Europe-Asia Studies* 69, no. 10 (2017): 1601–25.
5 In a text written several years ago, I addressed the issue of Europeanization of Balkan urban life by discussing mainly the influences on everyday reality from the point of view of the appropriation of some particular new commodities and modes of behaviour and then constructed on their basis new identities. See Dobrinka Parusheva, "*Orient-Expres*, or About European Influences on Everyday Life in the Nineteenth Century Balkans," *New Europe College Yearbook* 9 (2001–02): 139–67. Other colleagues from the region addressed similar issues too, i.e. Dubravka Stojanović, *Kaldrma i asfalt: Urbanizacija i evropeizacija Beograda 1890–1914* (Belgrade: UDI, 2008). However, the attitude of the people towards transport and communications in particular has not been studied in depth.

This position of being an imperial provincial capital reconfigured not only the political establishment, but also the commercial, economic, as well as cultural framework in which the citizens acted.

2 Modern, Modernity, Modernization: the Balkans and Europe

"Concepts such as modernity travel, and as they travel they change" is an insight from Jürgen Kocka.[6] I cannot but agree and since one of the central notions in the present text is "modern," I think it helpful to introduce the way I understand the terminology I will be using.

"Modern" is a term that first appeared in the sixteenth century, in its late Latin meaning of "now existing," "of this time." What people regard as modern and how they value it have differed over time. One can read modernity from the point of view of time, or from the point of view of style of life, or way of thinking about the life, etc. Although different opinions exist, the turn-of-the-nineteenth-century Europe may be thought of as a home of this phenomenon which stretched over social life, literature, and the arts. Modernity is most often considered a time period, but one may think of it as a model to follow as well. As to modernization, it became a central concept in the social sciences in 1950s and 1960s. I am fully aware of the different interpretations this term might provoke. Let me make it clear that I use it not as a polite allusion to an undeveloped society but rather to denote all diverse processes taking place during the transition from a traditional to a modern industrial society, from the point of view of social and economic history, history of technology, cultural studies, etc.

With the increasing emphasis on culture in the social sciences the paradigm has changed, and scholars nowadays prefer talking more about modernity and less about modernization. In addition, a move to the plural of modernity has been observed and the notion of multiple modernities was coined,[7] to express the scholarly conviction that no single country (or region) can provide a unique model for measuring the modernity of all others and that the concepts of modernization and westernization should be clearly differentiated.

---

6 Jürgen Kocka, "Multiple Modernities and Negotiated Universals," in *Reflections on Multiple Modernities: European, Chinese and Other Interpretations*, ed. Dominic Sachsenmaier, Jens Riedel, Shmuel N. Eisenstadt (Leiden: Brill, 2002), 119.
7 Shmuel N. Eisenstadt, "Multiple Modernities," *Daedalus*, 129, no. 1 (2000), 1–29.

Despite these new developments, however, modernization as a social process—or rather a set of processes—of becoming modern, or what was happening on the way to modernity always has meant Europeanization in the understanding of the contemporary Balkan people.[8] And the modernity which the Balkan societies wanted to emulate was European modernity. Europe has always been one of the key concepts in modern (and contemporary) Balkan history and the frustration of being "in Europe but not of it,"[9] has been pronounced.

The nineteenth century was the time of an omnipotent invasion of European influences of all kinds into the Balkans. After the Anglo-Turkish commercial treaty of 1838 and the Tanzimat Charter of 1839 (which provided the necessary institutions to foster the Western economic control that the treaty had made possible), the European impact on the Ottoman Empire and the Balkans in particular was increasing, slowly but irreversibly.

What did Balkan people perceive as Europe? We can observe a remarkable shift from the East (Orthodox Europe) to the West as a reference point in all Balkan lands during the nineteenth century. Despite the fact that Europe appeared to the Balkan people as something strange and foreign (they normally talked of "going to Europe"), in the eyes of most Balkan intellectuals, this foreign Europe was advanced, superior and worthy of emulation, a civilizing force which was stirring the passive Orient.

The West European influences used various channels to reach the southeast corner of the continent: by the end of the eighteenth century, interactions through other European peripheries, like Constantinople or Russia, dominated the direct communication and this situation mirrored the available networks: the Balkan lands were connected politically to the center of the empire and spiritually to the closest Orthodox land, which had powerful interests in the region. During the nineteenth century, and particularly from the mid-nineteenth century onwards, the European influences were already reaching the region directly. Yet, the changes coming from the West affected primarily the towns along the Danube River and along the railway line constructed by Baron Maurice de Hirsch (the two main channels of communication in the region) and the capital cities and some other large towns as well. The countryside remained impervious to European influences for a long time due to the lack of appropriate communication networks.

---

[8] In this text I use the Balkans for the lands that belonged, in one way or another, at one time or another, to the Ottoman Empire.
[9] Mark Mazower, *The Balkans* (London: Phoenix, 2000), 9.

3 Modernizing Infrastructure in the Balkans: Building the "Iron Militaris"

Building railways was one of the main features of the movement toward modernity all over Europe. Since railways, as a means of communication, were not only closely connected to the new understanding and experience of time and distance but also played a significant role in the development of the city of Plovdiv, it is necessary to pay some attention to their appearance and use in the region.

During the nineteenth century, in response to the Western challenge of the dual revolution of political and economic change, the Balkans adopted, at least to a certain extent, the fundamental institutions of modern capitalism. As already pointed out, the culture of modernity is intrinsically connected to the triumphant progress of science and technology, and of communication infrastructure in particular. The "modern wonders" had the potential to generate both public euphoria and technophobia. In the Balkans, the development of communication networks was often considered to be threatening to the existence of the traditional pre-industrial way of life. Having stepped onto the path of modernity, however, the Balkan people could not step off.

The construction of modern transport and communications networks already started during the time of the Ottoman Empire, although the empire came late to the railway age: in 1850 no line had yet been built anywhere in the imperial lands; the first tracks appeared only during the second half of the nineteenth century. The empire gradually engaged in railroad building in an attempt to reverse its economic and military decline, and this became particularly urgent after the opening of the Suez Canal in 1869. In response, the German-Austrian-Ottoman alliance was established, with an attempt to counter the British-French transport hegemony by building the so-called Berlin-Baghdad railway.[10] Although the project halted some 600 kilometers before Baghdad due to the dismemberment of the Ottoman Empire, the Vienna–Istanbul line was completed in 1888 and turned into an important trans-European railway axis.

The construction of railway tracks during the imperial period was of modest proportions. After the process had already started, one might have expected that it would have enjoyed some powerful momentum after the newly born Balkan states embarked on their independent development. Yet, what they achieved

---

10 Cf. Aristotle Tympas and Irene Anastasiadou, "Constructing Balkan Europe: The Modern Greek Pursuit of an 'Iron Egnatia'," in *Networking Europe*, ed. Erik van der Vleuten and Arne Kaijser (Sagamore Beach: Science History Publications, 2006), 27–8. The term "Iron Militaris" is adapted from this article.

in this area by the beginning of the twentieth century was actually not very impressive.[11] Communication networks were created very slowly, having to overcome many obstacles. One may claim that what Ivan Berend states for a neighboring region was true for the Balkans as well: despite all attempts, during the second half of the nineteenth century "[W]hile Western Europe rode a new express train, most of Central and Eastern Europe still ambled along in an old stagecoach."[12]

The Balkan governments' lack of success in constructing a communication system was a consequence of their limited freedom to decide on the location of the main infrastructure axes, which were generally imposed by the Great Powers. Other problems contributed to the poor performance of both the Ottoman Empire and the newly established modern nation states in the region during the second half of the nineteenth century: on the one hand, technology had to be imported, and that, together with the construction itself, required a huge amount of capital investments; on the other hand, specialists were needed who were familiar with this new technology, and since the region lacked such people, it depended on their import as well, at least at the beginning. The edu-

---

[11] The comparative data demonstrate the clear gap between Southeast and Western Europe at the time. Cf. e. g. Holm Sundhaussen, *Historische Statistik Serbiens 1834–1914: Mit europäischen Vergleichsdaten* (Munich: Oldenbourg, 1989), 517. For more information on railway building and related issues, see Halil İnalcık and Donald Quataert, eds., *An Economic and Social History of the Ottoman Empire* (Cambridge: Cambridge University Press, 1994), 2:804–15; Alexandre Kostov, "Les Balkans et le réseau ferroviaire européen avant la Première Guerre mondiale," in *Les réseaux européens transnationaux XIXe–XXe siècles: Quels enjeux?*, ed. Michèle Merger, Albert Carreras and Andrea Guintini (Nantes: Ouest, 1995), 48–60; Alexandre Kostov, "Entre l'influence occidentale et les efforts nationaux: Le choix des systèmes et du financement des chemins de fer dans les Balkans (1860–1912)," *Etudes balkaniques* 2–3 (2001): 11–20; Harald Heppner, ed., *Der Weg führt über Österreich: Zur Geschichte des Verkehrs- und Nachrichtenwesens von und nach Südosteuropa (18. Jahrhundert bis zur Gegenwart)* (Vienna: Böhlau, 1996). This is just a very small selection of the available historiography. The newest comprehensive account about the development of the transport and communications in the Balkans up to the First World War is provided in Kostov, *Transport i komunikacii na Balkanite*.

[12] Ivan Berend, *Decades of Crisis: Central and Eastern Europe before World War II* (Berkeley: University of California Press, 1998), 3. In fact, if for Central and Eastern Europe one may speak about "old stagecoach," in the Balkans we need to consider perhaps a "new" one, since a direct stagecoach line along the route to Istanbul was only created in the 1860s. Cf. Florian Riedler's chapter in this volume. In this section I follow the main ideas of my own discussion of the topic in Dobrinka Parusheva, "Europe Imagined and Performed: The Impact of Western Europe's Modernity on South East European Urban Space," in *Städte im europäischen Raum: Verkehr, Kommunikation und Urbanität im 19. und 20. Jahrhundert*, ed. Ralf Roth (Stuttgart: Steiner, 2009), 187–204.

cation of their own engineers and technicians took the Balkan states several decades.[13]

The railway construction reflected the struggles among the Great Powers, first, to control the Ottoman Empire better, and later, to dominate the newly liberated and already independent territories. The story of the building of the Baron Hirsch railway, from Constantinople to Belgrade through Edirne, Plovdiv and Sofia, is a good illustration: the construction was often interrupted by financial and political problems, including the uprisings in Bulgaria and Bosnia, and finally the Russian-Turkish war of 1877–78. That was why the famous Orient Express made its first trip in 1883 from Paris to Constantinople via Romania and, on the last part, with the help of the steam ship line from Varna across the Black Sea to reach its destination. A few years later the construction of the direct route was eventually finalized, and it represented a considerable percentage of Bulgarian and Serbian railway track up to the First World War. The track of the Oriental Railway (Chemins de fer Orientaux) was a result of military considerations, it encompassed c. 1300 kilometers of lines and connected Istanbul to Vienna via Edirne, Plovdiv and Sofia. According to one contemporary's opinion, when the Bulgarian capital Sofia was connected by railway to both Istanbul and Paris in August 1888, "all the people were giving their blessing to the precious Orient Express that could take them from the Rhodope Mountain to the East railway station in Paris in two and a half days!"[14]

The first Balkan railways were considered as offering important economic, political and military advantages. Yet, they did not make a profit for almost two decades after their construction. The principal articles transported along them, agricultural goods for foreign markets, were available only during the summer, and during the rest of the year the traffic was confined largely to passengers and mail. From a short-term perspective, the railways were not financially successful; their impact was expected to increase after the development of the trade traffic and stimulation of production for the market. As a contemporary Bulgarian demographer and statistician wrote at the beginning of the twentieth century, "[i]t is not because our production is large that we build our lines, but because we want to make our population start producing by connecting it to the market, to the export points on the sea or the Danube river, by diminishing

---

[13] İnalcık and Quataert, *An Economic and Social History*, 2:807–11. About the education of engineers in the Balkans before the First World War see Aleksandăr Kostov, *Ot zanajat kăm profesija: Inženerstvoto na Balkanite ot načaloto na XVIII vek do Părvata svetovna vojna* (Sofia: Paradigma, 2015).
[14] Robert de Bourboulon, *Bălgarski dnevnici* (Sofia: Colibri, 1995), 124–5.

the costs of the transport and offering an opportunity for higher margins."¹⁵ Despite this and other obstacles, including its slow expansion, the railway system in the region contributed, as it had done all over the world, to the further growth of urbanization.

4 Eastern Rumelia and its Capital: Impact of Railway vs. Borders

In June 1878, at the Congress of Berlin, the lands populated by Bulgarian people were divided: only one part of them formed the Principality of Bulgaria, and an autonomous province called Eastern Rumelia was created out of another part, while the region of Macedonia remained in the Ottoman Empire. The city of Plovdiv was nominated to be the capital of the new province of Eastern Rumelia. Now I turn my attention to the situation in Eastern Rumelia and its capital, in an attempt to sketch an overall picture of the economic and social life during the decades in question. I will do this, as already indicated, through the lens of the impact of communication and more precisely the railway infrastructure, taking into account as well the role of the borders in the development of the city and region.[16]

Situated on the military and commercial route connecting Istanbul with Belgrade and Vienna, the city of Plovdiv held a central position in the area for the whole Ottoman period. It played the role of an important administrative, military and trade center of the empire. During the last decades of the nineteenth century, where our attention is focused, two major factors contributed enormously to the development of the city. In chronological order, the first one was the open-

---

15 Georgi Danailov, *Našite železnici* (Sofia, 1902), 30–3 (quoted after Rumen Daskalov, *Bălgarskoto obštestvo 1878–1939* (Sofia: Gutenberg, 2005), 2:190.
16 Strangely enough, the city of Plovdiv still lacks a concise general history authored by professionals for the period from the end of the nineteenth to the early twentieth century. There are good scholarly written narratives about Plovdiv before 1878, but when one turns attention to the period after that, the existing narratives are dominated by the political history; only some aspects of the social and economic history of this second largest Bulgarian city have been covered up to now. For the Bulgarian Revival time cf. Nikolaj Genčev, *Văzroždenskijat Plovdiv: Prinos v bălgarskoto duhovno văzraždane* (1981, repr. Sofia: Iztok-Zapad, 2007) and Andreas Lyberatos, *Oikonomia, politiki kai ethniki ideologia: I diamorphosi ton ethnikon kommaton sti Filippoupoli to 19ou aiona* (Heraklion: University of Crete, 2009). For the period after 1878 see e.g. Manio Stojanov, *Kogato Plovdiv beše stolica* (1971, repr. Plovdiv: Kăšta Hermes, 2008); Vasilka Tankova, *Kogato Plovdiv ne e veče stolica* (Sofia: Sv. Kliment Ohridski, 1994); Spyridon Ploumidis, *Ethnic Symbiosis in the Balkans: Greek and Bulgarians in Plovdiv (1878–1906)* (Istanbul: Isis, 2016).

ing of the Baron Hirsch railway; the second was that in 1878 Plovdiv became the capital of the autonomous province of Eastern Rumelia. As a result, for the next seven years the city hosted some important political but also economic institutions, which came either to change or to substitute for the former Ottoman ones.

Establishing a railway connection to the Ottoman capital in 1873 and later on, in 1888, to the Bulgarian and Serbian capitals definitely enhanced the commercial importance of Plovdiv; it also connected the city to the Aegean Sea via the shorter but very important track running from Edirne south to the port of Dedeağaç (Alexandroupoli). On a different note, with the creation of the new province of Eastern Rumelia, the newly established borders also played a major role in the development of the city. How did they do this?

The fact that Plovdiv and the region remained for seven years, from 1878 to 1885, within the borders of the Ottoman Empire, albeit with an autonomous status, definitely had an impact on their development. The legal framework of Eastern Rumelia was defined by the Organic Statute adopted in April 1879. The province enjoyed significant administrative autonomy, but remained under the political and military jurisdiction of the Ottoman Empire, particularly with regard to foreign policy. Yet, the sphere which was most influenced by this political change was trade. The establishment of Eastern Rumelia resulted in a narrowing of the market for handcrafts such as soap, russet, furriery, etc. Their production, which had already been challenged by the gradually increasing import of manufactured goods, now had to cope also with the cost increase due to the custom tariffs introduced at the border with the Principality of Bulgaria (some of the raw materials came from there). In addition, a significant number of the Turkish population—who were among the main consumers of these products—emigrated. On top of that, the administrative support for the local handcrafts diminished compared with the situation in the Principality of Bulgaria, since the province's government (called the Directorate) had to follow the directions of the Sublime Porte and the Great Powers.[17]

Even the expansive imperial market did not compensate for these disadvantages, because at the time this market had already started experiencing the difficulties well-known to the researchers of the socio-economic history of the Otto-

---

[17] On the economic development of the province of Eastern Rumelia see Stojanov, *Kogato Plovdiv beše stolica*, 67–82, and particularly Elena Statelova, *Iztočna Rumelija (1879–1885): Ikonomika, politika, kultura* (Sofia: zdatelstvo na OF, 1983), 126–67. I do not refer to any industry, or at least to any manufacturing, due to the very low level of its development in the Eastern Rumelia province.

man Empire.¹⁸ It did not compensate for the problems in Eastern Rumelia and in Plovdiv in particular.

Another question can be asked with reference to the impact of the railway. When the building works started, the French version of the newspaper *Turquie* proposed the idea that crossing the state with railways would be enough to turn the Ottoman Empire into a true rival of the USA. At the same time, however, in an article published in the more skeptical Bulgarian edition of the newspaper *Turtsiya* Todor Ikonomov, a Bulgarian writer, journalist, publisher and politician who played a major role in the struggle for the creation of the independent Bulgarian Exarchate in the second half of the nineteenth century, claimed such hopes were not reasonable. While in the West, he explained, the railways emerged not as a basis of industry but, vice versa, as a result of its development, the situation in the Bulgarian economy (as a part of the imperial) was different due to very low productivity; indeed, the question could be raised as to who built such an ineffective railway? The line, Ikonomov insisted, did not belong to the Bulgarian people and was not connected to the lines in Europe. From the Turkish, i.e. Ottoman point of view, railways were detrimental, because they were an instrument of colonial power (that is, of the Great Powers).¹⁹ It would be an exaggeration to claim that the railway had no influence at all on the economic development of the region and on the development of the city of Plovdiv; yet there is no data seconding the opposite opinion either, that is, its impact was controversial and there were various reasons for this.

As already mentioned, in 1873 the city of Plovdiv was connected by railway to the imperial capital Istanbul. Yet, the Oriental Railway with its main concessionaire Baron Maurice de Hirsch retained all rights and privileges and paid neither taxes nor custom duties to the imperial government. At the same time, the company was charging very high rates for all goods transported. After 1878, the rights of the railway company were guaranteed by the Organic Statute of Eastern Rumelia: article 34 stated that all laws and regulations related to the construction and exploitation of the railways in the Ottoman Empire should remain valid also in the autonomous province of Eastern Rumelia.²⁰ Baron Hirsch was given the right to exploit 900 square kilometers of forest near the settlement of Belovo, and in order to use it he constructed—according to some contempo-

---

18 See for example İnalcık and Quataert, eds., *An Economic and Social History*.
19 Cf. Desislava Lilova, "Varvarite, civilizovanite i bălgarite: Definicii na identičnostta v učebnicite i pečata (1830–1878)," in *Balkanskijat 19 vek. Drugi pročiti*, ed. Diana Miškova (Sofia: Riva, 2006), 229–30.
20 Manio Stojanov, *Kogato Plovdiv beše stolica*, 70.

raries illegally—the track from Sarambey to Belovo.[21] In short, the company was acting as "an independent state in our state of Eastern Rumelia," as a contemporary stated it.[22]

The railway track of Baron Hirsch was not well constructed and hence of low quality. Attempting to maximize profit, the Oriental Railway not only introduced very high tariffs for transportation of goods but in addition did not take care of maintenance and did not guarantee the security of the goods carried. From the point of view of the authorities of Eastern Rumelia, the policy of the company resulted in an increase of the prices of Bulgarian agricultural and industrial goods and hindered the trade of the province. Since there were no other transport alternatives, the company in fact was re-directing the trade away from the more convenient Black Sea harbors and sending it to the Ottoman ports of Istanbul and Dedeağaç, serving this way the economic interests of the empire. All in all, the railway, while generally considered very important for the economy, in this particular time span failed to play the expected paramount role for the development of the city of Plovdiv and the province of Eastern Rumelia.

Yet, there is one more point to clarify and it concerns the custom fees and taxes which went hand in hand with the new borders established after the Congress of Berlin in 1878. The trade between the province and the Principality of Bulgaria was hindered by the custom regime introduced in 1879: according to the Organic Statute of Eastern Rumelia, customs were established along the border with the Principality. This customs border turned into a serious obstacle for active trade relations. Despite several attempts, it proved impossible to handle properly the need and wish of both sides to escape the custom fees. In 1881 an agreement was reached to free some goods from taxes but the problem persisted, because the most important goods for both sides, e.g., cattle, wine, and tobacco were not covered by the agreement.[23] I must underline, however, that pushing the Bulgarian state border to the south-east after the unification of the province of Eastern Rumelia with the Principality of Bulgaria in September 1885 (and particularly after 1886, when most of the issues were internationally agreed on) did not help much with regard to the economic development of Plovdiv either.

---

21 Ljuben Berov, "'Iztočnite železnici' v Bălgarija (1873–1908)," *Istoričeski pregled* 1 (1959): 85–9.
22 *Dnevnici ot Petata redovna sesija na Oblastnoto săbranie*, 19 October 1883, 50. Quoted after Statelova, *Iztočna Rumelija*, 142.
23 *Dnevnici na Postojannii komitet za 1881–1882*. Kn. III, dnevnik 4, 27 November 1881, 8–9. Cf. Statelova, *Iztočna Rumelija*, 148–151. More on this topic: *110 godini Plovdivska mitnica* (Plovdiv: Saloon, 1996), 7–19.

5 Europe in Plovdiv: Modernization of Everyday Culture

After shedding some light on the roles that transport infrastructure and borders played during the period of existence of the Eastern Rumelia province, I will briefly zoom in further and focus on some traits of modernity in the urban space of Plovdiv. By doing so, I will try to turn attention to the influence which both factors—transport infrastructures and borders—had on moving the city ahead in a wider sense, that is, not only in the realm of trade and markets. Because no matter how slowly the European influences reached the city, they definitely had an impact on and made changes to the life of the city. One of the main channels of these influences was the route we are focusing on. Due to the existence of the press, in addition to the presence of published and unpublished diaries, memoirs, photographs, etc. one can read the town and its life as a text and find signs of modernity.

As already pointed out, the process(es) of modernization had already started during the time when the Balkans and the Bulgarian lands in particular were still part of the Ottoman Empire. Quite a high urbanization rate was characteristic for the empire, which had always reflected the institutional structure rather than some kind of economic complexity. Exactly this was considered the reason for why some former imperial lands experienced deurbanization after gaining (or receiving) their independence.[24] There is no data which could make one claim that such a trend took place in Eastern Rumelia. Most of the prevailing small towns in the province did not experience big changes in the totals of their populations. For the city of Plovdiv, the available data show just a small decrease of the population in 1880: from 26,670 people in 1875 to 24,053 in the 1880 census; after that, a fast and impressive recovery was observed: in 1884 the population had increased to 33,442.[25]

---

[24] This is what Palairet claims for the Serbian case. Michael Palairet, *The Balkan Economies c. 1800–1914: Evolution without Development* (Cambridge: Cambridge University Press, 1997), 28–32.

[25] See *Oficijalna statistika na istočno-rumelijskoto naselenie* (Plovdiv, 1880), 88; *Rezultati ot prebrojavane na naselenieto v Istočna Rumelija na 1885 januarii 1. Kniga I. Plovdivskii okrăg* (Plovdiv, 1885), 2–3 and 102–3. Compare the data presented by John Lampe, "Modernization and Social Structure: The Case of the Pre-1914 Balkan Capitals," *Southeastern Europe* 5 (1979): 25–7.

Apart from the population rate, culture is another marker of the process of urbanization. The Ottoman model[26] had dominated urban life in the empire for centuries, but starting in the first half of the nineteenth century it endured some significant changes due to West European influences. The modernization efforts recast the traditional urban policies based on Islamic law and traditional arrangements, and replaced the urban institutions (in the widest sense of the term) with new ones adopted, or rather domesticated from Central and Western Europe.[27] During the nineteenth century, it was not difficult to spot the confrontation of the two models in the Balkan towns, including Plovdiv.

In 1878–1885, Plovdiv was the capital of the autonomous province. This, along with its position on the route, both contributed to gradually turning it into a modern city during the last decades of the nineteenth century. Signs of modernity were to be found everywhere and particularly in the public spaces, and contemporary observers wrote about these in both newspapers and their memoirs.[28]

Among the main features of modernity was the appearance of new modes of sociability, in the Habermasian sense of a bourgeois public, but also in the extensions of its understanding to include alternative publics of e.g. proletarians or women, which recent scholarship has demanded.[29] For example, the appear-

---

26 While using "Ottoman model" I think of the concept of "Islamic city." For further clarifications on this see Stéphane Yerasimos, "A propos des reformes urbaines des Tanzimat," in *Villes Ottomanes à la fin de l'Empire*, ed. Paul Dumont and Francois Georgeon (Paris: L'Harmattan, 1992), 17–32.
27 I have discussed the developments related to the cities' governance elsewhere: Dobrinka Parusheva, "Running 'Modern' Cities in a Patriarchal Milieu: Perspectives from the Nineteenth-Century Balkans," in *Who Ran the Cities? City Elites and Urban Power Structures in Europe and North America, 1750–1940*, ed. Ralf Roth and Robert Beachy (Farnham: Ashgate, 2007), 179–92.
28 In addition to several local newspapers (e.g. *Plovdivski ek, Plovdivski glas, Maritsa,* etc.) that can be used as important sources of information, quite a few memoirs and diaries offer interesting opinions with regard to the process of modernisation of the city, as for example: Robert de Bourboulon, *Bălgarski dnevnici* (Sofia, 1995); Ioakim Gruev, *Moite spomeni* (Plovdiv, 1906); Todor Ikonomov, *Memoari* (Sofia, 1973); Atanas Iliev, *Spomeni* (Sofia, 1926); Konstantin Ireček, *Bălgarski dnevnik*, 2 vols. (Sofia: Marin Drinov, 1995); Rada Kirkovič, *Spomeni* (Sofia, 1928); Mihail Madžarov, *Spomeni* (Sofia, 2004); Hristo Stambolski, *Avtobiografija, dnevnici i spomeni*, 3 vols. (Sofia, 1927–1931).
29 Jürgen Habermas, *Strukturwandel der Öffentlichkeit: Untersuchungen zur einen Kategorie der bürgerlichen Gesellschaft* (Darmstadt: Luchterhand, 1962); Nick Crossley and John Michael Roberts, eds., *After Habermas: New Perspectives on the Public Sphere* (Oxford: Blackwell, 2004); Douglas Kellner, "Habermas, the Public Sphere, and Democracy," in *Re-Imagining Public Space: The Frankfurt School in the 21st Century*, ed. Diana Boros and James M. Glass (New York: Palgrave Macmillan, 2014), 19–43.

ance of special places for walks in the late afternoons or evenings belonged to the new *savoir vivre*. For the citizens of Plovdiv the numerous gardens were a reason of pride: "Our city is encompassed in all directions by beautiful places for a walk: Bunardzhika, Pipinierata, Salashite along the Maritsa River, the King's garden, etc."[30] An interesting target for walks became as well the railway station, which was at the edge of the city in the late nineteenth century. People used to go there for a walk and to look at trains and locomotives; they themselves considered the railway as a channel for the European influences.[31]

Along with the novelties, the well-established places where people could spend some time together while having a cup of coffee or a drink, playing cards, reading newspapers, or simply chatting continued to exist, with their number of visitors growing. The coffeehouse was central to the organization of public life in the Balkans already in pre-modern times. During the nineteenth century it started playing a role in the process of political emancipation of the subjects of the empire. Hence, not surprisingly, some of these public places (and spaces) were ethnically marked. This was the case in Plovdiv too: at the end of the century Bulgarians, Turks, Greeks, and Armenians usually met at different places: so, for example, one could see the old Greeks in the coffeehouse named after its first owner Karmanos, next to the central mosque; Bulgarians had their places too.[32] Another characteristic of the coffeehouse of the time was that women were excluded from that public space for quite a while, at least up to the first decade of the twentieth century. In contrast, the salon—as a part of the public at the edge of the private space—was the women's way of taking part in the social life and gradually become visible. Women belonging to the higher social strata used to have their *jours fixes* on different days of the week, and it was a matter of prestige if some of the well-known citizens (of both genders) attended them.[33]

As another new form of entertainment, teachers and other people belonging to the Bulgarian intelligentsia enjoyed gathering at homes and discussing various subjects, or singing, or dancing. As the teacher Ekaterina Karavelova recalls, "[a] barrel music box with two people in change of running it was the usual type of music for our evenings in Plovdiv. [...] Both music box-runners were soon tired,

---

30 *Plovdivski glas* 21 (1899).
31 E. g. *Plovdivski glas* 17 (1899); *Plovdivski ek* 6 (1900).
32 Nikola Alvadžiev, *Plovdivska hronika* (Plovdiv: Hristo G. Danov, 1971), 35–6; cf. Spiridonos Ploumidis, "Social and Cultural Life in Plovdiv (1879–1906)," *Etudes balkaniques* 4 (2005): 129–39.
33 Sultana Račo Petrova, *Moite spomeni* (Sofia, 1992), passim.

but the guests had not yet had enough of dancing."³⁴ Such social gatherings were happening either in the professional communities or in circles of friends. All these new public places as well as private spaces used for public events provided the contemporary actors with a range of opportunities to perform different roles.³⁵

Other novelties coming from Europe at the end of the nineteenth century can also be read as markers of modernity: summer holidays for the family, for instance, which had been unknown in the Balkans before. The fact that people were going to different places, depending on the social milieu to which they belonged, deserves mention here, for this is perfectly applicable in the case of Plovdiv: in 1900, a newspaper reported that the local "aristocracy" was going to the village of Markovo near the city. Another village close to the city, Kuklen, was the place for the new "bourgeoisie"; the town of Hisarya was visited by sick and healthy of both strata, "while artisans and workers simply stayed in town and continued working hard."³⁶

At the end of the nineteenth and beginning of the twentieth century, there were a lot of indications for the presence of the West European commodities as well as West European practices in the local society. Newspapers reported about different new artefacts, most of them considered a luxury. All these things were quite expensive at the time, so only a few families could afford to buy them. This is an indicator that new, well-to-do social strata were appearing. Their existence can be considered a sign of modernity too, if one looks at modernity from the point of view of the economic culture. The link between modern urbanization and the process of embourgeoisement (or the rise of the middle class) can be taken as self-evident, as Peter Hanak points out, and as a result of this process, he claims, modern cities changed their functional structure and their social topography.³⁷ Whether or not one should refer to these strata as a bourgeoisie in the Bulgarian case, however, is a question with regard to which I am inclined to agree with Wolfgang Höpken who asserts in an article that the bourgeoisie

---

34 *Spomeni na Ekaterina Karavelova* (Sofia, 1984), 129. Ekaterina Karavelova was a teacher in Plovdiv for a short period in the early 1880s, when her husband Petko Karavelov (one of the leaders of the Liberal Party) and some of his followers left the Principality of Bulgaria after the state putsch in 1881. Most of these emigres from Sofia became teachers in Eastern Rumelia, mainly in Plovdiv.
35 More on the actors and their roles in Dobrinka Parusheva, "Evropejski vlijanija vărhu eždnevnija život na gradskija čovek," in *Godišnik na Istoričeskija muzej v Plovdiv* (Plovdiv, 2001), 52–6; and similar ideas, elaborated in more depth, in Parusheva, "*Orient-Expres.*"
36 *Plovdivski ek* 6 (1900).
37 Peter Hanak, *The Garden and the Workshop: Essays on the Cultural History of Vienna and Budapest* (Princeton: Princeton University Press, 1998), 3.

was an "inexistent class" in Southeast Europe. According to him there was no common cultural background to unite such a class, which would include a specific behavior (bourgeois habitus), a very high regard for education and, last but not least, shared values and norms.[38] Nevertheless, the start was given to a process of embourgeoisement in Plovdiv too, and that definitely resulted from the influence of the European goods and European cultural norms, or the impact of Europe in general.

6 Between the Social Telescope and Microscope: Modern or "Modern"?

No matter where exactly European culture was coming from and which ways it was used, it gradually found its way to the Bulgarian lands and to Plovdiv in particular. Meeting it was a challenge: people wanted to be modern, but did not know how to accommodate the coming modernity to the existing background, hence sometimes irrelevant performances were taking place. So, for instance, in the 1880s, Konstantin Jireček criticized "the particular childishness" of the Bulgarian society of the time. "Everybody runs and buys European furniture, things unknown until now [...]." Furthermore, Jireček noticed that "some politicians think *that you can found* [the new Bulgarian] *society through representation and dîners.*"[39] Exactly this was the main problem: the most noticeable changes, which imitated the European style, concerned people's outward appearance while the mentality was delayed considerably, that is, the form dominated the content.[40]

The Europeanization of the Balkans was considered a way for the region to become part of Europe, that is, the modern world. The Balkan people accumu-

---

[38] Wolfgang Höpken, "Die fehlende Klasse? Bürgertum in Südosteuropa im 19. und frühen 20. Jahrhundert," in *Transformationsprobleme Bulgariens im 19. und 20. Jahrhundert: Historische und ethnologische Perspektive*, ed. Ulf Brunnbauer and Wolfgang Höpken (Munich: Kubon und Sagner, 2007), 33–70.

[39] Ireček, *Bălgarski dnevnik*, 2:374; italic in the original text "dass man mit Repräsentation und dîners eine Gesellschaft gründen kann."

[40] Romanian intellectuals at the end of the nineteenth century talked about *formele fără fond* (forms without substance) while trying to explain the phenomenon related to the process of modernization in their country. Among the leading adepts of this theory was Titu Maiorescu, whose text "Against the Nowadays' Directions of the Romanian Culture" was considered programmatic. Cf. Titu Maiorescu, "In contra direcţiunii de astăzi a culturei romane," *Convorbiri literare II (1868–1869)*, 375–81.

lated knowledge about Europe and created an image of Europe which they tried to imitate. However close this image might have been, the attempts to implement West European models were not quite successful. The performance was, in fact, very poor. As one of the reasons, the appropriate communication networks, lacking for centuries, should be listed. Especially, the scarcity of modern infrastructure was of crucial importance.[41] The newly established Balkan states, while trying to enhance economic development, had to reckon with the rules of a political cartography designed by the Great Powers for the region in the course of the nineteenth century. Hence, despite the momentum with which each newly established state developed its communication networks, infrastructural projects that were carried out did not exactly follow the economic logic of these states and as a result gave rise to a hopelessly insufficient and outdated infrastructure which has been a long-standing negative symbol of the region.

At the level of the everyday life, the communication of ideas and knowledge and the appropriation of technological novelties, that is, material artefacts, turned out to be not an easy enterprise. Nevertheless, what they had achieved at the time could be labelled "modern," rather than what is modern from a current perspective. If one takes into account the accumulated cultural experience and its divergence from the model(s) they tried to emulate, the Balkan people made some progress on their way to modernity during the last decades of the nineteenth century.

The fact that the processes of modernization and urbanization were given a start was of great importance for the city of Plovdiv and its citizens. At the same time, the presence of continuity should be underlined. Plovdiv was an old city and its short period as a capital and the years afterwards up to the end of the nineteenth century were nothing but a continuation of the previous development, since the city had always been a center of a large and rich province. The proximity to Istanbul definitely had an impact on the entire way of life, and on the local society. In March 1884, Konstantin Jireček wrote about the newspaper *Maritsa*, the herald of the city's media landscape at the time: "*Maritsa* is very weak, it is languishing and remains behind the new times."[42] Similarly slow was the pace of the city and it fitted well to its fame of possessing a "relaxing calmness," so described by both its citizens and foreign visitors. On the other hand, there is no doubt that time was needed to accept and give momentum

---

[41] The circulatory system of Ottoman command mobilisation was a dromocracy and it was not its function to articulate a web of commercial relations independent of command, i.e. to produce a system favourable to market economy. Cf. Traian Stoianovich, *Balkan Worlds: The First and Last Europe* (New York: Routledge, 1994), 99.
[42] Konstantin Ireček, *Dnevnik, 1879–1884*, vol. 2 (Sofia, 1995).

to the progress being made. Bearing this in mind, one may claim that exactly the slower pace was more appropriate for a society which had just escaped (or had it yet?) the shadow of the all-embracing understanding and practice of *yarın* (tomorrow). Perhaps if the Bulgarian political elite had approached the introduction of the undoubtedly necessary changes with more caution in Sofia, too, the result would have been better for the Bulgarian state and its population. For, if moving more slowly, in a more "oriental" way, we all would have had enough time for reflection and for correcting the mistakes, instead of repeating them constantly even though in a new mode. In 1885, alas, Plovdiv, while gaining and celebrating its unification with the Principality of Bulgaria, had lost the possibility of imposing on the Bulgarian people and state its tempo of moving towards modernity.

Nenad Stefanov
Tsaribrod, a Dot on the Line: A Microhistorical Approach to Societal Change along the Route in the Nineteenth and Twentieth Centuries

1 Introduction

The transformation of the Belgrade–Istanbul route in the second half of the nineteenth and into the twentieth centuries went hand in hand with a general change in Balkan societies. This can be understood as a profound societal change, in which former patterns of organization of power and control transformed slowly but steadily. Since the 1860s, both in the Ottoman imperial frame of the Tanzimat period as well as in the context of the new national states since the 1880s, the protagonists of the new states sought to modernize all aspects of societal life. The transformation of imperial space to national territory affected also this communication line. In this chapter, the central issue is the relation between this route as a line of communication and the new borders of the national states. I will present the example of Tsaribrod, an emerging border town approximately in the middle of the route between Istanbul and Budapest; I do this in order to focus particularly on the relationship of the local actors towards the transformation of the road and the emergence of a new obstacle, i.e., the Serbian-Bulgarian border.

The general contradiction between more or less unbounded communication and borders as new obstacles is the key issue characterizing the route in this epoch. This dichotomy can be illustrated by focusing on a particular region between Niš and Sofia, which some of the previous contributions have also analyzed. The focus on a concrete local context can provide insight into the relationship between new modes of domination and the changes in communication. The actors in this local context were, on the one hand, the officials from the new centers such as Sofia and Belgrade and, on the other hand, the local actors whose region changed from an imperial province to being on the periphery of a nation state. Their relationship reflects (in a condensed way) power-society relations—the border, what in accordance with Jürgen Osterhammel could be called the condensation of political rule (*Verdichtung von Herrschaft*): "Political boundaries are therefore concrete: physical reifications of the state, symbolic and material condensations of political rule (since the state is constantly tangible there on a day-to-day basis)."[1]

The analysis will proceed in three steps. Firstly, we will look at lines of communication in a regional space within an imperial frame. Secondly, the chapter will examine the process of drawing borders as an interrelated process between the local, the regional (the establishment of new national states) and the global dimensions (the Congress of Berlin in 1878). Necessarily connected with this bordering process is the changing quality of the paths of communication. Our route changed considerably with the construction of the railway line from Central Europe to Istanbul, which had an effect on the local context. Thirdly, the tension of "bounded space"[2] and transgressing communication will then be analyzed in its different constellations in the second half of the twentieth century. Here, the chapter will focus on the new possibilities of mobility under the changed conditions of territoriality and loyalty in socialist Yugoslavia.

Why actually Tsaribrod? Of course, it is a coincidence that this small town of all places was meant to be the place where the border between the Serbian and the Bulgarian states would cross the "Stambulskoto džade" (Istanbul Road) as it was called in the local language. But in comparison to other border towns in the region, Tsaribrod is also peculiar: it is the only town which came into being as a border town and has stayed a border town for the rest of its existence until today. Only the towns on the Danube between Rumania and Bulgaria are exceptions to this, however they emerged as commercial centers and not as border cities. Since the nineteenth century, state-borders in the Balkans have often changed their positions. With advancing territorial expansion of the new nation-states, the first border towns of Romania, Bulgaria, Serbia and Greece found themselves later on deep within national territories. In the recent violent break-up of Yugoslavia, this process of moving borders and changing border towns repeated itself yet again. Also, the border line between Serbia and Bulgaria changed, but for Tsaribrod the border remained a crucial feature of the town throughout its existence. Until 1920, when the town was in Bulgaria, the border was situated to the northwest, afterwards, when it became part of Serbia, it ran in southeasterly direction; in each case the border was close by (within a distance of six kilometers), except for the period from 1941–1948 when it was not functioning.

In 1952, the name of Tsaribrod was changed to Dimitrovgrad. In this way, the Yugoslav communists tried to demonstrate their principal attachment to Yugo-

---

[1] Jürgen Osterhammel, *The Transformation of the World: A Global History of the Nineteenth Century* (Princeton: Princeton University Press, 2014), 110.
[2] Charles S. Maier, *Once within Borders: Territories of Power, Wealth, and Belonging since 1500* (Cambridge, MA: Harvard University Press, 2016), 3.

slav-Bulgarian friendship even in times of confrontation during the conflict between Tito and Stalin. Nevertheless, the local population still calls the town Tsaribrod. There were two attempts to reinstate the old name, but finally the town assembly decided that a renaming would be too costly and not necessary, given that Tsaribrod was used by the public, anyway.

In sum, Tsaribrod's permanent function as a border town as well as the fact that it was contested between Bulgaria and Serbia offers an opportunity to examine the dialectics between bordering and communication from a *longue durée* perspective.

2 Nationalism, Territory, and Borders

As Bernard Lory noted for Bitola, a city today in North Macedonia which had been contested between Greece and Bulgaria since the end of the nineteenth century, the disputed areas themselves were of little interest for the intellectual and political elites at the centers of the new nation-states.[3] The areas only became relevant as future "components" or "pieces" of the national territory, which had to be assembled from the "hereditary mass" of the Ottoman Empire. This perception and practice were also particularly pronounced in the region being discussed in detail in this chapter. The area between Sofia and Niš was disputed between the nation-states of Serbia and Bulgaria and it symbolized age-old military confrontations between the two states; any phases of peaceful cooperation appear as exceptions. The area, when finally incorporated in one of the nation-states, turned afterwards into an irrelevant space on the fringe of the national territory.

In the Balkans—and of course not only there—ethno-national demarcations became meaningful in the course of the emergence of national states. Nation was and is understood as a community of descent, independent of the subjective state of mind and the will of the individual. Such an "objective" understanding of nation[4] (as opposed to a "subjective") was primarily a politically defined com-

---

[3] Bitola, the Ottoman Monastir or Manastır (in the process of the emergence of the new nation states) belonged to those cities whose future territorial affiliation was most fiercely disputed. Bulgarian, Serbian and Greek nationalists apodictically asserted how existential Bitola's future territory was. When, after 1913, it was allocated to one of the new nation-states (Serbia), a process of decline of this former regional center to a city on the periphery began. Bernard Lory, *La ville balkanissime: Bitola 1800–1918* (Istanbul: Isis, 2011).
[4] Holm Sundhaussen, "Ethnonationalismus in Aktion: Bemerkungen zum Ende Jugoslawiens," *Geschichte und Gesellschaft* 20, no. 3 (1994), 402–23.

munity and was based on the idea of an ancestral community with clear limits independent of the will of the individual, and it constructed society as a homogeneous ethno-national or ethno-confessional community.

In the nineteenth century, the protagonists of the national idea usually defined nationality according to "objective" criteria such as language or religion. In Bosnia and Herzegovina, for example, following such an "objective" understanding, Catholics became Croats and those of Orthodox confession became Serbs. It is a peculiarity of the Central Balkan region being discussed here that the state border newly drawn in 1878 itself was the crucial factor in producing differences among a local population, which now suddenly found itself on either side of a new dividing line. Religion, language, as well as cultural practices were the same on both sides of the border and still are today. There was simply no "objective" criterion to serve as an anchor for a clear dividing line.

Nationally minded politicians, intellectuals and scholars in the two new states were well aware of this, so they made no effort to impose some sort of artificial ethnic dividing line on these two groups as they materialized on a state border. However, this did not encourage tolerance. On the contrary, the Serbian and Bulgarian nationalisms were structurally congruent; they functioned as mirror-images of one another. Both were determined by an integral nationalism: of course, there were no differences (as said on the Serbian side); after all, the people even to the east of Sofia were all Serbs. The Bulgarian variant corresponded with this: After all, the people to the south of Niš were without exception Bulgarians, as old travel descriptions and historical maps proved.

Only in recent decades has a—still small—current emerged among geographers and historians in Serbia and Bulgaria, which has set itself apart from such interpretations. In their opinion, the people of this region form their own ethnic group, which can be defined by the local language, which differs from both the Serbian and Bulgarian standard languages. This group called Shopi was separated by the border just shortly before the development of an ethnic self-awareness. The demarcation had halted and broken off the process of ethno-genesis; the people had then adapted to the Serbian or the Bulgarian ethno-national context.[5]

This last interpretation refers to the time before the founding of the nation-states to explain the identical language, cultural practices and cult of saints on both sides of the Bulgarian-Serbian border. Although challenging current ethnic

---

5 Jovan Ćirić, "Šopluk: Jabuka razdora ili most spajanja na Balkanu?," in *Granice, izazov interkulturalnosti*, ed. Božidar Jakšić (Belgrade: Forum za etnicke odnose, 1997); Stefan Dečev, "Granici i identičnosti: Ot 'seljani' i 'hristijani' do 'bălgari' i 'sărbi' (1877–1918)," *NotaBene* 21 (2011): http://notabene-bg.org/read.php?id=221, last accessed 25 November 2019.

classifications, this interpretation does not consistently question ethno-national categories as social constructs. It tries to acknowledge the specificity of the region but does not free itself fully from the established shapes of ethno-national "groupism" (Brubaker) by taking the observed ambiguity seriously in order to question the concept and practice of ethno-national classification as such.

3 Space and Infrastructure in the Late Ottoman Period: The Kaza Şehirköy/Pirot

Before turning to the central issue of this chapter, we have to reflect on the place and meaning of Ottoman infrastructures in the middle of the nineteenth century. This is important in order to demonstrate that, in the Balkans, it is problematic to equate modernization[6] with the national states. Transformations in state organization and particularly improvements in infrastructure took place before the new national states emerged, as will be demonstrated by a short but close look at regional roads. We also have to take into account the relationship between the local inhabitants and the infrastructures established by the center, the meaning and relevance the local acquired in the central plans and constructions, and the factual importance these infrastructures developed within the local context. This has also to be kept in mind when we deal with the period when national states were emerging. And, finally, to better understand the development in the post-Ottoman period, we will examine the structure of local space, concretely the micro-region around Tsaribrod, before the emergence of national states.

The village Tsaribrod, as described in Tatjana Katić's chapter, was a *menzil* on the Tsarigrad Road. As such it was part of the *kaza* (district) Şehirköy/Pirot. In 1525, Pirot was designated a *kaza* and its perimeter does not seem to have changed until 1878. The *kaza* included the territories of the present-day municipalities of Babušnica, Bela Palanka (Turk. Ak Palanka) and Dimitrovgrad

---

6 Despite the criticism of the term modernity/modernization, it will be used here, first and foremost as a descriptive term. But one should also keep in mind that the contemporaries used this term to criticize the existing circumstances and demand changes. This is not only true for the protagonists of nationalism, but also for the reformers in the Ottoman Empire, to whom the term was not unfamiliar, as the gazette of the Vilayet Tuna/Dunav shows. Cf. Michael Ursinus, "Gazette and Independent: Early Disputes between Ottoman Newspapers: Metropolitan versus Provincial," in *Querelles priveés et contestations publiques: Le rôle de la presse dans la formation de l'opinion publique au Proche Orient*, ed. Christoph Herzog, Raoul Motika and Michael Ursinus (Istanbul: Isis, 2002), 99–114.

(Tsaribrod) in today's Serbia as well as Trn (Znepolje/Iznebol), Dragoman and Godeč in today's Bulgaria. Since around 1525, Pirot was as "Nefs-i Sehirköy in the Liva [sub-province] Sofya, always a kaza in the Paša-Sandžak Rumeli."[7] For a long time Sofia was the center of the Paša Sandžak, the administrative unit that comprised a large part of Ottoman Europe (Rumeli), the seat of the Beglerbeg (governor) of Rumelia. In the 1830s, Sofia lost its central position when Monastir/Bitola became the new capital of Rumelia. In the 1840s, the *kaza* Pirot became part of the *sandžak* of Niš, which in 1864, like the *sandžak* Sofia, became part of the new Tuna/Danube Vilayet (province).[8]

The *kaza* comprised a considerable territory, approximately the size of today's Luxembourg. The Stambul Road, following for the greatest part the Nišava river, virtually cut the *kaza* in two halves, which were also characterized by distinct geographical and ecological features. The right riverbank is predominantly a karst area, dominated by high planes which gradually rise to the peaks of the Stara Planina range in the northwest with an average height of 2000 meters. This part is characterized by extensive pastures which reach until the ridge of the Stara Planina. In this part, livestock breeding was almost the exclusive occupation of the rural population. On the left riverbank, breeding was also the predominant occupation, but the structure of the landscape is different. This part is dominated by hills, varying in height from 1200 to 1600 meters, and lies under the Ruj mountain at 1900 meters in the southeast. There are only very narrow valleys with a dense vegetation mostly of oak trees. In contrast to the Zabrđe and Visok region, the villages in the Burel, a region southeast of Tsaribrod on the left bank of the Nišava river, are characterized by scattered hamlets, where one village can cover two to four square-kilometers.

The different micro-ecologies were interrelated to the regional and supra-regional traditional lines of communication. In the center of the *kaza*, the Stambul Road followed the Nišava river from the southeast to the northwest. On the right bank in the Visok region, the local roads followed the east-west directions

---

[7] Hans-Jürgen Kornrumpf, *Die Territorialverwaltung im östlichen Teil der europäischen Türkei vom Erlass der Vilayetsordnung (1864) bis zum Berliner Kongress (1878) nach amtlichen osmanischen Veröffentlichungen* (Freiburg: Schwarz, 1976), 312.

[8] The terminology changed several times. Until the 1860s, *sandžak/sancak*s were small provinces that then were combined into bigger ones called *vilayet*. Kornrumpf, *Territorialverwaltung*, 312. In 1613, for example, a sultan's *ferman* to the *beglerbeg* (governor) of Rumeli and the *kadı* (judge) of Sofia spoke of the "Nahija Šehirköy in the Pascha-Sandžak of Sofia." Cf. Galab Galabov und Herbert W. Duda, eds., *Die Protokollbücher des Kadiamtes Sofia* (Munich: Oldenbourg, 1960), 191. In 1647, a diocese existed which included the "districts of Sofia, Breznik, Šehirköy and Iznebol." Ibid., 364.

of the high plains along the foothills of the central range of the Stara Planina. In the Burel region, despite the difficult terrain, since Roman times regional roads followed the hilltops in a north-south direction and connected the Nišava valley with the Stambul Road. With this as the background and with respect to our topic of routes and infrastructures, I will now sketch the changes in the second half of the nineteenth century.

From the 1850s, the reform policy in the Ottoman Empire was characterized by the attempt of the central power to strengthen its influence in the provinces.[9] Particularly the *kaza* Pirot was the focus of such policy. As part of the *sandžak* of Niš, it became part of the new Tuna/Dunav Vilayet, which was a blueprint for a new administrative model for maintaining central power. The renowned reformer Midhat Pasha,[10] whose infrastructure policy is also discussed in the chapter by Florian Riedler, was *vali* (governor) of the *sandžak* of Niš, before he was nominated to be head of the new province. It is remarkable that this attempt at strengthening the central power of the empire also resulted in a new kind of visibility and institutionalization of the provinces themselves. Not only considering the various new administrative bodies on the regional level, which had the task to mediate and formalize power structures in the provinces, but also in a very material dimension, to concern itself with the infrastructure of the region.

As in other parts of the *vilayet*, in this region roadbuilding was also one of the visible effects of Midhat Pasha's time in office. One impulse for roadbuilding was that the borders of the autonomous Serbian Principality blocked the traditional routes from Niš to the Ottoman ports on the Danube. Therefore, two particular new regional roads were built connecting Niš via Pirot with the Danube ports of Lom and Vidin (Fig. 2). But there were not only strategic reasons for this impressive road-building program. They were also designed to strengthen intra-regional networks. Thus, the connections within the *kaza* of Pirot were re-established. Particularly in those areas at the periphery, such as the *nahija* (Turk. *nahiye*, sub-district) of Trn, it was reconnected with a modern macadamized road to Pirot. The Trn–Pirot route mentioned above is impressive for its course through a rocky terrain at 700 to 900 meters above sea level until it connects with the main route in the Nišava valley. Such roads were constructed by engineers from Belgium following the then most advanced methods of roadbuilding. Even after the end of Ottoman rule, Serbian officials, usually not that enthusiastic about the "uncivilized Asiatic Turkish tribe," were full of praise

---

9 Maurus Reinkowski, *Die Dinge der Ordnung: Eine vergleichende Untersuchung über die osmanische Reformpolitik im 19. Jahrhundert* (Munich: Oldenbourg, 2005).
10 About Midhat cf. Hans-Jürgen Kornrumpf, "Midhat Pascha, Ahmed Şefik," in *Biographisches Lexikon zur Geschichte Südosteuropas*, (Munich: Oldenbourg, 1979), 3:192–4.

for the—from their perspective—unexpectedly good shape of these regional roads, which were better than those in the Serbian Principality.[11] The road-building program could not be achieved without compulsory labor, which affected the whole population along the route. Every town or village along the road was obliged to participate in the construction works by building bridges, digging trenches, etc.[12]

These new intra-regional roads were accompanied by an infrastructure offering security and modest comfort for the travelers. Approximately every ten kilometers a *kula* (Turk. *kule*, tower) was build. Also, a dense net of khans, in the local language *anove*, was revitalized. Although today they seem to be at the end of the world, in Ottoman times they were vital points of traffic. As mentioned above, particularly the border drawn in 1920 (which ran parallel to the Trn–Pirot road and crossed it several times) led to a sharp decline in traffic and later on to a massive depopulation of the area. Since 1948 it separated anti-Stalinist Yugoslavia from the People's Republic of Bulgaria within the socialist camp and became part of the European Iron Curtain with a particularly strict border regime.[13]

At the end of Ottoman rule, the *kaza* Pirot had a road network that, beyond the intended effect of strengthening the ties with the central power, also had (possibly not foreseen) benefits for the region. These new roads strengthened the ties within the *kaza* between the separate micro-regions and provided good communication for trade with the neighboring *kaza*s and regions, like Leskovac, Samokov and the Danube ports.

---

[11] Staniša Vojinović, "Rukopis dnevnika Mite Rakića sa puta po krajevima oslobođenim 1877–1878," *Leskovački Zbornik* 18 (2003): 48–86.

[12] Cf. Milen V. Petrov, "Everyday Forms of Compliance: Subaltern Commentaries on Ottoman Reform, 1864–1868," *Comparative Studies in Society and History* 46, no. 4 (2004): 730–59. In traditional terms this obligation was called *kuluk* (compulsory work without payment) by the local population. The word is derived from the Turkish *kul* meaning servant or slave. Concerning street-building, it is remarkable that this word remained in use among the local population until socialist times. The commitment to "voluntary work" and "in the service of the socialist community" regarding the maintenance of roads was still stubbornly referred to as *kuluk* by the local population—as if from the perspective of the people not much had changed in terms of rule.

[13] Other roads from this period survived longer, e.g., the section of the Orta Kol from Niš to Bela Palanka built in 1862 by Midhat Pasha was in use until 1964, when the new motorway (*autoput*) through the Sićevo Gorge was built. This means that it was still in use in a time when transport by car had become important. Olga Zirojević, *Carigradski drum od Beograda do Sofije (1459–1683)* (Belgrade: Istorijski muzej Srbije, 1970), 36.

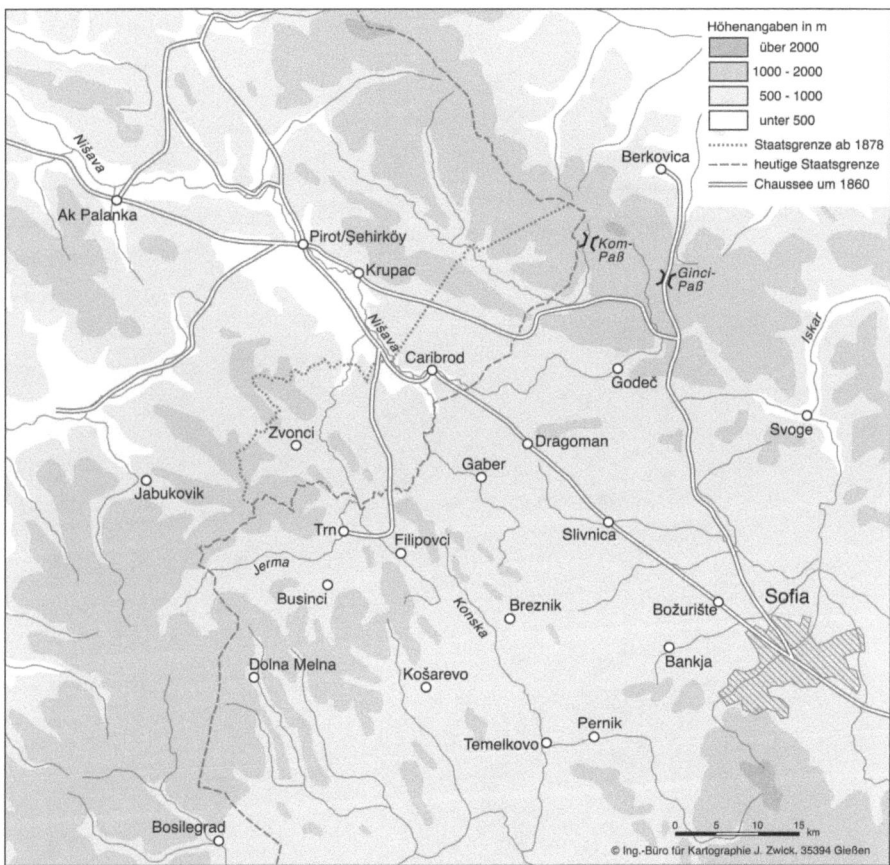

Fig. 1: Borders and Communications in the Region 1. The map shows elevation in meter (*Höhenangaben in m*), state borders after 1878 (*Staatsgrenzen ab 1878*), current state borders (*heutige Staatsgrenzen*), macadamized roads around 1860 (*Chaussee um 1860*). Cartography by J. Zwick.

Since the 1830s, Christian merchants from the region profited from the interplay of these new regional roads and the Stambul Road for regional and empire-wide communication. These traders mostly originated from the peripheral micro-regions and were successful in Pirot as the biography of Mali Rista[14] illustrates.

---

14 Saška Velkova and Mila Panajotović, *Mali Rista i njegovo vreme* (Pirot: Muzej Ponišavlja Pirot, 2014).

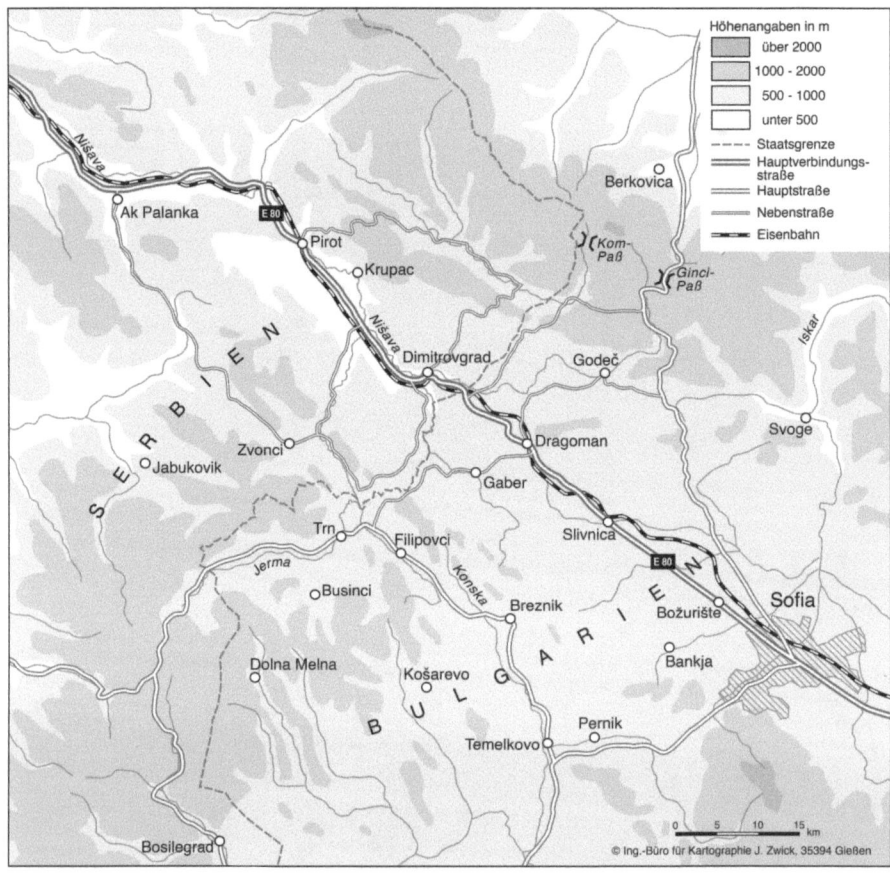

Fig. 2: Borders and Communications in the Region 2. The map shows elevation in meter (*Höhenangaben in m*), state borders (*Staatsgrenzen*), main connecting roads (*Hauptverbindungsstraße*), main roads (*Hauptstraße*), secondary roads (*Nebenstraße*), railways (*Eisenbahn*). Cartography by J. Zwick.

He came from the sheep-breeding villages of the Stara Planina and entered the business of butter production and livestock trade, selling on the level of the *kaza* in neighboring regions like Leskovac and Sofia. On the next level, provided with enough capital, Mali Rista entered the tax-farming business. This was not possible without support from the *saraf*s (bankers) in Istanbul. Mali Rista developed a close business connection with Hristo Tapchileshtov, who was a wealthy merchant and *saraf* as well an influential person within the emerging Bulgarian national church movement.¹⁵ One of Mali Rista's assets was his extraordinary familiarity with the region and excellent ties with merchants and people of power from both Muslim and Christian backgrounds. This enabled him to act on a supra-regional level with merchants like Tapchileshtov in Istanbul. Because of the information on regional matters that Mali Rista provided, Tapchileshtov could bid very precisely on particular tax-farms in Pirot as well as in the neighboring *kaza*s. Mali Rista received a share from these tax-farms and was also obliged to collect the money. Mali Rista's career-path literally reflects the interrelatedness of the material paths, i.e., the "great" Stambul Road and the new regional roads. The mobility of the new class of merchants existed before the road program of Midhat Pasha, but the building program reflected intensified mobility between regions and the center. Traditional historiography usually underestimates the societal change that was taking place within the Ottoman Empire.

4 Drawing Borders and the Effects on the Region

The networks of communication and trade that developed in Ottoman times were torn apart by the decisions of the Congress of Berlin in 1878 to have the border between the now sovereign Principality of Serbia and the newly created Principality of Bulgaria run right through the *kaza* Pirot. This marked the beginning of a profound transformation of the region, which can be illustrated also from a spatial perspective: The relations between center and province were being newly formed. An Ottoman province in which new infrastructural networks had been developing for three decades now became a nation-state periphery. At the edge of the newly formed nation-state territory, as it were, a new border cut through the traditional communication networks and structures. The usual nation-centered view sees in this just a "natural process" of a gathering of *terre irredente*—areas finally redeemed from "alien suppression." In such a perception, any difficulties on the newly created borders were caused by the local populations on both sides. That the border itself could create these difficulties, such that the local population clashed with the new officials and guards at the

---

15 SS. Cyril and Methodius National Library (Nacionalna biblioteka Sveti Sveti Kiril i Metodii, from now on NBKM), Sofia, Bulgarian Historical Archive (Bălgarski istoričeski arhiv, BIA), IA 2786, Hristo Tăpčileštov. Cf. also Svetlana Janeva, *Bălgari – otkupvači na dănăci văv fiskalnata sistema na Osmanska Imperija* (Sofia, Izdatelstvo na Nov bălgarski universitet, 2011); Evguenia Davidova, *Balkan Transitions to Modernity and Nation-States through the Eyes of Three Generations of Merchants (1780s–1890s)* (Leiden: Brill, 2013).

border, did not come to the minds of the protagonists of this new kind of territoriality of the nation-state. The new border confronted the local society with unknown difficulties, conflicts and new obstacles. This new, delimiting dimension, the experience of the border, will be briefly outlined here in two dimensions: Border demarcation and local obstinacy.

This new border stood in contradiction to the traditional use of space and regularly produced situations in which the officials seemed to be completely baffled by the practices of the rural population. Challenging the traditional orientation and use of space by cutting through the village markings, the pastures, the defined places of wood supply, led to a reaction by the rural population. Shortly after the war of 1885 between Bulgaria and Serbia, the Belgian economist Emile Laveleye (1822–1892) travelled the region and remarked, when he crossed into Bulgaria at the customs house of Sukovski-Most: "You can see that here neither historical nor geographical circumstances, but just the stipulations of a treaty have drawn the border. And with the exception of two posts, there are no other indications of the border crossing."[16] Many villagers, particularly in the Visok region, decided not to change their settlements, but to change the border line in order to maintain the full use of their lands. Thus, for years, during the night the trench marking the border between Serbia and Bulgaria was filled up by the rural population and dug out again in places which seemed to be more appropriate for the villagers—often in agreement with the villages on the other side of the border. The border-guards had to "correct" this "mistreatment of the borderline" as it was called in the official correspondence and to re-dig the trench back again to the "right" place. Until the Serbo-Bulgarian war in 1885, officials on both sides of the border could not stop such practices.

The border was primarily a new and formerly completely unknown obstacle. It was cutting through the familiar everyday space of the local inhabitants, literally separating the yard from the house, or transforming the main road of a settlement into a delimiting line.[17] As no ethnic or confessional criteria were at hand, the border commission concentrated on the canonized criteria of drawing border lines by employing natural limits such as watersheds and mountain ridges as the basis for delimitation. Thus this commission, like the others in the twentieth century to follow, searched the area for suitable border lines. It appears from the minutes of all the commissions that the inhabitants and their settlements were only unpleasant obstacles in their work. But the outcome of this

---

[16] Emile de Laveleye, *Die Balkanländer* (Leipzig: Reissner, 1888), 2:48.
[17] This is true particulaly for the villages Planinica (in the micro-region Burel) and Preseka (in Derekul). Cvetko Ivanov, *Planinica, Gornja i Donja* (Dimitrovgrad, 2016).

quest for natural delineations was everything else than natural. Because of the arbitrary nature of bordering itself, these as well as all other borders were highly artificial. The local population had to accommodate itself to these new obstacles —sometimes creating new paths over the border line by obstinately adhering to traditional orientations and directions of mobility in the local space, despite the existence of the border.

The borders not only affected local space, but also the larger region. The former connection to Plovdiv and Istanbul, so vital for Pirot and its merchants, was now cut. Customs check points collected particularly high tariffs, because from the beginning Serbia employed a protective tariff policy. The long-term effects on Pirot were sobering. The town suffered a serious decline in trade and stagnation for half a century. From the perspective of the Pirot merchants, there existed no comparably intensive trade exchange in the direction of Šumadija, the core region of Serbia, to which the city now belonged. The perspective of the center on the new periphery was similar. The Serbian officer Todor Popović was convinced that the area he was sent to as a Serbian official (*načalnik*) had little in common with Serbia proper:

> The Pirot district has nothing in common with Šumadija. This is the consequence of such powerful facts, that I have good reason to doubt that there will ever be a time in which Pirot and its characteristics will not be like a tumor for the Serbian organism. First, its geographical position, separated from Serbia by a chain of mountains, its horizon opens in the direction of Sofia. Then its political situation. Until liberation, the handful of Serbian people were for centuries in a close organic relationship to another ethnic element, in which all manly feelings and the beautiful Serbian language ceded their place to a stubbornness and to a barbaric dialect.[18]

Moreover, the overall trade of Serbia was directed almost completely towards Austria-Hungary. The exchange with the Ottoman Empire was maintained through the Morava valley on the Serbian-Ottoman border near Ristovac, connecting Serbia with the port of Salonica. Pirot on the old route towards Istanbul remained detached from these new important commercial lines of communication in a north–south direction which emerged in the Morava-Vardar valley. Also, in the newly formed Bulgarian state, the old Belgrade–Istanbul route was now of lesser importance. Bulgarian statistics document the low amount of duties that were collected from passage of the Bulgarian-Serbian border in comparison to the Danube ports and Varna. The amount of trade on the old route remained practically irrelevant. However, it has to be stressed that the numbers of the national statistics should not be retrospectively applied in

---

18 Todor Popović, *Blede uspomene mog života*, ed. Borislava Lilić (Pirot, 1996), 58.

order to get an idea of the amount of transregional trade in the Ottoman era. The regional networks, which were the basis of the prosperity and the careers of the local merchants in the period between the 1830 and 1870s, now came to an end.

5 Drawing Borders and New Lines of Communications: The Building of the Railroad in Serbia and Bulgaria

The Berlin Treaty of 1878 marked the reinforcement of a new era of territorial organization in the Balkans. It acknowledged sovereign nation-states and thereby new kinds of spatial delimitation. But at the same time, the Berlin Treaty also produced a new dialectic of bordering and communication: new borders were drawn, and at the same time new lines of communication were imposed by the treaty. In the treaty, the new states were obliged to build a railway through their territories, which would connect the Near East with Central Europe. Serbia and Bulgaria were to add the missing link to this route, which, in the decade before, the Ottoman government had started to build. In 1880, Austria reached an agreement with the Serbian government to build connections in the direction of Bulgaria and the Ottoman Empire. Two years later, agreements defining the obligations of Serbia and Bulgaria were reached by a *conférence à quatre* consisting of Austria-Hungary, the Ottoman Empire, Serbia and Bulgaria; the meetings had begun working on this in 1881, discussing the construction of railway lines connecting Istanbul with Central Europe.[19]

But these demands enforced by Austria-Hungary were not met with enthusiasm by either of the governments in Belgrade and Sofia. As in the previous decade in other parts of Europe such as France or Prussia, railways were increasingly seen primarily as a means of strengthening ties within the national territory—or even to develop this territory.[20] The dimension of transnational connectivity was of secondary importance. This was the way that the political elites in Belgrade and in Sofia also looked on the matter. The Serbian government was primarily interested in a stable railway connection to Salonica and thus were oriented towards building a railway to Ottoman Macedonia through the Morava val-

---

19 Klaus Reisinger, "Österreichs Eisenbahnwesen als Bindeglied zwischen Zentraleuropa und den Balkanländern," in *Der Weg führt über Österreich*, ed. Harald Heppner (Vienna: Böhlau, 1996), 130–1; Momir Samardžić, *Roads to Europe: The Railway Issue and Serbian Politics 1878–1881* (Pisa: Edizioni Plus, Pisa University Press, 2010).
20 Maier, *Once within Borders*, 185–205.

ley. In the deliberations of the political elite in Belgrade, the connection towards the new Bulgarian state or the Ottoman capital Istanbul along the classical route was of no relevance.

The Bulgarian government wanted railways not just to strengthen the connection within the established territorial frame, but also to create the preconditions for new territorial aspirations towards Ottoman Macedonia. In the eyes of the Bulgarian nationalists, Macedonia was part of the Bulgarian heartland that by ethnic and historical roots belonged to Bulgaria. In both states, Bulgaria and Serbia, the economic aspect of railways was given lesser significance. If a connection between railways and commerce was made, it was about gains in the future. Bulgarian economists who defended the building of railways argued that, although in the moment there was no commercial necessity for them because there were not enough goods to be carried, the railway infrastructure would accelerate the process of economic modernization and would create the preconditions for increasing commercial traffic. In this perception, railway infrastructure was intended to become the generator for the development of capitalism, following an argumentation from North America under completely different circumstances.[21] The Belgian economist Laveleye had similar high hopes for the railroad when he was traveling this area and complained about the high existing tariffs. A railroad would be a remedy for only a small amount of trade:

> The ride is incredibly long and expensive, so that you will welcome the railway with joy. Until now, Serbia keeps collecting very high customs duties, which amount to three to five per cent of the value and it is also leveled on exports. Bulgarian duties are higher and have a protective character. For one oka wine (1.02 kg) it amounts to 25 centimes, so that the wine that costs 20 centimes in Pirot ends up costing from 80 up to one franc in Sofia. The customs officer told me that imports from Serbia to Bulgaria mainly consist of butter and cheese, which go as far as Constantinople. But hemp and ropes are also imported. In 1882, the goods imported via Sukofski-Most had a value of 2,500,000 francs; in the same year, the total commerce between Bulgaria and Serbia amounted to 4,500,000 francs for both imports and exports. Of course, there is a close connection between these very low figures and the difficult transportation situation, and I am tempted to speak of a Wall of China that separates the two countries.[22]

But first and foremost, the railway was to serve future territorial expansion. In the context of the *conférence à quattre*, the government of the new Bulgarian

---

21 For the transfer of ideas from the American context concerning railways cf. John R. Lampe and Marvin R. Jackson, *Balkan Economic History, 1550–1950: From Imperial Borderlands to Developing Nations* (Bloomington: Indiana University Press, 1982), 208.
22 Laveleye, *Balkanländer*, 2:49.

Principality did not agree with the concept of transcontinental interconnection. There were even fears on the part of Bulgarian politicians that the existence of a railway would encourage a Serbian attack on Bulgaria, as Konstantin Jireček ironically noted in his diary. The Serbian army could then simply go by train to Sofia.[23]

As Jordan Dančov in one of the first studies about the Bulgarian railways summarized, the Bulgarian government claimed that it was only obliged to build the railway (which the Ottoman government had already committed itself to build in a treaty with the Oriental Railway Company owned by the famous entrepreneur Maurice de Hirsch) i. e., consisting of the line Belovo–Sofia–Kjustendil up to the border at Egri Palanka (Kriva Palanka) for a connection to Skopje (Üsküb). According to Dančov, the Bulgarian government followed national interests, creating a connection to Ottoman Macedonia and also stressed that the question of the connection under article ten of the Treaty of Berlin was formulated exactly in this direction. It pointed out that the connection via Kjustendil was also of high relevance, "especially since the connection of the Serbian railways with the Macedonian railways near Vranje meant a serious threat to the national interests in Macedonia." Vienna insisted on the Belovo–Sofia–Pirot route defined by the Treaty of Berlin, which the Ottoman Empire had committed itself to as early as 1875.[24]

Finally, after several meetings of *conférence à quattre* between 1881 and 1882, the government in Sofia gave in and committed itself to building a railway line by 15 October 1886, which would connect to the Serbian line Niš–Pirot. However, at the same time in 1882, as a sign of the political priority of a "national railway construction," a law on the construction of a railway line Svištov–Sofia–Kjustendil was passed, which was supposed to allow a connection to Macedonia.[25] Here the politics of symbols compensated for the lack of possibilities of the new nation-state to realize the ideas of the enlargement of national territory. After all, construction of the line from Radomir to Kjustendil did not begin until 1905 and was only completed in 1910. There was no connection to the Ottoman rail network.[26]

It is therefore not surprising that neither Serbia nor Bulgaria prioritized a railroad that would connect both new states along the traditional communication line of the Belgrade–Istanbul route. In both cases the political elites wanted to acquire new territories, which in essence meant creating new borders and not

---

23 Konstantin Ireček, *Bălgarski dnevnik*, 1879–1884, (Sofia, 1995); 171.
24 Jordan Dantschoff, *Das Eisenbahnwesen in Bulgarien* (Leipzig: Parlapanoff, 1917), 6.
25 Ibid., 11.
26 Ibid., 34.

creating connections across borders. It is remarkable that the region of Tsaribrod (so bitterly contested by nationalist claims in both states) played no role in the idea of a national road and communication network. For both sides, it was a dead end. At least the Great Powers forced both states to build the remaining section of the railway between Niš and Sofia and in this way to complete the missing part of a transnational connection. For the local population, this reactivated or more exactly continued the experience of living on a route that connected not only European regions, but continents, albeit of course under completely different conditions. The effect of this new experience on the region will be discussed below.

6 The Emergence of a Border Town: Tsaribrod in the Nineteenth and at the Beginning of the Twentieth Centuries

Independent of the plans of the political elites in Belgrade and Sofia about new lines of communication, the local actors in Pirot and Tsaribrod still relied on the old route as their most important connection. As the border remained in place, despite the aforementioned attempts of the rural population to move it, the merchants from Pirot became mobile themselves. Many of the wealthy families left Pirot.[27] The motif was to maintain the commercial ties to the regions which were now part of Bulgaria and the Ottoman Empire.[28] Many settled in the village Tsaribrod, at the border crossing point on the Bulgarian side, to keep close ties to Pirot and organize their business without the border as an obstacle. In the Bulgarian national narrative, the migration to Tsaribrod, which turned the village into a small town, was the proof for the patriotic spirit among the Pirot merchants, who allegedly refused to live under "Serbian domination" as it is reiterated in nearly all publications on this matter.[29]

---

[27] The exact number is difficult to estimate, but it can be said that among the higher strata of the urban population the majority left the city. Also leaving were those from the younger generation, who up to then attended the local school in the Bulgarian language and wanted to complete their education in Sofia. NBKM, BIA, fond Spas Vacov IA 227.
[28] The semi-autonomous Bulgarian Principality had to keep Ottoman tariffs and taxes until 1908, being still under the suzerainty of the Sultan.
[29] In Serbian historiography this is strongly downplayed; there is only talk of "a few exarchist families." Borislava Lilić, *Istorija Pirota i okoline (1804–1918)* (Pirot: NiP Hemikals, 1994), 2:270.

Another group of new inhabitants that transformed Tsaribrod were Bulgarian officials of the new state, such as administrators, custom officials, civil servants, military staff, and finally teachers. All of them brought their families from all parts of the Bulgarian Principality, and also from Wallachia, Black Sea ports like Odessa, Ottoman Macedonia and other regions. Both groups, Pirot merchants and Bulgarian officials, gradually changed the character of the former village. In 1882, the village of Tsaribrod was declared a town, forming an *okolija* (rural district) within the *okrăg* (district) Trn.

Thus, the village with its tiny *čaršija* along the Stambul Road (*stambulskoto džade*) developed gradually into a border town. In 1885, Emile Laveleye described Tsaribrod in this way: "The little market town consists of a single large street, which passes by wooden houses and the low and open Turkish shops. But also here there are the first one-story brick houses, and it is a joy to see a new school—a good sign for the future!"[30]

The decisive turn, however, came in 1888 when the railway track, which connected Niš and Sofia, was completed. As noted above, the obstinacies of both national states about the direction in which their railway networks had to develop was the reason for the delay of this last part of the connection. Another serious obstacle was the Serbian-Bulgarian war of 1885, which mostly took place in the region between Pirot and Slivnica. As a result, it took one decade until this particular article in the Treaty of Berlin, i.e., the building of the railway line, was finally realized and Tsaribrod, the former *menzil* station on the route, also became a border railway station. This combination of communication and barrier had a decisive impact on the development of the town. Around the turn of the century, a Serbian traveler wrote about the railway station in Tsaribrod: "At the entrance to Tsaribrod there is a large railway station. At first glance, you see a whole series of beautiful two-storied houses so spacious and comfortable that the visitor, judging by the station, might think he is coming to a modern European city. The station is spacious and in the other buildings there are a police station, a restaurant, a customs office and rooms for storing railway material."[31]

As the first railway station on the route through Bulgaria, the border and customs officials were now joined by the railway staff. Tsaribrod thus stood out clearly from the other few border crossings between the two countries. In 1889, according to the first journal of the city, *Domašen Učitel*, the city already had 400 houses, with 500 to 600 families said to be living in Tsaribrod at that time. According

---

30 Laveleye, *Balkanländer*, 2:51.
31 Paun Spasić, "Biljani Petak," *Iskra* 12 (1898): 186–9, quoted from Ilija Nikolić, *Pirot i Srez Nišavski: Arhivska građa* (Pirot: Muzej Poništavlja, 1981), 3:223, doc. 1371.

to the journal, 300 of these families lived from agriculture. At the end of the 1880s, a vivid picture of the small town was already emerging: eight restaurants, 43 taverns, 22 grocery stores, five manufacturers, 13 guesthouses, three of which were run as hotels: Hotel Europa, Hotel Sofija, and Hotel Vidlič (named after the dominant mountain in the area). The large number of taverns (*mehanas*), newer and traditional hotels (*hans*) as well as craftsmen shows the focus on services for travelers and especially for the growing number of civil servants. With the turn of the century, the development of the city received a new upturn. In contrast to Trn, whose population stagnated at 2,000, Tsaribrod quadrupled its population between 1882 and 1910 from 1,074 to 4,485 inhabitants.[32] At the turn of the century, Tsaribrod had the institutional and infrastructural characteristics of a city: a hospital, an extensive complex of barracks and a large railway station, a library, three hotels and a secondary school.

Tsaribrod was literally a *frontier* town, a place where new inhabitants were thoroughly convinced that they were bringing civilization into this remote part of the country, where everything was beginning from zero with the uncivilized half-wild Shopi population.[33] This odd combination of *Kulturträgerschaft*, the central European version of the *mission civilisatrice*, and an US-like frontier mentality among the new officials was also visible in their spatial presence in the town: This was materialized not only in the new administration buildings, but also in the representative and comparably large private houses, which were erected starting at the end on the century within the town. The two-story buildings stood out from the townscape which still had its dominant traditional Ottoman domestic architecture, and the new taller buildings demonstrated the distinctiveness of the new power-holders in the changing social space.

As research has shown, a decisive turn in the post-Ottoman development of large cities like Belgrade or Sofia happened in the end of the 1890s. This was the time when the development of infrastructure gathered pace. Only with the beginning of the new century, did electrification, trams, and a new building infrastructure begin to dominate the new national centers.[34] Interestingly, a place like Tsaribrod, obviously due to its function as a border town and a crossing point for the railway line to Istanbul, was not peripheral in all respects: indeed, urban infrastructure developed in exactly the same period there as in the capitals.

---

[32] *Spisăk na Naselenite Mesta* (Sofia: Sofijska Dăržavna Pečatnica, 1921), 519.
[33] On the Shopi discourse, see Nenad Stefanov, "Schopen," in *Lexikon zur Geschichte Südosteuropas*, ed. Konrad Clewing and Holm Sundhaussen (Vienna: Böhlau, 2016), 878–9.
[34] Milan Ristović, "Beograd, glavni grad na granici," in *Gradovi Balkana – Gradovi Evrope: Studije o urbanom razvoju postosmanskih prestonica 1830–1923*, ed. Marko Dogo and Armando Pitasio (Belgrade: Clio, 2018), 85–114.

Fig. 3a: Tsaribrod between the centuries. View from the southeast. Postcard ca. 1900, collection of Nenad Stefanov.

For a considerably long time, the administrations on both sides of the border accepted the uncontrolled mobility of the Pirot merchants across the border to Tsaribrod, and their unclear status concerning citizenship in Tsaribrod. This shows that people did not leave Pirot all at once and forever in the direction of Tsaribrod, as the Bulgarian national narrative suggests. There were various motives for the move to Tsaribrod, about 25 kilometers away, and there was a wide range of forms of migration. Some, especially the merchants, first purchased a plot of land in Tsaribrod as a precaution in order to observe the extent to which the old trade relations might actually be better maintained by relocating to the new city. Others moved to Tsaribrod, but as a hedge they did not give up their property in Pirot. In other families, it was decided that one part would move to Tsaribrod, while the other would remain in Pirot to take full advantage of the new situation. The Džadžini brothers, who changed their names into Džadžić (following the Serbian linguistic standard), and Džadžov (following the Bulgarian linguistic standard), opened shops and inns in both towns. In the early years, continuous movement in both directions was the rule.

Fig. 3b: Tsaribrod between the centuries. View from the northwest. Postcard ca. 1900, collection of Nenad Stefanov.

Apparently, the Serbian authorities did not appreciate the lively communication between the two places on both sides of the border immediately after its establishment. The complaints by merchants from Pirot, who lived in Tsaribrod in Bulgaria, that they were being harassed when crossing the border into Serbia, became more frequent. When in 1880 a number of travelers from Tsaribrod had their Bulgarian travel documents taken from them and were arrested in Pirot, the Bulgarian Foreign Minister, Dragan Cankov, protested against this action with the Serbian representative in Sofia and demanded that the owners of valid travel documents not be molested.[35]

Another conflict arose from the fact that the former inhabitants of Pirot did not need Bulgarian citizenship to run for electoral office on the communal level. Many of the people from Pirot were experienced in municipal affairs through their work in the Ottoman city councils in Pirot and successfully continued such offices in Tsaribrod. In the late 1890s, a coalition of some people from Tsaribrod who did not want to see the rapid rise of their neighbors, and some civil

---

35 Serbian Embassy Sofia to Foreign Minister Jovan Ristić, 12 May 1880, Archive of Serbia (Arhiv Srbije, from here on AS), Belgrade, Minitry of the Interior (Ministarstvo Unutrašnjih Dela), MUD-A, F. 11, r. 140.

servants from other parts of Bulgaria who were uncomfortable with the fact that Serbian citizens filled important electoral posts at the municipal level, protested against this practice. Despite protests and petitions, the Bulgarian courts upheld the practice, which was not legally codified. One motive on the part of the central state might have been the hope that Bulgaria would become increasingly attractive for the people from Pirot who remained in Serbia, but in practical terms this contributed to the maintenance of an ambiguity, which had to be eliminated from a central state perspective.[36]

However, the difficulties continued. In particular, the assessment of what valid papers were, or more precisely who had the authority to issue them and whose subjects these people were, was controversial between both states. This became particularly obvious when 79 families from Pirot applied for release from Serbian citizenship via the Serbian envoy in Sofia; the Serbian Minister of the Interior, Milutin Garašanin, rejected this request. The reason given was that according to article 74 of the Law on the Establishment of Liberated Territories, "[e]veryone who lived in one of the settlements concerned at the time of the liberation or who is now a former inhabitant of those settlements shall remain a Serbian citizen (*građanin srpski*)." Accordingly, the 79 families who had moved from Pirot were to be regarded as Serbian subjects.[37]

As these examples show, despite the material nature of borders, e.g., as trenches in the landscape, the new states were not able to set up undisputed control on societal "movement." Even in the most exclusive state matter, citizenship, we can see how the local actors created a space in between two citizenships and used it for their own benefit. Obstinacies, or more exactly the persistence in and the insistence on the previous practices of mobility in local space became visible in two dimensions: Firstly, as local people re-moving the border in order to maintain traditional uses of space as in the case of the Visok villages and, secondly, as obstinate commuting between Pirot and Tsaribrod across the border along the traditional route, which in the eyes of the new officials implicated ignorance concerning the new rules of citizenship.

Here a novel approach by the protagonists of the nation-state towards the mobility of local actors becomes visible. Both in the local as well as in the trans-local space, the new principle of fixing "belonging" was conveyed, while ambiguous, multiple loyalties were something suspicious. The fixing of belonging correlated with the fixing of state territory, in which contrary to imperial

---

[36] Nenad Stefanov, *Die Erfindung der Grenzen auf dem Balkan* (Wiesbaden: Harrassowitz, 2018), 224.
[37] Minister of the Interior to president of the Council of Ministers, 26 Jan. 1882, AS, MUD-P, F. 21, r. 201.

times no intermediate spaces were allowed. Belonging was interpreted as belonging to a certain community of descent from which nobody could leave, as Milutin Garašanin's decree shows. As Philipp Ther has shown, this identification of ethnic belonging and territoriality set in motion an ill-fated dynamic of creating unambiguity through violence.[38] In the area described here, this occurred with the outbreak of the Second Balkan War and later with Bulgaria's entry into the First World War, when Serbia and Bulgaria fought on different sides. The pressure for unambiguity, confinement and control became increasingly intense, the confrontations increasingly violent and, as a consequence, in-between-spaces for obstinate action shrank, but never totally disappeared.

7 Obstacles to Communication and Mobility: The Dynamics of Coercion to Unambiguousness, 1920–1956

For a better understanding of the context, I will briefly outline the background of the border changes in the focus area as a result of the power constellations after the First World War. Serbia was part of the Entente, while Bulgaria had joined the Central Powers. The motive for the Bulgarian government's decision was its claim to Macedonia as a natural part of the Bulgarian nation, but which had been assigned to Serbia by the peace treaty after the Second Balkan War in 1913. After the Bulgarian government had declared war on Serbia, the Serbian front against Austria-Hungary collapsed, Serbian troops withdrew from Serbia, and the country was divided among Austria-Hungary and Bulgaria. Bulgaria was awarded the eastern part of Serbia, the so-called Morava-Bulgaria including the cities of Niš, Pirot and Vranje as well as Macedonia. After the defeat of the Central Powers in 1918, the Paris Peace Conference restored Serbia to the borders of 1913. However, the Serbian government also demanded a "strategic expansion" of its territory at the expense of Bulgarian territory, namely territories that had belonged to Bulgaria since the founding of the state in 1878. The Belgrade government argued that a relocation of the borderline was necessary, in order to secure its railway lines against a potential Bulgarian attack. But Bulgaria should also be sanctioned for its "betrayal." Despite the fierce resistance of the new Bulgarian government, which sought reconciliation with Serbia and a closer

---

38 Philipp Ther, *Die dunkle Seite der Nationalstaaten: 'Ethnische Säuberungen' im modernen Europa*, (Göttingen: Vandenhoeck & Ruprecht, 2011).

relationship with the new southern Slavic state, the Neuilly Peace Treaty handed over the two cities of Tsaribrod and Bosilegrad to Serbia. As a result, many inhabitants, among them mainly civil servants, began to leave Tsaribrod for Bulgaria.[39] Many merchants, nevertheless, returned after some time, when they had the impression that the disadvantages of the border shift for their trade were limited. Nevertheless, between 1923 and 1934 there was a dynamic of violence when a "liberation movement" founded in Sofia called Vrtop[40] carried out bomb attacks on the border, in Pirot, as well as on the railway line to Istanbul. It was following the example of and was supported by the IMRO, the much bigger and more "famous" organization operating out of Sofia, which was fighting for the accession of Macedonia to Bulgaria.[41] The Serbian security forces declared the rural population responsible for helping Vrtop. With the rapprochement between the two states, the Bulgarian government dissolved this "liberation organization," but the government and large sections of the public demanded as part of the rapprochement that the "western territories" (Zapadnite Pokrainini, a standing term in Bulgaria) also be returned. After the occupation of Tsaribrod by Bulgaria during the Second World War, which was regarded as a liberation by some of the inhabitants, the border between the two communist brother states remained open until 1948, until it was hermetically closed similar to the border between West and East Germany, because of the conflict between Yugoslavia and the Soviet Union.

However, the new border line did not change the character of the city as a railway and border station. In contrast to before, the border no longer ran to the northwest of the city, but to the southeast. What was new for the inhabitants was the coercion to loyalty in public space: all inscriptions in Bulgarian had to be removed and the use of the standard Bulgarian in public conversations was prohibited. With regard to family names, only the Serbian variant on -ić and

---

[39] Krsto Mančev and Bogdan Nikolov, "Caribrod: Prosveta i Kultura na Granica meždu Skarani Državi," in *Jubileen Sbornik: Izsledvania v čest na 80-godišninata na prof. Krsto Mančev* (Sofia: Paradigma, 2006).
[40] Vrtop is a characteristic regional toponym, which was also used for the local organization with the official name VZRO Vrtop (Vătrešna zapadnopokrajinska revolucionna organizacija).
[41] Internal Macedonian Revolutionary Organization: A successor organization from the 1920s to the liberation movement in Macedonia, which emerged at the turn of the twentieth century and fought for the independence or autonomy of Macedonia, which at that time was part of the Ottoman Empire. It sought to achieve this by means of guerrilla warfare, assassinations and bomb attacks. After 1920, the IMRO committed itself to a separation of Macedonia from the Yugoslavian state, and in cooperation with the fascist Ustaša organization executed the murder of Yugoslavian King Aleksandar Karađorđević in Marseille in 1934. Cf. Keith Brown, *Loyal Unto Death: Trust and Terror in Revolutionary Macedonia* (Bloomington: Indiana University Press, 2013).

no longer on -ov was valid. Letters that were "incorrectly" addressed in this sense were returned to the sender.

In the period between 1878 and 1914 the border was above all an obstacle with regard to trans-regional commercial exchange, which led the Pirot merchants to the decision to settle in Bulgaria. This obstacle did not limit mobility and communication as the supporters of the nation-state had hoped. Obstinate paths crossing between both sides still existed and were difficult to close by the authorities of both sides. The former region was of course cut by the border, but the dividing line also acquired the quality of a contact zone for both separated halves.

However, this changed after 1920 when these territories became the new Kingdom of Serbs, Croats and Slovenes. Between 1923 and 1934 in particular, the area on the border turned from a contact zone into a conflict zone. The border area was transformed into a specific space, which was primarily occupied by actors who were bound to the ministries of the interior on the respective sides, such as Serbian gendarmes, the military, and the members of the aforementioned "liberation organization," which was supported by the Sofia Ministry of the Interior. Thus, actors of both governmental and non-governmental agencies were active in this area, setting in motion an escalating dynamic of violence. It mainly affected the villages, which above all were characterized by land ownership on both sides of the border. The permanent closure of the border meant that the traditional routes were gradually abandoned. Mobility now took place on a larger scale: many inhabitants of this conflict zone left their villages and moved to Bulgaria, hoping to benefit from a special aid program for refugees that had been developed there with the support of the League of Nations after the First World War.[42]

The closure of the border did not have the same effect everywhere. Wealthy city dwellers could continue to travel by train to Sofia. With a few exceptions, the international railway lines were not affected by the blockade of the border, which mainly concerned road traffic. But overland traffic consisted almost without exception of the local carriages of those who were landowners on both sides of the border, called *dvuvlasnici* (double owners). In their work, they were affected by more than the blocking of the border. The security authorities of both states observed them suspiciously, since it was assumed that they were also involved in smuggling or in the activities of Vrtop. Therefore, both governments did everything in their power to remove what they now considered to be a major obstacle

---

[42] Krsto Mančev and Mariana Gudeva, "Zapadnite Pokrainini i Bălgarsko-Jugoslavskite Otnošenija," *Istoričeski Pregled* 7 (1990): 3–16.

to comprehensive border control. This was to be achieved by exchanging land ownership[43] on both sides of the border. However, it took until the 1950s for this to be implemented.

After 1948, the situation again changed and the border was turned into a hermetically sealed barrier, which went along with an unprecedented control of local society by the state. The background for this extreme hardening of the border regime was the growing confrontation between the Soviet Union and Yugoslavia. Stalin rejected the independent policy of the Yugoslavian communists around Tito as e.g., in the project of a Balkan federation. Yet, the massive Soviet economic pressure and the military threats did not lead to an immediate breakdown of Tito's leadership. On the contrary the tensions intensified, consequently also with Bulgaria as a Soviet satellite, so that the former close relation between the two sides was abandoned step by step up to a point when in 1950 the Yugoslav embassy in Sofia had to be closed.[44]

In 1948 the Yugoslav-Bulgarian border was closed and became part of the Iron Curtain. From now on, the border zone was a mediating space in the power struggle between the two sides. The area close to the border was restructured: Land ownership on both sides was no longer permitted and the peasants had to give up their fields in the immediate vicinity of the border. Here, the military and the security organs moved in and installed loudspeakers to relay insults and propaganda messages to the opposite side. In this period, the border acquired the character of a space of confrontation totally controlled by state actors. Although the border installations were less imposing than in other parts of the Iron Curtain, in its effect on the local population, the Yugoslav-Bulgarian border resembled the border between East and West Germany.

There were also long-lasting effects on local society. Primarily this concerned the Bulgarian minority in Yugoslavia, which had been officially recognized just a few years earlier. The Yugoslav security organs viewed this minority with suspicion as a potential ally of pro-Stalinist Bulgaria. In the prosecutions of so-called Stalinists from 1948 to 1956, many individuals in the Tsaribrod area were subjected to long periods in prison and labor camps. Especially those families with members who had fled across the border to Bulgaria were forced to work

---

43 The demarcation of the border often meant that the new dividing line ran right through the agricultural property of several farmers. For a long time, the agreement between the two states was that those who had land on the other side of the border (these were called dual owners) could continue to cultivate it, and could also cross the border beyond the checkpoints with a special identity card. Cf. Stefanov, *Die Erfindung der Grenze auf dem Balkan*, 335.

44 Petar Dragišić, *Jugoslovensko-Bugarski odnosi 1944–1949* (Belgrade: Institut za noviju istoriju Srbije, 2007), 228.

for the police as informants. This policy resulted in a climate of fear and possible denunciation, which until today has not been adequately treated in public media or the academy. Individuals who were children at the time still suffer from the trauma.[45]

On the whole, this situation resulted in new practices for demonstrating loyalty to and conformity with the state. While previously, there had been single acts of denunciation, in the years after 1948 the whole local society was forced to conform to a degree that was not common in other parts of Yugoslavia where there existed many niches for non-conformist behavior. Those who did not want to comply fled to Bulgaria where the situation was similar. It can be said that in this period of increased control, the relation between center and periphery was turned around. While before, the periphery had been hard to read and control from the center, now it was observed and controlled to a degree that was untypical even for the population of the center.

In sum, the epoch between 1878 and 1956 was characterized by declining micro-regional communication, stagnating transregional communication, and the experience of the rise of transcontinental communication, which stood in a dialectical relationship to the growing limiting character of the border. These general trends are characterized by three stages: during the first stage until 1915, the border was an obstacle for trade, but only an obstacle, not an unsurmountable barrier. Between 1920 and 1941, it grew from an obstacle to a significant barrier with periods in which the border area transformed from an area of limited communication to an area under full state control and violence. In the third phase after 1948, the border zone acquired all the characteristics of the Iron Curtain, similar to the inner-German border. In these times, the definitively limiting effects on local communication became manifest (see Fig. 2). But despite everything, the bitter times of the Cold War did not necessarily mean the complete disruption of lines of communication, as will be discussed later.

---

[45] The writer Detko Petrov has dealt with these experiences in a literary form, which his short story collection bears witness to: Detko Petrov, *Granica* (Belgrade: Književna Zajednica Petar Kočić, 1972). In the last years a process of rehabilitation of the victims of the repressive measures between 1948 and 1956 was initiated, which also resulted in a greater willingness to talk about this period by the descendants of the victims, who experienced this difficult time as children.

8 Mobility beyond Boundaries: Transnational Traffic and Local Actors

As mentioned above, the trains on the route ran, while, in the most difficult periods, the double owners waited at the border and could not pass. Was this a general experience, since the Orient Express as the most famous international train used this route? Did the trains only roar past the people living near the tracks? Did the locals outside and the passengers inside the train only look at each other while passing by, or did the people in Tsaribrod and the surrounding area get on the train?

After the borders were drawn in 1878, in the view of the representatives of the new state institutions, the traditional local and regional trade routes were being transformed into illegal smuggling pathways. But this was not the only form of movement across the border that was neither welcomed nor tolerated by the center. Even beyond the new commercial side paths, in everyday life obstinate forms of communication developed which crossed the border.

One example is the Blagi Petak or Biljani Petak, which was originally a holiday celebrated in Pirot during the week after Easter. With the already described migration of many families from Pirot to Tsaribrod, they took their holiday along with them. Until then it had been celebrated as a large picnic on the Barje, a partly drained swamp area near Pirot. Now the families, those who had settled in Tsaribrod and those who had stayed in Pirot, met directly at the new border on the Bulgarian side, in the village Željuša near to Tsaribrod. At first, the "wandering holiday" (now celebrated at a different location) had been initiated by the people of Pirot and Tsaribrod. But after some years, the state and church institutions also got involved. At the latest, starting in 1889 the Pirot clergy took part in the celebrations. At the beginning of the 1890s, both states recognized this holiday. In 1896 the border was opened at Željuša for three days so that it could be crossed without identity cards.

The state participation caused an increase in mobility: people could use the railway to reach the location of the "wandering holiday." Since the opening of the rail link between Central Europe and Istanbul, its local significance became apparent exactly on this spot. The radius of the visitors expanded considerably. The holiday was no longer celebrated exclusively by the Pirot families on both sides of the border, but it turned into a big fair with brass bands, marching bands and other amusements.

It is unclear when the railways started to be used, but as the report of 1896 shows, it was majorly important for the holiday. There was a real rush to the Pirot railway station where over 8,000 tickets were sold. On this day, local trains operated continuously between Pirot and Tsaribrod. Many people used this holiday as an opportunity to travel on to Sofia or to Niš in the opposite direction. From the Serbian side alone, there were over 12,000 people who rode the rail that day.[46]

On these journeys the focus was not on the comfort of travelers, but on sheer transport. The Promenade Trains (*Spazierzüge*) consisted mainly of second- and third-class cars. Similarly to Western Europe, the third class at that time consisted mainly of wagons without seats and with very few windows.[47] Between Pirot and Tsaribrod even cattle wagons were used as a third class, as the writer Aleko Konstantinov amusedly reports in a satire about the celebrations at the border:

> Five hundred people, men, women and children, tried to descend from the wagons. At the same time, thousand tried to get on. Every wagon, which was built for eight head of cattle, was crowded with thirty humans. When cattle get on or off these wagons, a little wooden bridge was provided; but not for the humans. From the door of the wagons it is one and a half meters to the ground. Now, try to imagine all these people in their close-fitting Sunday dress, who while descending are pressed by those who are in the process of jumping off and being obstructed by those who are hopping up into the wagon.[48]

In the satirical description of the festive joy and tumult, two things come to light: curiosity about what lies beyond the border, but also about the new means of transport itself. Even though railway lines had already existed in the Ottoman Empire for a long time (since 1866 there was the line from Ruse to Varna, and since 1873 the line from Istanbul to Belovo near Pazardzhik in Bulgaria, as well as from Salonica to Kosovska Mitrovica since 1873), in this region, the railway was something new and it could be tried out at a reasonable price on this occasion. This experiment also had another result: inhabitants of Sofia traveled far across the new border and people from Serbia traveled in the opposite direction to Sofia. Here the dialectical relationship between border and communication becomes visible: modern statehood implied a new quality of bounded space, but also new possibilities for communication now represented by the railway.

Uncontrolled movements across the border were not only of a commercial nature as in the case of smuggling. The circulation of cultural goods was also

---

46 "Biljani Petak Spasić," quoted from Nikolić, *Pirot i Srez Nišavski*, 3:223, doc. 1371.
47 Ralf Roth, *Das Jahrhundert der Eisenbahn: Die Herrschaft über Raum und Zeit 1800–1914* (Ostfildern: Thorbecke, 2005), 136–8; Aleko Konstantinov, "Do Željuša s Goveždi Vagoni," in id., *Săčinenija* (Sofia, 1957), 1:390–3.
48 Ibid., 1:392.

part of it, particularly at such "wandering holidays." For example, there were popular songs and hit songs, which aroused suspicion among patriotically minded subjects, because of their linguistic and thematic ambiguity: They were sung in dialect about mundane topics such as love and spectacular stories. In the local newspaper *Nišava*, which was printed in Tsaribrod, some readers repeatedly complained about the lack of national awareness that was expressed in the singing of such songs. For most inhabitants of Pirot and Tsaribrod, it seemed completely irrelevant whether these songs were "Bulgarian" or "Serbian." This indifference was probably what most angered the author of the article in the weekly *Nišava*.[49]

In this local context, too, the railway stood for a different, better future, for a new kind of connectivity, as expressed during the "wandering holidays," or when patriotic choral societies from Pirot went on tour to Sofia,[50] thus creating connections even among the nationalist protagonists who were in favor of demarcations.

In contrast, the road itself stood for the past. When the already mentioned Belgian economist, Emile Laveleye, travelled through these areas in 1885, particularly over the section from Tsaribrod to Dragoman, he was struck by its neglect and poor maintenance:

> The route follows the river on its way through the canyon. It is in very bad condition and is not protected against the water, which has undermined it and partly washed it away. Here, you had to walk through the riverbed and at another place, further uphill, there was only a small strip of the way left, so that the third horse had to be unharnessed. [...] [This is] the main road, which leads from Serbia to Sofia and Constantinople and should be [developed into] the most important traffic artery of the Balkan peninsula. Midhat constructed it and trade, mail, the administration, the army, in short everything, remains dependent on it. Just weeks ago, a storm caused this destruction, but nothing had happened yet to repair the damage. Suddenly you understand that Bulgaria does not seem to be too keen on an easy traffic connection with its neighbor.[51]

As already mentioned at the beginning, the road had long since lost much of its transcontinental significance. With the introduction of the railway, the sparse transregional trade shifted to freight trains. Now, at the beginning of the twentieth century, the railway line stood for transcontinental connectivity as one of the essential characteristics of this route. It was not until seven decades later

---

49 *Nišava* 25, 20 February 1910, 3, section "chronicle."
50 The exchange of cultural societies such as men's choruses and gymnastics organizations increased in the first decade of the twentieth century.
51 Laveleye, *Balkanländer*, 2:55.

that the road, under completely changed forms of mobility, would experience an enormous increase in significance, as will be discussed later.

The question remains as to how relevant was the railway for the people of Tsaribrod and the surrounding area in the last decades of the nineteenth century? As already mentioned, the local communication networks and roads remained decisive, even if the border disrupted the previous road networks or made mobility more complicated. In fact, the turn of the century appears to be the time when things began to move. This applies to the aforementioned intensification of urban infrastructure development in the province and especially in the new metropolises. The construction boom in Sofia led to increased seasonal migration of many peasants from the Tsaribrod area and even from the Serbian side of the border, who could not live from their small plots, and hired themselves out in Sofia as construction workers, carpenters or woodworkers.[52] They stood in the tradition of the *pečalba*, seasonal migration across larger distances e. g., to the Danubian Principalities for agricultural work on the large magnate estates, or to Istanbul as day laborers. This form of labor migration had existed for almost the entire nineteenth century and was only made more difficult by the new borders, or directed to other closer regions, such as Sofia. It therefore gave a new impetus to mobility along the old route. It is difficult to say to what extent the descendants of such *tajfe* (the groups of men who together undertook the *pečalba*) used the railway on their way to Sofia also in the time before the First World War.

At least it becomes clear that there was a relatively full timetable between Tsaribrod and Sofia beginning at the turn of the century. There were four daily connections, one of them the luxurious Orient Express, which, since summer 1889, ran twice a week in each direction, (Tuesdays and Fridays in the direction to Istanbul, Wednesdays and Saturdays from Istanbul).[53] In 1914 there was a daily service of the Orient Express. Additionally, there was the *Konvencional* (conventional train) between Berlin and Istanbul with first and second class, as well as a *Pătnički Vlak* (Passenger Train) with all three classes, and a "mixed" train with freight cars and third class only.[54] The Orient Express would certainly not have been used by seasonal workers, because the ride was of course not affordable for them. But it created a particular atmosphere, when the luxurious train was standing for a longer time at the station, and

---

[52] Jelenko Petrović, *Pečalbari naročito iz Okoline Pirota* (Belgrade: Tipografija, 1920).
[53] Nenad M. Govedarović, *Pruge Jugoistočne Srbije 1884–2014* (Niš: Mašinski fakultet, Društvo ljubitelja železnice, 2014), 76–7.
[54] *Pătevoditel za Železnicite i Parahodite za 1914 god* (Sofia, 1914), 4. Timetable for the route Tzaribrod–Sofia–Philippople–Svilengrad.

the passengers stretched their legs on the station platform or took a drink in the restaurant of the station. As Dobrinka Paruševa describes it for Plovdiv, the railway station was transformed into a favorite place for Tsaribroders, who wanted to catch a glimpse of the international flair of the Orient Express passengers, reading international newspapers and enjoying a cup of coffee in the same restaurant.

The fact that many pupils from Tsaribrod attended grammar schools in Sofia and returned at the end of the week shows the increase in the use of the railway even into the interwar period.[55] Research has also shown that many better-off people from Tsaribrod regularly used the railway for stays in the former capital, although they were now separated by a border. In particular, there were former Bulgarian officers and retired teachers who had been in Bulgarian service until 1920 and collected their pensions there. Although the border was often closed, this did not affect the railway since some of them were international trains.

For their travels to Sofia, the inhabitants of Tsaribrod above all used the *Konvencional*, as well as the mixed freight-passenger trains, which had only a third class, as biographical information as well as the fares suggest. The *Konvencional* remained relevant for travelers from Tsaribrod also in the interwar period, now for their journeys within the new national territory, to Pirot, Niš, and to the new capital Belgrade.

In the interwar period, a pair of express trains, four normal passenger trains and another international train stopped here, in addition to the Simplon Orient Express, also called the Direct Orient, which started in Paris and went via Italy and Yugoslavia to Istanbul.

After the Second World War, traffic on the railway line again intensified, especially toward the end of the 1950s, at which point eight passenger trains rolled on the Niš–Pirot–Tsaribrod/Dimitrovgrad line. Until the 1948 break between Yugoslavia and the Soviet Union, Tsaribrod also remained connected to the Bulgarian rail network. As timetables show, the station was integrated into the Bulgarian regional net, although the city was outside the national territory. This changed after 1948: instead of Tsaribrod, Dragoman became the last stop for regional trains before the state border with Yugoslavia.[56] In addition, two lines of divided Europe came together here, each traveling from west and east towards the southeast: the so-called Pannonia Express from Berlin (east) (Berlin–Beo-

---

[55] The effect of this commuting between Tsaribrod and the former capital was among other things a surprisingly numerous circle of young communists in Tsaribrod, who were politized in the turbulent first half of the 1920s at their grammar schools.
[56] *Pătevoditel za Železnicite za 1952 god.* (Sofia, 1952).

grad–Niš–Sofia) and the Istanbul Express (Frankfurt–Beograd–Niš–Istanbul) from West Germany.[57]

9 Mobility in the Time of the Iron Curtain

Of course, none of the locals could afford to ride the Orient Express. They could only wave to the heads of state such as Aleksandar Stambolijski, Tsar Boris, King Alexander of Yugoslavia, and after the war the communist leaders Josip Broz Tito or Georgi Dimitrov, who passed in this or similar luxury trains through Tsaribrod. From the 1960s, however, many in Dimitrovgrad (as the town was called since 1952) literally got on the moving trains, which brought migrant workers from Turkey to the West.

Since 1956, after the end of the comprehensive blockade of Yugoslavia imposed by the Soviet Union along with its satellites including Bulgaria, the people from Dimitrovgrad could travel more easily to the areas on the other side of the Iron Curtain that were once part of the micro-region of *kaza* Pirot where many had relatives living. However, a legal agreement on local border traffic between Yugoslavia and Bulgaria was not concluded until 1973. In this agreement, an area of 20 kilometers on both sides of the border was defined as the area to which the rules of local border traffic were to apply. Its residents could cross the border without a visa and using special identity cards, called *Propusnica* (identity document only valid for the border passage), which allowed them to traverse the border twelve times a year.

The growing but still "unsatisfactory" number of identity cards, as assessed by the joint Yugoslav-Bulgarian Border Commission, was certainly also due to the small quantities of goods that could be taken across the border: allowed were two liters of beer, ten packages of cigarettes, 200 grams of coffee, 300 grams of the local cheese speciality, Kačkavalj, which enjoyed great popularity on both sides as an important *meze* (small dishes, usually accompanied by *rakija*), and surprisingly 500 grams of biscuits and other pastries. In contrast, four kilograms of fresh fruit or three and a half liters of non-alcoholic beverages were allowed. Here it becomes apparent that particularly in the case of scarce goods, especially in Bulgaria, the exchange was subject to strict limits.

But not only the limited border traffic shaped everyday consumer life. The people on the Yugoslav side set themselves in motion in completely new directions. At the end of the 1960s, shopping tours to Trieste became popular for

---

[57] Govedarović, *Pruge Jugoistočne Srbije*, 86–7.

young people from Dimitrovgrad. Trieste, apparently so remote, was only a day's journey away due to the good trans-European train connections through Dimitrovgrad. Jeans and other modern clothing from Trieste were prestige items throughout Yugoslavia, including Dimitrovgrad.

In the 1980s, Trieste was replaced by Istanbul as the most important shopping destination. "The hustle and bustle that existed ten or more years ago on the Italian border," wrote the local weekly *Bratstvo* in 1986, "has now migrated here, and Istanbul is for Yugoslav citizens today what Trieste meant to them years ago." With chartered buses the people from Dimitrovgrad now also travelled to the former capital of the Ottoman Empire to buy leather clothes and above all fake brand clothes from Ellesse to Lacoste. At the peak of this new trend, in one year 1.2 million Yugoslav citizens crossed the border towards Istanbul as *vikendaši* (weekenders) and *šoping turisti*. Bratstvo soberly stated that apparently neither high inflation nor high petrol prices would prevent Yugoslavs from such shopping tours.[58]

Of course, smuggling also belonged to the small border traffic. It can only be dealt with very selectively here. As was shown in conversations during my research, smuggling resumed immediately after the end of the hermetic closure of the border in the mid-1950s. Obviously, the people involved were not afraid of the enormous risk which accompanied smuggling during the most pointed confrontation between the two states at that time. It is noteworthy that it was mainly people from the wealthier villages who entered into such enterprises, as well as those who had made careers within the institutions that were part of the central authorities and now used their old family networks for such purposes. In addition, there seem to have been very persistent cross-generational networks. Gavrilo Vidanović shows that at the village of Radejna it was initially the wealthy inn owners who shaped the smuggling of 1878–1920, then they continued this business even after the relocation of the border, because they had sufficient experience and their networks persisted. The interviews also showed that money was the condition for success in this profession, which was motivated not by poverty, but by the wish to make more money or for advancement within local or even state administration. Another central prerequisite was having cooperative connections with both the police and the authorities at the Ministry of the Interior.

---

58 *Bratstvo* was the publication organ of the Bulgarian minority in Yugoslavia, especially for the two municipalities Dimitrovgrad and Bosilegrad, and so it was published in Bulgarian. "Kontrol na nad 4,5 miliona pătnici," *Bratstvo*, 28 February 1986, 10.

The motives of the *šverceri*, as smugglers were called in Yugoslavia, for this cooperation with the authorities varied; on the one hand the decisive impulse was to gain protection for other already existing illegal practices. On the other hand, this cooperation was often linked to the fact that the authorities at the Ministry of the Interior tolerated smuggling in individual cases but demanded from the smugglers that they report on relatives and acquaintances when traveling to Bulgaria. In any case, smuggling essentially was almost impossible without the tacit support of police and authorities. Opportunities for promotion, such as a post in the apparatus of the authorities in the capital, arose from close cooperation with the police as an informant, which at the same time made successful smuggling possible and provided good recommendations for promotions. This parallelism of illegal practices and at the same time close cooperation with representatives of official institutions thus proved to be profitable in two ways: firstly, the money generated by smuggling per se, and secondly, the career opportunities for oneself, family and relatives from the close connections with the authorities. It can be assumed that in principle the Bulgarian police did not handle this differently. Thus, the only risk that remained was being caught by the authorities on the other side who were not part of the patronage network. This entanglement of spying services with smuggling still makes it difficult to talk about today. Only a few people are willing to give information about this time of smuggling under the conditions of extreme control imposed by the Iron Curtain. Although the increasing exchange across borders also led to a reduction in risk and thus greater scope for smuggling, the relationship described remained structurally dominant until 1989.

Smuggling could also take the form of private barter transactions. Certain consumer goods that came to Yugoslavia from the West and became an increasingly natural part of the consumer culture were in great demand in Bulgaria. People in the interviews remember how in the early 1970s, right in the center of Sofia, they were asked about their jeans and whether they would want to sell them. Trains, however, were the most popular place for such transactions. Bulgarian travelers, who used the Pannonia Express and were on their way back from Poland or Czechoslovakia, saw the train itself (while passing through Yugoslavia) as an opportunity for consumerism. One of the interviewees reports on a quite common exchange at the end of the 1960s: a Bulgarian fellow traveler liked her shoes. It turned out that the shoe owner traveling to Sofia from Yugoslavia had the same shoe size as the daughter of the interested Bulgarian. They then arranged to meet at the market in Sofia for an exchange. Before that, the Yugoslavian interlocutor had already bought some cheap Bulgarian sandals.

From the late 1960s onwards, with increasing transnational mobility, a new dimension of smuggling arose, since the connection between Istanbul and Central Europe was an important route for the booming drug trade between the Middle East and Western Europe.

10 From "the Threshold of Europe" to "the Gateway to the Middle East"

Over a long period of time until the mid-1970s, most travelers who crossed the border experienced passport control in a moving train. The James Bond film *From Russia With Love* is reminiscent of this fact. The journey on the former Orient Express leads the main character on the route from Istanbul via Greece to Belgrade and passport controls serve as an impulse for as many action scenes as possible during the train journey. The train was thus a fascinating place of simultaneity of trade and control, of contact between people who otherwise had little opportunity to meet under the prevailing rules, as demonstrated above in the example of the shoe exchange. The train was used to smuggle simple goods, as the weekly *Bratstvo* called it, from cassette recorders to textiles. The *Bratstvo* reported exhaustingly about an unusually large number of headscarves that were carried by a Bulgarian tourist returning to Bulgaria from his holiday in Czechoslovakia. In addition to the aforementioned Pannonia Express, which connected East Central Europe with Bulgaria, it was especially the Istanbul Express, which departed daily from Istanbul to Munich, that shaped life at the Dimitrovgrad railway station. As told in the interviews I conducted in Dimitrovgrad, the young, almost exclusively male passengers with fine mustaches and in Sunday suits drew the attention of the people at the two railway barriers in the city and at the station. Obviously, the destination was promising, when so many people from distant Turkey, dressed so solemnly, set off for the equally distant Germany.

Possible wanderlust was mitigated by the fact that the station was on the border and paradoxically was also a place of communication. Although only a small station on this long route, the trains stopped in Dimitrovgrad for as long as they did at the main stations. "When trains arrive, it becomes an 'international oasis.' You can hear conversations in all European languages in the restaurant," the *Bratstvo* wrote.[59] Since 1964 the Dimitrovgrad railway station was a joint Yugoslav-Bulgarian border station and was therefore "unique in the Balkans."[60] Prior to this, passport controls were carried out in Dragoman and Dimi-

---

59 Bogdan Nikolov, "Njakoj pătnici ne poznavat svojite prava," *Bratstvo*, November 1962, 7, 19.
60 "Tri godini obšta gara v Dimitrovgrad: Družba na Delo," *Bratstvo*, 25 May 1967, 2.

trovgrad respectively, resulting in delays in train services.[61] Afterwards, however, customs and railway personnel from Bulgaria also worked at the Dimitrovgrad station, something which in view of the often rather bad relations between the two states under the conditions of the Cold War also contributed to the uniqueness of the station for the people from the editorial staff of *Bratstvo*. Now it was no longer just statesmen who waved their hands from the train in passing or during a short stop, as in the interwar period, but people from the region themselves were participating in the new mobility.

The border crossing on the road connecting Central Europe with the Middle East was hardly much used until the mid-1960s. Afterwards, it developed into Yugoslavia's most important border crossing alongside Spielfeld on the Austrian border. It was only in 1963 that the road between Niš and Dimitrovgrad (which was a simple macadam road) was asphalted as a part of the Yugoslav Autoput program. In the following three decades, the entire infrastructure on the border grew from what was initially a small building with a tollgate to an area of several hectares. As early as 1965, the Slovenian tourism company Kompas, the "largest tourist-gastronomic company in the country," as the weekly *Bratstvo* regularly called it, acquired a very large property on the border.[62] However, it took almost a decade and a half before a small motel, duty-free shops and restaurants were opened. Nevertheless, since the mid-1960s, a tourist infrastructure gradually developed on the border. A large motel above the city with the only bar between Niš and Sofia that was open all night, can serve as an example. It was built completely in the elegant international style of the 1960s, and a new hotel was built in the city itself.

While rail travel remained constantly high, from the end of the 1960s onwards, car traffic in the summer months also rose significantly. Contemporaries were amazed by this fact. The *Bratstvo* reported about 200,000 travelers and 15,000 cars. "In summer there were days when up to 400 automobiles crossed the border in both directions."[63] The number rose from 116,180 passenger cars in 1960 to 369,706 in 1965, of which 80 per cent were foreigners.[64] In 1968 there were estimates of 1.6 million travelers crossing the border in both directions by car or train, almost one million of them by car.[65]

---

61 "Uredba o Ratifikaciji Konvencije između Srbije i Bugarske o Regulisanju Pograničnog Železničkog Saobraćaja," *Službeni list SFRJ* 9 (20 July 1964): 730–3.
62 "Kak da se uredi prehodat pri selo Gradina?," *Bratstvo*, 20 October 1966, 2.
63 Ibid.
64 "Kak da se uredi," 1966. In 1967, transit travelers exchanged 600 million dinars at the border; Nikolov, "Uspehi," 1968.
65 Nikolov, "Uspehi," 1968.

Fig. 4: Dimitrovgrad at the end of the 1960s. Postcard ca. 1969, collection of Nenad Stefanov.

Passenger traffic was lower than at the borders with Italy, Austria and Hungary, but higher than that with Albania, Romania and Greece.[66]

Local statistics between the 1960s and 1980s show a growing number of overnight stays, which was otherwise unusual for a small town. These growing numbers were mainly caused by Turkish migrant workers and the increase in freight traffic from Turkey and the Middle East since the 1970s. Particularly in the summer months, Turkish migrant workers crossed the border, no longer commuting between their old and new homelands with the Istanbul Express but with their own cars, which were often from the same factories in Cologne or Rüsselsheim in which their owners worked.

In the 1980s, Gradina, the road checkpoint at Dimitrovgrad, alongside those five border crossings to Italy and Austria in Slovenia, developed into the most important border crossing point for transit traffic in Yugoslavia, which is reflected in the strong contrast to the other border crossings to Bulgaria.[67]

---

[66] Stevan Stanković, *Geografija Ponišavlja* (Pirot: Sloboda, 1997), 104. This is also shown by the figures for 1985: Bulgaria 5,659,950 travelers; Albania 57,569; Romania 3,135,178; Greece 4,484,469; Hungary 7,824,330; Italy 22,423,390, Austria 25,759,546. Ibid., 111.
[67] Ibid., 123.

Tab. 1: Border passages by road at Dimitrovgrad Gradina and rail at Dimitrovgrad station according to Stanković, *Geografija Ponišavlja*, 106, 172.

Bordercrossings	Yugoslav		Foreigners		Total	
	Number	%	Number	%	Number	%
Dimitrovgrad Gradina 1975	423.524	48,9	3.880.077	83	4.303.611	77,8
Dimitrovgrad station 1975	58.849	6,8	585.817	12,5	644.666	11,6
Dimitrovgrad Gradina 1985	1.121.558	53,9	3.220.433	89,9	4.341.991	76,7
Dimitrovgrad station 1985	29.697	1,5	276.317	7,8	306.014	5,4
Dimitrovgrad Gradina 1990	1.284.020	54,5	5.160.546	67,7	6.444.566	64,6
Dimitrovgrad station 1990	80.482	3,4	572.969	7,5	653.451	6,5

As can be seen from the table, Gradina and the Dimitrovgrad railway crossing accounted for 92.8 per cent of total border traffic to and from Bulgaria in the 1970s. At the same time, the border station on the road (Gradina) had definitively replaced the railway station (Dimitrovgrad) as the main border crossing point.

In the 1980s, movement across the border stalled. On the Yugoslav side, this was primarily for economic reasons. The over-indebted state tried to prevent what it saw as an uncontrolled outflow of urgently needed foreign currency caused by Yugoslav consumption abroad. Therefore, the state introduced deposit payments, which meant that every citizen now had to deposit the sum of 10 Deutschmark on leaving the country, but this was not repaid.[68] In 1982 and 1983, the number of Yugoslav citizens among the travelers decreased drastically. Whereas in 1981 it was 951,642 and in 1982 716,087, in 1983 it fell to only 123,959, in 1984 it grew to a modest 375,939 travelers, then in 1985 it rose again to 1,052,301, when these payments were abolished in the face of growing dissatisfaction. In 1985, Dimitrovgrad customs statistics recorded the control of 4,600,000 persons crossing the Yugoslav-Bulgarian border in both directions, which was the average of the 1980s.[69]

On the Bulgarian side, it was primarily political motives and the will to control the border that led to a restriction of movement. In the mid-1980s, the Bulgarian authorities decided that foreign travelers could only travel via the border crossings at Gradina (road) and Dimitrovgrad (railway); all other crossings were to be reserved for Yugoslav and Bulgarian citizens only. The rail and road cross-

---

68 Ibid., 112.
69 "Kontrol na nad 4,5 miliona," 1986.

ings at Dimitrovgrad and Gradina including Delčevo on the Macedonian part of the border were also the only ones to be open 24 hours a day thereafter.[70]

Between 1965 and the beginning of the 1970s, new ways of positioning and locating the city on the border emerged. When Tsaribrod belonged to Bulgaria between 1878 and 1920, the local newspaper with some pride talked of "our threshold to Europe," which all the goods, people and crowned heads of the country had to cross on their way to Europe.[71] In the interwar period under Serbian/Yugoslav rule, Tsaribrod became "our bastion on the border" as it was called in the Belgrade press in martial language, and the inhabitants were certainly not asked whether they shared this impression. In the socialist "new era" following the real-socialist jargon, Tsaribrod was to become a "bridge between the two states," and the basis of Yugoslavian-Bulgarian friendship, as Georgi Dimitrov put it. It was precisely at the height of the conflict with the Soviet Union that the city was renamed Dimitrovgrad to demonstrate to Stalin and his allies that, unlike them, Yugoslavia was clearly in favor of international friendship. But the official bridge metaphor faded away beginning the 1960s in the face of new experiences.

The new quality of traffic at the border, the growing importance of the infrastructure for the city with gastronomy and customs, where many well-paid jobs were found, also broadened horizons, standards and mental maps in the local context. Following the non-aligned policy of Yugoslavia, which operated in global dimensions, the city and the border were increasingly referred to as the "gateway to the Middle East." The neighbor, Bulgaria, which was present before in the metaphor of Dimitrovgrad as the connecting "bridge" between Yugoslavia and Bulgaria, was now simply overlooked. The view extended from Turkey to Iran where the continuation of the European Highway E-80 finally ended. This description became common starting in the 1960s:[72] The weekly *Bratstvo* talked about the "international road Belgrade–Sofia–Tsarigrad" on which "our city is

---

70 Stanković, *Geografija Ponišavlja*, 124. Every foreigner who entered the border zone in Bulgaria was violating the law. Possibly, this was an attempt to stop refugees from socialist countries going via Bulgaria to Yugoslavia.

71 Bulgarian politicians made important first statements when leaving the country, then again on the way back from political negotiations, and final statements at Tsaribrod station, which was especially decorated on such occasions. This tradition of speeches at the Tsaribrod railway station gained a macabre note in 1919, when in Paris the surrender of Tsaribrod to the new Yugoslavian state was negotiated. Along with Prime Minister Stambolijski, the Bulgarian Foreign Minister announced this declaration on the outward and return journeys to and from Paris, and ironically his electoral constituency was in Tsaribrod itself.

72 Nikolov, "Njakoj pătnici," 7.

fortunate to be situated,"[73] one of the most important "gates of our country" through which travelers from west and east pass.[74] The importance of this line of communication is also illustrated by the contrast with the Bosilegrad-Ribarci border crossing further south, where "on some days not a single traveler crossed the border." It was only a locally relevant Yugoslav-Bulgarian border crossing without a trans-regional road connection.[75] The diminishing proportion of Bulgarian travelers at the Dimitrovgrad border crossing in relation to Turkish labor migrants, Iranian truck drivers as well as German, English and Dutch students traveling to Turkey with Interrail was also a reason why the self-perception of the city at the border and of the border itself changed significantly.

With its initial demarcation in 1878, the tension between the border and the communication lines, the railway route to Istanbul, further increased in the 1950s. On the one hand, the border became almost hermetic as part of the Iron Curtain. On the other hand, the intensity of the traffic at the border with the motorway and the Istanbul Express created a new regional self-image. Trieste and the Middle East were now the coordinates of a changed expectation horizon of a "good life" that was linked to them.

In addition, the lines of communication, be it a railway or the famous Autoput (the Yugoslav highway connecting nearly all republics) became important for the new ways of consumerism. Dimitrovgrad, at least since 1920 on the periphery, in this consumerist respect underwent a transformation, becoming a part of a transnational network. The two endpoints of this shopping route, Trieste in the West and Istanbul in the Southeast, as centers of Yugoslav consumer tourism since the 1960s, illustrate vividly the specificity of Yugoslavian socialism with regard to possibilities of mobility, surmounting the political boundaries of the Cold War. It seems paradoxical that precisely in an epoch in which borders divided Europe into two parts, socialist Yugoslavia created new possibilities for transnational mobility for the inhabitants of Tsaribrod/Dimitrovgrad.

Wolfgang Höpken mentions for the period of the "Golden Sixties" a negative loyalty on the part of Yugoslav citizens to their state. Negative loyalty means that this loyalty was mainly created by comparison with the other socialist states, where the supply situation was much more modest and travel to Western countries was impossible.[76] The concept of negative loyalty can also be used to ana-

---

73 Kiril Trajkov, "Meždunarodnijat păt i našijat Dimitrovgradčanin," *Bratstvo*, 30 March 1967, 5.
74 Bogdan Nikolov, "Uspehi koito zadălžavat," *Bratstvo*, 17 April 1968, 7.
75 "Pri Mitničarite," *Bratstvo*, 6 June 1969, 5.
76 Wolfgang Höpken, "Durchherrschte Freiheit? Wie autoritär (oder wie liberal) war Titos Jugoslawien?," in *Jugoslawien in den 1960er Jahren*, ed. Hannes Grandits and Holm Sundhaussen (Wiesbaden: Harrassowitz, 2013), 39–65.

lyze the transformations in the region discussed here. In addition, there was also an active identification with the Yugoslav state and what being a Yugoslav implied. It was the possibility of articulating different close affiliations beyond the old compulsion to unambiguity, e.g., to be at the same time a member of the Bulgarian minority and a Yugoslav. Negative loyalty had its starting point in daily comparisons with the living conditions of friends and relatives in Bulgaria, but at the same time participation in a larger non-national whole, i.e., in Yugoslavia, and this provided an experience which created a positive loyalty. In contrast to the regimes that were dominant between 1878 and the end of the Second World War, socialist Yugoslavia did not force its citizens to identify unambiguously with only one ethnic group. It is certainly no coincidence that this form of new loyalty, which permitted ambivalence for the first time since the end of Ottoman rule was formed in a state structure that was not nationally founded.

After 1989, the end of the Cold War did not mean the comprehensive removal of all barriers; their function as obstacles only changed direction as conditions on the border were reversed. Yugoslavia disintegrated and, in 1992, sanctions were imposed on Serbia in the war for ethnically homogeneous territories. These sanctions severely affected the previous mobility of the people of Dimitrovgrad. On the other side of the border, in Bulgaria, 1989 was a real breakthrough in the sense of free mobility, which increased rapidly until the country joined the EU in 2007. In contrast, the mobility of Yugoslavian and later Serbian citizens was increasingly restricted until visas became necessary for entry into Bulgaria. Today the former section of the Iron Curtain is again part of a transnational border organization, now the EU's external border. For the people in today's Serbia, the EU is thus also in the East. While they were previously relatively privileged in their mobility, since as Yugoslav citizens they needed visas neither for the West, e.g., to go to Trieste, nor for the East, e.g., to go to Istanbul, the following two decades have meant a noticeable restriction of their mobility. But also, under these new circumstances, people from the region are once again appropriating opportunities for mobility through citizenship as they had a hundred years earlier by productively exploiting the ambiguity of ethno-national affiliation. Although this ambiguity was an impertinence in the eyes of the central state and the protagonists of ethno-national homogeneity as described above, the local actors back then were able to make use of it and pursue their business and interests for a long time between Pirot and Tsaribrod on both sides of the border. Today, a hundred years later, the people of Dimitrovgrad, as members of the Bulgarian minority, have the right to Bulgarian citizenship, which at the same time makes them citizens of the EU. In this way they have the opportunity to regain the mobility that threatened to be completely lost in 1990.

11 Conclusion

This chapter has demonstrated the dialectics between borders and mobility in the case of Tsaribrod/Dimitrovgrad from a long-term perspective. Borders prove highly permeable, even hard borders such as the Iron Curtain, given that people could travel from Dimitrovgrad to Trieste or to Istanbul. Frequently and under completely different conditions, local actors were able to reconstruct communication routes across the border. At the same time, the Iron Curtain had devastating effects on the micro-regional communication which came to a standstill for decades. Until 1989, the relevance of transregional communication between the Yugoslav-Bulgarian border regions was exceptionally low as compared to the border-regions of Yugoslavia with Italy and Austria.

Once local space was intersected by the border, it gradually lost its significance as a communication network. In the last third of the nineteenth century up to the First World War, this local road network, mentioned in the introduction of this chapter, was still visible despite the demarcation of borders and it continued to be part of local everyday life. Between 1920 and 1953, violence—at times open, at times structural—became a new factor that transformed the border zone into a space dominated by state actors (military, police, underground organizations). This process culminated in the Cold War period in a hitherto unknown hermetic quality of the border. As in other places along the Iron Curtain, space that had been part of work and village life (fields, pastures, hamlets) was transformed into a new, alien border zone, in which completely different rules applied from those previously known. The state, in the person of the military, the police, and employees of the Ministry of the Interior, was present, both quantitatively and qualitatively, in a very special form, controlling people's lives. But in contrast to other Cold War border zones, the route, which still crossed the border, made the essential difference.

Mobility, or more precisely, obstinate mobility across borders, is an integral part of border systems. Such obstinate mobility arises from the tension between the usual patterns of work and everyday life and the borderline that runs counter to these patterns. The balance between the possibilities of obstinate mobility and its limitation changes constantly. In the concrete case of the city of Tsaribrod/Dimitrovgrad the field of tension between mobility and its restriction was and still is defined by the route with its very special transnational dimension, which cannot simply be cut off or rerouted by a single state. Its relevance in the national and local context is certainly subject to change. As the chapter has demonstrated, the local population initially could not use the railway, through which the old route regained its transnational capacity. But under changed social conditions, people became again part of transnational mobility along the route. Beginning in the 1960s, the meaning of the route changed, when local lines slowly faded and the trans-local participation in the route was reinstituted similar to imperial times: the route seems now to be reemerging in a form reminiscent of the Ottoman Orta Kol.

Precisely the intertwining of border and route—e. g., as a border crossing especially for road traffic—produces a new quality, a completely new resource for the local population and highlights the *differentia specifica* to other border-regions. Be it through new job opportunities in the border authorities, such as customs and police, be it in hotels and restaurants, or as a not entirely legal possibility to exchange goods. This new quality has emerged from the renewed transnationalization of the lines of communication, but also from the transnationalization of the border. It is not just any point on the border between Yugoslavia and Bulgaria with a small sleepy border post. Rather, the border here was above all part of the Iron Curtain that divided Europe, and this part of the border in turn was essentially determined by the route as a section of the transversal between Central Europe and the Middle East. Both the border and the route gain a new transnational, even transcontinental quality and therefore reflect the change in the mental map: from the threshold to Europe to the gateway to the Middle East. What is special here is not the region as "just another border-region" with its cultural specifics, which produces an equally specific reaction to the demarcation of borders. What is special here is that at this very concrete point, a nation-state border is crossed by a transcontinental route, which then literally counteracts the usual effects of such border demarcation. A route that significantly influences the region, at least as much as the border. And, even more: the route also shapes and models the border landscape itself, as we could see in the creation of one of the largest border crossings in Yugoslavia, transforming this border area into something new, which does not simply mean in to a crossing between two states, but contains an essential transcontinental dimension.

In all its transformations and re-appearances, the route remains a constant challenge to nation-state territorialization and demarcation. The people at this point of the route not only participate in this challenge, they also constantly reproduce it.

Nenad Stefanov
Park ve Restoran: About Oblivion, Obstinate Mobility and Temporary Infrastructures on the Road

1 Introduction

At noon, a group of travelers entered the Turkish restaurant. They were wealthy pensioners with a secular, middle class background who obviously liked traveling and could afford it. To me they looked like engineers with their wives enjoying their retirement and the leisure time that comes along with it. The group ordered the cheapest set menu, a classic of Turkish cuisine. The big restaurant fitted with dark wood, a white fake marble floor and chairs upholstered in red velvet was quite busy. The group of pensioners, other couples and smaller groups of men, probably truck drivers, waited for their meals while drinking tea. In the corner, on top of a glass cabinet, a TV showed the latest news from the capital. Below, a couple of books showing the scenic landscapes of the Turkish Black Sea coast were on display. The service staff bustled about taking orders and occasionally disturbed the perfect scene of a Turkish restaurant somewhere on the Black Sea coast by talking in Serbian to the women in the kitchen.

In fact, I was not on the Black Sea coast, where in some unexpected way Serbs make a living as kitchen staff, but rather in Serbia. The restaurant is located at the outskirts of Pirot, on the European Motorway 80, the old road to Istanbul. Considering where we were on this road, which for centuries connected Anatolia with Central Europe, the perfectly Turkish scene in Serbia becomes less surprising. We can understand the restaurant with the telling name Tiha Noć (Quiet Night) as a practical expression of this route. But against the background of a world of nation-states with their national languages and national cuisines, the restaurant is an oddity. From the perspective of transregional traffic, it is something normal. The following chapter will focus on this tension.

From a nationalist perspective, the state as a social space is usually perceived as a clearly bounded territory with impermeable borders. Any communication or everyday practices which go beyond these borders have no significance from such a state-centered perspective. For the protagonists of the nation-state, such phenomena are literally peripheral. This is certainly not an exclusive feature of the Balkans. But there it was particularly pronounced in the period when nation-states were being created between the end of the nineteenth and the first half of the twentieth centuries, and cities that once formed regional centers such as Bitola (Monastir) in the Ottoman Empire or Subotica (Maria-Theresiopel) in the Habsburg Monarchy, suddenly found themselves on the periphery of the new Yugoslavian state territory. The same applies to the town of Pirot, which, after 1878, transformed from a regional center in the Ottoman Empire into a town on the new Serbian-Bulgarian border.

Yet it is precisely these supposed peripheral locations that deserve greater attention, since from such a de-centered perspective the relationship between the center and the local, between state-power and everyday life can be grasped more precisely. In particular, what can be adequately analyzed is what happens with those practices of local everyday life which ignore the newly drawn borders. If in these former regional centers contacts of various kinds are maintained within the former region, i.e., now across state borders, then from the perspective of the new central state this tends to be regarded as disloyal behavior. The maintenance of kinship relations across the border, the adherence to former religious festivals that took place on the other side of the border, but above all commercial ties are, from the perspective of the center, acts which tend to undermine the state authority and disrespect the new borders. Especially inter-regional trade, which had to cross state borders, was quickly denounced as illegal smuggling. In general, actors do not consciously reflect on such practices as a kind of resistance against the new obstacles. For them, they are self-evident and not explicitly articulated as guiding principles.

This chapter will focus on the road between Pirot and Dimitrovgrad as a location where cross-border practices such as trade, commercial activities and traveling can be observed. Both cities are located close to the Serbian-Bulgarian border on the Serbian side; from 1878 to 1919 Dimitrovgrad, which was called Tsaribrod until 1952, was part of Bulgaria. The chapter will examine symbolic and material practices which reveal "transgressive" ambiguity along the route, and will do this in three steps: Firstly, it will focus on how cross-border connections along the route faded into oblivion; secondly, on the construction of specific spaces and the infrastructures of new transnational connections; and thirdly, on the symbolization of this particular area of action.

The chapter is interested in cross-border practices along the route, on what has faded into oblivion as well as made a reappearance under completely changed social conditions of certain practices or infrastructures, since they are frequently part of processes of persistence. Such processes have been discussed in the context of "phantom borders," focusing on the reappearance of certain structures, discourses and practices. "In the study of phantom borders and phantom spaces, the primary question is how and why varied social, historical, and imagined heritages mutually influence each other. Here, they not only can combine to create something new, but also persist over a more or less extended period of time."[1] In this approach, there is a systematic interrelation between persistence and situativity, which is of central importance especially for the context dealt with here. Disappeared spatial structures do not simply re-surface following mysterious laws. Rather, examining processes of persistence "aims to arrive at a situational understanding of how the characteristics of a region establish and reproduce themselves, the circumstances under which they survive specific historical periods, and why they disappear."[2] The situational approach also implies an actor-centered perspective in that processes of persistence are put into relation to the situated, concrete, possibly obstinate strategies of the actors.[3]

2 Oblivion

The consciousness of past transnational communication disappeared particularly in those areas and their urban centers which were transformed into the peripheries of new nation-state. For those places, such as the town of Pirot on our route, as mentioned in the previous chapter, the protagonists of the national idea and its version of space advocated for its incorporation into the central narrative. They perceived the lack of definitude as to where they belonged in these new peripheries as a defect. Since Pirot was a trading town with many contacts to all parts of the Ottoman Empire, there was an excess of flaws and shortcomings according to this centrist perception. To prove exclusive belonging to the new nation-state center, all ambiguities had to be concealed and, over the decades, they would eventually be forgotten.

A fragment in which this forgetting becomes visible is the cooperation of Muslim, Jewish and Christian merchants even after the end of Ottoman rule in this area. In the national narrative, which is still dominant today, such cooperation in principle could not exist, because all Muslim inhabitants had immediately left Pirot when the Serbian army entered the town in 1877.[4] The disappearance of the Muslim urban population, the "Turks," (as they are called even today), means the definitive natural correction of a centuries-long anomaly.

---

[1] Béatrice von Hirschhausen et al., "Phantom Borders in Eastern Europe: A New Concept for Regional Research," *Slavic Review* 78, no. 2 (2019): 371–2.
[2] Ibid., 372.
[3] Michael G. Esch and Béatrice von Hirschhausen, eds., *Wahrnehmen, Erfahren, Gestalten: Phantomgrenzen und soziale Raumproduktion* (Göttingen: Wallstein, 2017), 18.
[4] For the dominant narrative cf. Borislava Lilić, *Istorija Pirota i okoline (1804–1918)*, 2 vols. (Pirot: NiP Hemikals, 1994).

However, recent research paints a more differentiated picture.⁵ Neither did all the families leave the cities conquered by the Serbian army overnight, nor did they stay away forever. Rather, it was a longer process. The 1878 Treaty of Berlin, which legitimized these conquests, obliged the two new states, Serbia and Bulgaria, to recognize the Muslim inhabitants of the newly acquired territories as citizens.⁶ It is true that the newly established local authorities used legal chicanery to drive away those Muslims who still regarded Pirot as their hometown. But they succeeded at a much slower pace than they had planned. Moreover, the experience of such forced migration in large part did not result in a cutting of all links to the old homeland. On the contrary, relationships were even re-established, and the route played a decisive role in this. Despite the difficult conditions, Pirot Muslims continued to maintain good contacts with their old neighbors. This can be seen in the correspondence between the merchant Abedin Efendi, who emigrated from Pirot to Istanbul, and three other inhabitants of Pirot: Aleksa Hristić (the son of the wealthy Mali Rista, who had previously lived in Istanbul for a long time), Jovan Džadžić, and Mair S. Beraha. In 1890 all three founded the trading company Džadžić, Hristić and Beraha, which worked together with Abedin.⁷ Even twelve years after the incorporation of the region into Serbia and its de-Ottomanization, the contacts to Istanbul and the relations between Jewish, Muslim and Christian merchants from Pirot were still so stable that they decided to found a joint enterprise. The company specialized mainly in trading cotton products, Pirot kelims (carpets), dried plums, and butter to Istanbul. Beginning in 1892, Abedin ordered kelims as well as butter and the famous local cheese Kaškaval. At the same time, Abedin intended to supply the Pirot side with raw material such as wool from Anatolia for the kelims.⁸ This exchange was facilitated since the end of the 1880s by the railway line that connected Pirot to Istanbul.

This cooperation along the route is only mentioned here briefly as an example for those practices which fell into oblivion.⁹ It is very likely that, in the same

---

5 Florian Riedler, "Communal Boundaries and Confessional Policies in Ottoman Niš," *Journal of the Economic and Social History of the Orient* 61 (2018): 726–56.
6 Wolfgang Höpken, "Der Exodus: Muslimische Emigration aus Bulgarien im 19. und 20. Jahrhundert," in *Osmanen und Islam in Südosteuropa*, ed. Reinhard Lauer and Hans Georg Majer (Berlin: De Gruyter, 2013), 303–432.
7 Cf. Ilija Nikolić, *Pirot i Srez Nišavski: Arhivska građa* (Pirot: Muzej Poništavlja, 1981) 2:822, doc. 1161.
8 Abedin Efendi to Gospoda Džadžić, Hristić, Beraha, 10.5.1892, in: Nikolić, *Pirot i Srez Nišavski*, 2:822, doc. 1161.
9 Field research has shown that there are no traces of memories of such collaborations, even though one of the companies belonged to one of the city dwellers respected by the new central

period, there were numerous such enterprises in other post-imperial cities.[10] But in the eyes of the protagonists of the new nation-states, these were an anomaly, a problematic legacy from the past. As a consequence of the major break in relations during the Balkan Wars (1912–13) and the First World War, such cooperation along the road was forgotten. Forgotten above all, because there was no space for telling stories about it to keep it present. After all, in a border region, national attributions or independently articulated affiliations could quickly be compromising: From the perspective of the state authorities, it was important, especially in the border area, to ensure the unambiguous loyalty of the population. Particularly teachers and civil servants had to pay attention to the stories that the children brought to school from home. The officials listened attentively to the stories told in the taverns and the gossip that was passed on, which had the potential to damage the reputation of the state, especially here on the border, and to allow the infiltration of "harmful," a-national attitudes from "over there." Telling stories here signifies the passing on of experiences from the other side of the border, of grandparents' memories of "good old Turkish times," or of experiences of inter-confessional cooperation, which might undermine the official narrative of the Muslim oppressor and the Christian victim. This diminished the space for stories that did not correspond to the standard nationally centered master narratives, since there were increasingly fewer people to whom they could be told who were not already nationally prejudiced. Borders—be they state borders, ethno-national b/ordering, or simply those of practiced conformism—even blocked any overarching stories, which could communicate ambiguity and might make connections where they were denied by the national narrative. And this is precisely why these stories were suspect. A good example is the business relationship between Christians, Jews and Muslims from Pirot who, despite the drastic effect of the border, were able to maintain their connection over the distance of 660 kilometers to Istanbul by means of the old line of communication. Abedin Effendi had left Pirot, because of the border and all the negative effects for Muslim subjects of the Ottoman Empire that were associated with the establishment of the nation-states. So, he lived in Istanbul, yet the connection to his homeland Pirot was not lost. Mair Beraha, Jovan Džadžić and Abedin Ef-

---

power. Such episodes were not further narrated. Only a part of the preserved commercial correspondence gives an idea of the cooperation.
10 Evguenia Davidova, *Balkan Transitions to Modernity and Nation-States through the Eyes of Three Generations of Merchants (1780s–1890s)* (Leiden: Brill, 2013).

fendi were not the only ones, as can be gleaned fragmentarily from customs documents, yet in the local context such stories were not retold.[11]

3 Spontaneous/Provisional Infrastructure along the Route

Ambiguity, represented by the traffic and the communication line, is also associated with obstinacy. Such obstinacy repeatedly undermined officially standardized and declared boundaries, be they material barriers, or be they the attempt by the state to define which and whose stories were the right ones.[12] Even more than a century after the aforementioned enterprise, which was still based on a common experience within an imperial context, cross-border contacts developed again, mostly spontaneously and for a certain period of time.

On the section of the route between Niš and the Yugoslav-Bulgarian border, a remarkable phenomenon occurred beginning in the 1980s. Self-made company signs with Turkish inscriptions *Lastik-Tamir* (tyre-repair) became a natural part of this section of the E-80 motorway. At Niš, the E-80 went down to a single-lane in each direction and until 1988 it led through the villages and towns along the route until local bypasses were built. In the summer months, this meant kilometers of traffic jams from the Yugoslav-Bulgarian border crossing to the center of Pirot, through which the old Stambulsko Džade (Istanbul Road) passed. This section of the route is particularly interesting in view of the phenomena described. Several factors favored the emergence of a "spontaneous" infrastructure of car repair shops, service areas and restaurants. First, this section is approximately the middle of the route between the Federal Republic of Germany and central Turkey. Second, the single-lane with open roadsides made it possible for local actors to set up small private enterprises, which were tolerated in Yugoslavia in contrast to state-socialist Bulgaria. Third, especially Turkish working-migrants traveling in the direction of the Federal Republic of Germany were only permitted transit passage through the People's Republic of Bulgaria as

---

[11] This is particularly true of the Jewish community of Pirot, whose deportation during the Second World War by the Bulgarian occupying power (to Nazi extermination camps) has only been the subject of attention in recent years. Saška Velkova and Mila Panajotović, *Šalom iz Pirota* (Pirot: Muzej Ponišavlja Pirot, 2015).
[12] For obstinacy (*Eigensinn*) as a concept cf. Alf Lüdtke, "Geschichte und Eigensinn," in *Alltagskultur, Subjektivität und Geschichte: Zur Theorie und Praxis von Alltagsgeschichte*, ed. Berliner Geschichtswerkstatt (Münster: Grennwood Press, 1994).

part of the Warsaw Pact, similar to the situation in the GDR for West Germans. This meant an approximately 500 kilometers long trip through Bulgaria with only a few stops and resting places. On the Yugoslav side, this led to numerous accidents due to the fatigue of the drivers. The necessary resting places were created without the specifications that would have come from the traffic authorities and the motorway maintenance authorities, and it developed because of the residents' initiatives on this section of the E-80.

Such a private initiative was not possible on the sections from Belgrade to Niš, as the two-lane motorway remained separated from the surroundings by a fence. In any case, the operation was reserved for state-owned companies, mostly Yugoslav petrol station chains, which were able to take over and finance the entire infrastructure of service station complexes.

On the way between Niš and the Bulgarian border, car mechanics who owned a house on this part of the Yugoslavian Autoput began to set up workshops and erect signs, which in addition to the words *Lastik-Tamir* were also intended to inspire confidence by painting the names of West German car brands on large signs in large letters, or by advertising their services in a peculiar pictogram language they had developed themselves.[13] At the end of the 1980s, a relatively dense network of such (after-work) garages had developed between Niš and the Yugoslav-Bulgarian border crossing.

Todor Todorović, who opened his workshop on this part of the route between Pirot and Dimitrovgrad in 1982, can be cited as an exemplary case in point for the emergence of such spontaneous infrastructures. Todorović had chosen this location because of the frequent damage to cars as well as accidents which occurred on this section of the route. A second reason was that the place was exactly halfway between Pirot and Dimitrovgrad.[14] The garage was positioned almost in the same place as an Ottoman inn, to which we will come back later.[15]

In the following years, Todorović added a towing service to the repair shop and finally gained a license from the West German automobile club ADAC. This was particularly lucrative. Todorović earned up to 3000 DM for towing services to Turkey or the Federal Republic of Germany and was regularly on the road in both directions.[16] In the meantime, he continuously expanded his property, which

---

13 Compare the discussion of this particular art work in: Malve Lippmann and Can Sungu, eds., *Sila Yolu: Der Ferientransit in die Türkei und die Erzählungen der Autobahn* (Berlin: bi'bak, 2016).
14 Interview with Todor Todorović (real name changed), camping site Carski Drum, 4 May 2019.
15 Interview with Todor Todorović, camping site Carski Drum, 4 May 2019.
16 He also worked for other European insurance companies and went with his tow truck to Holland, Belgium and France. In the summer months, Todorović was on the road day and night working in the garage or towing cars. The Turkish "guest workers," because of their few and

today covers more than one hectare, by buying up the surrounding meadows and fields. Today, the entire property extends from the old Autoput to the tracks of the railway line and thus connects both communication lines between Central Europe and Anatolia. Initially, Todorović set up a workshop for cars. Then a garage for the tow truck, as well as a workshop for repairs on trucks. Finally, he added a camping site with the meaningful name Carski Drum (Sultan's Road) and the breeding of peacocks.

Todor Todorović's business almost collapsed during the 1990s sanctions imposed by the international community against Serbia for its role in the war in Bosnia-Herzegovina. This meant that the section of the route, which since 1960 was the main corridor for cars between East and West and which led through Yugoslavia, was now blocked by the war in Croatia and Bosnia-Herzegovina. While the international traffic shifted to other routes, this route was now only used by migrant workers from Serbia. Apart from the war, which kept most Turkish "guest workers" from their previous route, it was an enormous financial burden for the few who still dared to use it. As an attempt

Fig. 1: Billboard at the entrance of the car workshop and restaurant. Photo by Nenad Stefanov, 2019.

---

therefore very precious holiday days, literally wanted to have the repairs done as quickly as possible at any price. Interview with Todor Todorović, camping site Carski Drum, 4 May 2019.

to compensate for the financial losses caused by the halt of transit traffic, the Serbian government charged astronomical sums for car insurance and road tolls. The route of the labor migrants, whose destination in the summer was Turkey and who were still dependent on cars, shifted. They went from Italy by ferry to Greece, and there generally along the other old route, the Via Egnatia, to Istanbul. The truck drivers usually went via Hungary, Romania and Bulgaria.

It is remarkable that these alternative routes did not prevail in the long run. A few years after the end of the wars in the now former Yugoslavia, the volume of traffic on the old line gradually began to reach the level of the early 1990s again. Todorović now did not have to count on the few long-distance drivers who had decided against the detour via Romania or the more expensive route by ferry via Greece to Italy. On the contrary, transit traffic increased in the 2000s to such an extent that Todorović decided to create a half-hectare truck park with a restaurant.

The visual appearance of his business and above all the advertising had changed considerably compared to the previous decades. It was no longer the improvised billboards mentioned earlier that radiated a self-made aesthetic appeal, but modern illuminated signs in Turkish. In addition to Carski Drum, inscriptions such as *Vatan* (Fatherland), *Bayburtlunun Yeri* (The place of those from Bayburt) and *Avrupa Halal* (Europe *halal*) appeared. At Todorović, the Carigradski Drum campsite was now joined by the truck driver restaurant *Park ve Restoran Vatan – Karadeniz* (Parking and restaurant Fatherland – Black Sea). As with the other rest stops mentioned, the tenants of the restaurant came from Turkey, the staff spoke Turkish and the guests without exception were Turkish long-distance drivers and in the summer months also many German-Turkish "guest workers."

The owner was in contact with many potential tenants through the networks he had built up over the years (the ADAC trips resulted in ever-new acquaintances in Turkey, some of whom developed into steady business relationships). It was precisely through these networks across Bulgarian and Turkish borders that he was able to win Turkish tenants for his Park ve Restoran, which developed into a highly frequented service area for truck drivers. The result was a wide-ranging service area infrastructure, including everything from a spacious truck parking lot to a small prayer room, a mescid, constructed from a typical "real-socialist" kiosk.

Speaking with Todorović, he conveys an idea of the Autoput, the highway, as anything but a "non-place," i.e., a space that can only be passed and which has

Fig. 2a: Socialist kiosk ...

Fig. 2b.: ... transformed into a mescid. Photos by Nenad Stefanov, 2019.

no further meaning beyond the brief transit.[17] In contrast, one senses a panorama of entanglements, actors and institutions along the route, which remain in constant interaction with each other; through this a social network of relations along this section of the route becomes visible. All the actors, public and private, are networked along the route: from the police, customs, border officials, the owners of private petrol stations, who are remarkably numerous on the Bulgarian side around Dragoman, the driver of the towing service, the truck driver, etc.

In Todorović's stories, these networks reveal their true border-crossing character all the way to Istanbul. Everyone knows each other, exchanges information. Todorović was often called to Bulgaria for towing, because hardly any of his Sofia colleagues wanted to drive in the direction of the border. During the constant crossings of the border, the owners of the towing services and the authorities on both sides were no strangers to each other. Finally, cooperation with the police resulted from the fact that it was mostly police officers on both sides of the border who reported damaged vehicles to him. Cooperation also existed over long distances, for example, when one of the owners of service areas was looking for new Turkish tenants, or when someone wanted to buy a new location for a restaurant. These relations between the protagonists of state territoriality such as the police and customs officials and the protagonists of mobility such as Todorović and his customers were not free of conflict. But here, too, there were transitions, for example in the form of previous customs officials on the Bulgarian side becoming owners of petrol stations.

The fact that the road is anything but a non-place also applies to the travelers, for example the migrant workers from Turkey, for whom this route was and still is charged with a very special meaning, and is expressed in the expression *sıla yolu* (reunion way). It is not only the entire route that is marked by a peculiar fascination for its users, as the numerous videos of the journey uploaded to YouTube currently convey.[18] The individual stages also play a special role, and this simultaneously at different levels of temporality. First, with regard to the temporal experience of the journey itself, which is structured by its successive stages, e. g., of the restaurants mentioned, but also of the changing landscapes, which convey that one is getting closer to the destination. Secondly, the journey has something cyclical in that it takes place every year or every second year and is

---

[17] Fabian Engler, "Sommer, Sonne, Autobahn: Die Ferienstraße in die Türkei und das Erfahren von Heimat(en)," in *Sıla Yolu: Der Ferientransit in die Türkei und die Erzählungen der Autobahn*, ed. Malve Lippmann and Can Sungu (Berlin: bi'bak, 2016), 16–27.

[18] Some examples: https://www.youtube.com/watch?v=cqNr-xVtbIA; https://www.youtube.com/watch?v=-yBghjAIKNA&list=RDQM1yqf2Tx72gU&start_radio=1, last accessed 24 October 2020.

at the same time particularly affectively charged as a regularly repeating journey, not simply as an abstract, arbitrary holiday destination, but as being on the road between two homelands. This applies not only to the labor migrants from Turkey/Germany, but of course just as much to those from the former Yugoslavia, as well as more recently to the labor migrants from Bulgaria. In addition to this annual cycle, in which the journey on "our route" or *sıla yolu* has a very special meaning,[19] there is the biographical dimension of temporality. Most of those who travel this route also carry their memories of all the previous trips in different periods of their lives with them. Remembering how they used to travel this route in both directions as children, as young people, as workers, how the speed changed because of new motorways, but also the borders, dissolving and then re-appearing again as obstacles. So even the travelers, who literally only seem to rush through this route, have a very specific relationship, as it were a biographical relationship, to it.

4 Symbolisms

At first glance, the practice of creating spontaneous/provisional infrastructures, which rest on a business model that crosses borders and transgresses official regulations, seems to indicate a cosmopolitan self-understanding. However, in reality the relationship between everyday practice and self-understanding is often fractured and characterized by paradoxical forms of mediation, which becomes particularly apparent at the level of the symbols along the way.

This can be illustrated by the example of another garage with a service area. The Pension Murat, almost directly at the Yugoslav-Bulgarian border crossing Gradina/Kalotina, was one of the first such facilities in the 1980s. At this service area and workshop, a fascinating conversion between the rising new ethno-nationalism in Serbia on the one hand, and completely different obstinate intentions of action on the other hand could be observed.

The owner of the car workshop and pension aimed his focus mainly at Turkish truck drivers (all year round) and the Turkish "guest workers" in summer as customers. He was familiar with the name Murad, which to him seemed to be typical Turkish and very meaningful, because of the many series and feature films on television about the anniversary of the battle of Kosovo in 1389. In the 1980s, the battle had become the central topos of Serbian ethno-nationalism. According to legend, Sultan Murad, one of the protagonists of the Kosovo myth,

---

[19] Lippmann and Sungu, eds., *Sıla Yolu*.

was stabbed by a Serbian knight after the end of the battle and thus found death on the battlefield. The owner of the pension thought the name Murat was particularly suitable for his business idea, as in his eyes it was a typical Turkish name easily recognizable by the Turkish customers he wanted to win.

Of course, "Murat" had nothing to do with a conscious appreciation of the Ottoman past, yet in the mind of the owner the similarity of the two names was his (misguided) attempt at suggesting a common heritage that would connect Turkish migrants and truck drivers with the people living here. At the symbolic level, it was in fact the opposite: the new businessman made use of a world of characters borrowed from the Kosovo myth that had just become fashionable in Serbia, which developed into the symbolic legitimation of a new ethnic community in the context of rising populism.[20] While the real-socialist symbolic world (*Prvi Maj, Progres, Svoboda* etc.) had long since lost its appeal, the political symbolism of the new ethno-nationalism unfolded with commercial success.[21] Sultan Murad was one of the figures from this merchandising world of the Kosovo myth. They were names from a very distant past, which now stood for a promising future.

At the same time, however, Murat in this very concrete context, as the eponym for a truck boarding house on E-80 in the immediate vicinity of the Serbian-Bulgarian border, practically stepped out of the new mythical symbolic space and interacted with the people from a wide variety of contexts who were on the road.

The contradiction, however, between the everyday practical meaning of this name for business purposes and its origin from a symbolic world remained and, as Ivan Čolović said, it was marked by the renewal of an alleged permanent struggle between "fanatical Muslims" as the "centuries-long Turkish oppressors" against Slavic Orthodox Christianity. This past was now projected on Muslim Bosnians and Kosovans.[22]

The possibilities of dealing with this contradiction between official narratives and individual action, the experience and reflection of this experience

---

[20] Ivan Čolović, "Die Erneuerung des Vergangenen: Zeit und Raum in der zeitgenössischen politischen Mythologie," in *Bosnien und Europa: Die Ethnisierung der Gesellschaft*, ed. Nenad Stefanov and Michael Werz, (Frankfurt: Fischer, 1994).
[21] From a commercial point of view, there was a broad spectrum of "merchandising": from elaborately produced full-length TV-series, comics, booklets reminiscent of Panini albums with sticky pictures of the various "teams" and legendary figures, to chocolate boxes decorated with historicist paintings of the Kosovo-Polje theme. Even cosmetic products adorned themselves with the memory of the Battle of 1389.
[22] Ivan Čolović, "Die Erneuerung des Vergangenen," 92.

Fig. 3: Motel Murat. Photo by Nenad Stefanov, 2019.

can be seen in the relation to the very concrete ambivalent legacies of the late Ottoman epoch. Only a few meters from the current car workshop of the previously introduced Todor Todorović, as well as the Park ve Restoran, there was an inn (*han*) in the Ottoman period for the travelers on this route. Some years later, the customs station on the Serbian-Bulgarian border between 1878 and 1920 was built very close by, surrounded by other inns. They were quite profitable until the opening of the railway line in 1888 and then completely lost their importance, as the traffic on the road decreased abruptly. About a hundred years later, the large complex of Todorović's car park, restaurant and camping site is now located here. This shows graphically how in very different constellations and (at different times) infrastructures can persist. Even the border as a contradiction of mobility and the protagonists of the nation-state and its border regulations reproduce the infrastructure of the road by placing infrastructures of the border such as a customs station here and not directly at the border.

In addition, on the site there was also part of the Circassian settlement, Zaganica, one of those founded along the road to Istanbul by the governor of the province of Niš after the Circassians had fled from the Russian Empire in 1867. More precisely, it was the Muslim cemetery of the settlement that was located directly on the estate of Todor Todorović. He discovered this when he wanted to level a meadow for the future truck parking lot and came across the skeletons of those who had been buried there up to 1878.

Todorović learned about this background of his discovery, the past of this environment, as accidentally as he had discovered the Muslim cemetery. When he bought the meadow to build the truck parking lot, he saw that this area was entered in the cadaster as Ćerćesko Selo (Circassian Village). He became interested in this background and heard some of the history of *Ćerćezi* in this village from old people. During these conversations he also learned that there was once a watchtower and a customs station here. In the end he discovered that under his property there was a cemetery.[23]

It was rather scattered and vague information that the owner of Park ve Restoran received. The just mentioned list contains references to quite different epochs: The *kale*, the watchtower, could date from late antiquity or the Ottoman period. The a*nove*, the inns, probably from the Ottoman period, until the opening of the railway line. The *presretači* who demanded customs were officials of the border between Serbia and Bulgaria that existed here between 1878 and 1920. Todorović's everyday working life went on, perhaps leaving him no time for further discussions or reflections on this kind of information. When asked whether the Turkish truck drivers knew what was under their resting place, Todorović spontaneously replied: "You know, I wasn't so interested in that and neither were the drivers." A moment later Todorović added: "I don't know, I told them

---

[23] Interview with Todor Todorović, camping site Carski Drum, 4 May 2019.

Fig. 4: Parking and cemetery. Photo by Nenad Stefanov, 2019.

about it, while having coffee (*ovako uz kafu*), I told them that it was a *ćerćesko selo*, the 500 years that the Ottomans were here and they know that, and because our mentality is very similar, the food is very similar, many words. And I can tell you, when I have driven the Turks somewhere, then they have always invited me to stay overnight. They provided us with clothes, always made sure that we had enough to eat; I can say that the Turks are very emotional and generous people. They like to negotiate and then find a price together (*da se pogode*). Unlike the Westerner who tells me 'drive me there and there,' then sign, Ciao and work done. Many friendships. It's a nice feeling when you help someone, and it is appreciated."[24]

5 Conclusion

It is remarkable how a story that is clearly negatively charged and taboo in the official narrative is here transformed by a subjective perspective into a completely different relationship to the Ottoman past. At the same time, it is amal-

---

[24] Ibid.

gamated with personal experiences that give this past a new meaning, in which the shared dominates and the ambivalent divisiveness of the official narrative recedes into the background.

Here it becomes clear once again, as emphasized at the beginning, that there is no institutionalized public knowledge in the region about the recent past under Ottoman rule. Individual, divergent memory has no systematic, institutional place. In addition, there is the fundamental fragility of ever-threatened subjective remembrance under authoritarian conditions. With the disappearance of the earlier generations, these remnants finally and irrevocably dissolve. If subjective remnants of experience, fragmentary episodes about the past still circulate, then only in a very limited, private space.

Here it is remarkable that an unorthodox subjective appropriation of the past appears, mixing the official narrative with the opposite: an affirmative relationship towards ambiguity. This emerges from a practice that unconsciously ties in with that of a hundred years ago.

Persistence, which was mentioned in the beginning, does not therefore lie in the artefacts of the past, but in the relationships which acting individuals and social groups develop under completely changed social conditions, and yet still link to constellations from the past without consciously doing so. At the same time, there is a commonality with similar forms of action in the past: such examples of cooperation have remained contested since the end of the nineteenth century; from the perspective of domination, they do not form a natural component of social action and are not accepted as such. But it is also self-evident for the actors, be it a hundred years ago or in the present.

"I've been working here for 35 years," says Todor Todorović, "I talk to them [he speaks a little Turkish, but mostly German], they stay with me when I fix the cars, the importance this trip has for them. They live for this day, the whole year they save. This road was made for the Turks, without them it is dead."[25]

---

25 Ibid.

Sandra King-Savić
Voices of the Via Egnatia: Deliberating Migratory Pull-Factors along the Roman Road in the Western Balkans

1 First Steps on the Egnatia: Beating the Heat

It was midday when we walked into Mesochori. This Greek town bordering North Macedonia seemed to house more tumbleweed than humans, which, plausibly, might have been due to the unrelenting heat that kept people indoors. This was our sixteenth day on the Via Egnatia, the old Roman road that connected Byzantium and Istanbul respectively, with Rome. Thirsting for ice cold drinks and some respite from the sweltering heat, we entered the first bar-café on the main-square and struck up a conversation with the only three customers in the run-down, but cozy café. Seeing that we were only a hop, skip, and jump from Bitola, North Macedonia, I tried my luck and introduced the two of us in Bosnian/Croatian/Serbian/Montenegrin (BCSM).[1] We sat with the three elderly men for a while, and learned that one of them had left Greece for Germany after completing his compulsory military service. Thinking he would go to Germany for just a couple of months to earn some money as a labor migrant, he eventually married, had kids, and ended up living in Germany for about thirty years before returning to Greece on his own. *My kids did not come back with me*, he said, adding, *I am here, they are in Germany. There is hardly anybody left in this town... what can I say?*[2]

This was not the first, nor was it the last time that we walked into either completely or partially abandoned hamlets on the Egnatia, which stands symbolically for the regional volume of the rural to urban- and/or international outmigration. Looking for employment and more choices compared to the possibilities found in the countryside, people from rural areas flock to the cities, or else abroad. Preferred destinations for Macedonian *émigrés* include Germany (86,626), Italy (68,714), Serbia (61,315), Switzerland (57,907), and Australia

---
[1] Many people in Macedonia understand the Bosnian/Croatian/Serbian/Montenegrin (BCSM) language, especially older generations.
[2] Fieldnote, Sandra King-Savić and Joshua King, Niki, Greece, 4 August 2016; also published as a blog entry under: *Voices of the Via Egnatia* at https://voicesoftheviaegnatia.wordpress.com, last accessed 5 February 2019.

https://doi.org/10.1515/9783110618563-010

(53,225).³ Germany (238,220) also serves as the preferred destination for Greek émigrés, followed by the United States (147,498), Australia, (136,221), Turkey (87,690), and Canada (83,910).⁴ Albanians, meanwhile, emigrate most often to Greece (574,840), Italy (449,657), the United States (84,665), Germany (31,969), and North Macedonia (25,400).⁵ Why is this the case, and what motivates people to up and move? Impending poverty, low average salaries, and unemployment drive the outmigration, according to Siniša Jakov Marušić who stated that more than ten percent of the North Macedonian population resides abroad, for instance.⁶ Indeed, by 2017, the official unemployment rate stood at 22.4 per cent in North Macedonia, 13.8 per cent in Albania, and 21.5 per cent in Greece.⁷ Yet, this is only half of the story. How, one might rather ask, do people live before they migrate to parts yet unknown, what are their specific plans before setting out, and might common narratives go beyond mere economic pull-factors that entice people into emigrating? My husband, Joshua E. King, and I hiked the stretch of the Via Egnatia between Durrës, Albania, and Thessaloniki, Greece, to find out.

2 Slowing Down: Doing Fieldwork on Foot

Our journey did not start on foot. Instead, we started out on tracks as we boarded the train that brought us from Switzerland to Bari in Italy. From there, we crossed the Mediterranean on the Rhapsody Ferry, an enormous ten-storied vessel not suited for the faint of heart. The Rhapsody has clearly been downgraded from whatever purposes it used to serve in its previous life. While there was a pool, it had, however, no water in it. No band or other source of entertainment be-

---

3 UNICEF, The former Yugoslav Republic of Macedonia (North Macedonia), International Migrant Stock, DESA, Population Division Migration Section, Migration Profiles Common Set of Indicators, last accessed 31 January 2019 at http://esa.un.org.
4 UNICEF, Greece, International Migrant Stock, DESA, Population Division Migration Section, Migration Profiles Common Set of Indicators, accessed 31 January 2019 at http://esa.un.org.
5 UNICEF, Albania, International Migrant Stock, DESA, Population Division Migration Section, Migration Profiles Common Set of Indicators, last accessed 31 January 2019 at http://esa.un.org.
6 Sinisa Jakov Marusic, "Macedonia Population Drained by Emigration, Report Says," *Balkan Insight*, May 15, 2013, https://balkaninsight.com/2013/05/15/report-macedonia-drained-by-migration/, last accessed 14 September 2020; see also Mark Rice-Oxley and Jennifer Rankin, "Europe's South and East Worry More About Emigration Than Immigration – Poll," *The Guardian*, 1 April 2019, https://www.theguardian.com/world/2019/apr/01/europe-south-and-east-worry-more-about-emigration-than-immigration-poll, last accessed 14 September 2020.
7 CIA Factbook, https://www.cia.gov/library/publications/resources/the-world-factbook/.

mused the audience from the existing, though now empty stage. One was able to go outside, and yet, the combination of flimsy rails and slippery surfaces appeared too perilous for an evening stroll on deck. The kids, to be sure, neither minded the slippery deck nor the flimsy rails. They played and chattered with their, perhaps, newly won friends in English, various forms of the German language, Italian, and switching to Albanian when turning to their parents. By overhearing Swiss-German spoken between two kids, we met a young couple who regularly travel this route to visit family and friends in southern Macedonia, or, as the man in his late thirties said, *a place some people consider to be Greece.*

Families were over-proportionally present that day on the Rhapsody, perhaps because summer break had just begun in many Central and Western European states. Most of the families lugged around enormous suitcases and bags—no doubt gifts and souvenirs for their family and friends, scenes with which I am intimately familiar being a daughter of labor migrants, or so-called *Gastarbajter*, myself. Like these families, my parents either packed the car to the brim, or else we hauled giant suitcases on the train each time we visited our family in the former Socialist Federal Republic of Yugoslavia (SFRY). I held a passport from SFRY until the age of 15, when I turned into a Swiss citizen. Back then, this seemed to me like some sort of magic—you go to bed a Yugoslav and wake up a Swiss citizen. As a result, I introduced myself as being from Switzerland—a country in which I was born, whose language I speak fluently and accent free, and a country I call home. The BCSM language was, nevertheless, the first one I learned to speak, and a language I used regularly to communicate with interlocutors along the Egnatia. A number of the people we met along the Egnatia, meanwhile, insisted on my Serbian background. This made for intriguing discussions about migration, identity and belonging. Dimitar, one of our interlocutors whom we met near Sopotsko, North Macedonia, emphasized:

> Dimitar: Your parents were *Gastarbajteri*, yes...? Now, you pretend to be Swiss.
>
> Me: Well yes, what else should I be? I was born a Yugoslav citizen, but Yugoslavia no longer exists. That is why my parents applied for Swiss citizenship for me.
>
> Dimitar: O.k., but you cannot change. You can live there, in Switzerland, you can become a naturalized citizen, but you can never become Swiss. You can never become a real Swiss girl. You can't, because of your genes. Your genes don't allow it. You have to understand that.[8]

---

[8] Dimitar, interviewed by Sandra King-Savić, (in the vicinity of) Sopotsko, Macedonia, 5 August 2016, Atlas.ti transcript/quote no. 8:1.

At first sight, Dimitar appears to be a man with nationalist inclinations. And yet, I would like to suggest that, while clearly displaying an essentialist understanding of nationality, Dimitar's statement must be contextualized.

Dimitar is an elderly, stout and very gentle man with a long, white beard and disheveled hair. Once an engineer, he lost his job following the closure of the nearby factory. Breathing heavily while speaking, he told us about his sister during our time spent in the village. *My sister left Sopotsko 30 years ago to get some experience abroad*, he explained. Like the elderly man in Mesochori, Greece, Dimitar's sister left the former SFRY with the intention of returning after a couple of years of working abroad. She, however, did not. *She stayed in the U.S.*, Dimitar explained. *She has a good job there. She works in some IT company. But she visits together with her kids. She teaches her kids our language; they are Macedonian, you know.* Attributing my background as immovably Serbian might be interpreted as a protective mechanism that cemented Dimitar's own continuous bond between himself and his sister's family against the backdrop of the former SFRY's disintegration, the closure of his former employer's factory, and the slow but clearly visible dissolution of his village. *There used to be some 200 kids who went to school in this town, now there are maybe six*, Dimitar said. His friends, plus the clerk in front of whose store we sat, had meanwhile joined us. They all nodded and pointed toward the large, though dilapidated school building. One might argue that families present a constant pole in a region in which individuals cultivate a protracted sense of history. This might be one of the reasons as to why interlocutors like Dimitar perceived me as one of their own. People along the Egnatia, in other words, often narrated stories from a "we perspective," perhaps expecting that I would understand the question of migration intrinsically—that is from their perspective.[9]

Dimitar's perception of, and articulation regarding my background illustrates that interlocutors scrutinize anthropologists. They are often curious why researchers might be interested in them. Like anthropologists who habitually analyze how their presence influences interviews and participant observation, so do informants who, too, seek to bridge potential asymmetries and/or find commonalities between anthropologists and themselves. The above example, moreover, demonstrates how informants react to an ethnographer's "inside/outside status" as Dimitar placed me within a national, linguistic, and cultural frame that was familiar to him. Dimitar perceived me as a second-generation migrant from the former SFRY, and reacted accordingly. This short example illustrates that people, to put it in Corinne Squire's words, tell stories "that are situated

---

9 Fieldnote, Sandra King-Savić and Joshua King, Kičevo, Macedonia, 29 June 2016.

in particular contexts, [while] working strategically to resist those contexts."[10] People perceived us to a greater extent as "insiders" in North Macedonia and Greece, most likely due to the BCSM language use, and less so in Albania where we communicated with interlocutors in English, German, and Spanish.

We recorded eight interviews, equally divided between men and women. All of the interviews lasted between one and three hours and took place in people's homes and third places.[11] Four interviews were held with only the interlocutor present; four interviews took place in the presence of at least one additional person—usually family members. Reconstructed, casual conversations and field notes taken during our trek on the Egnatia, which took place between 19 July and 13 August 2016, are not enumerated but equally important.[12]

Fieldnotes, interviews, and participant observation figure prominently in ethnographic accounts. Ethnographic accounts in which walking represents the central practice, are less common. According to Tim Ingold: "Once (they) [ethnographers] come to write up their results, (however, it) [walking itself] tends to be side-lined in favor of what really matters, such as the destinations toward which people were bound or the conversations that happened on route."[13] Conversations on route were as important as slowing down to learn and experience the everyday the way locals along the Egnatia do. Doing ethnography on foot allowed for us to slow down, to look at bridges that date back to Ottoman times, to touch the materiality of amphitheaters off the beaten path. Pierre Bourdieu maintained that material conditions endow social actors with "schemes of perception" in an *Outline of a Theory of Practice*.[14] Trailing Bourdieu, we thus embarked on the Egnatia to learn how locals imbue heritage sites with perceptions from their daily lives. Like the Egnatia that bares traces of both the present and the past, so do locals who share cultural traits that blur national differences despite the Euclidian lines that politicians and diplomats drew between them around the turn of the century. Making use of this *common*, as opposed to the rather divisive national past, it was our attempt to learn

---

10 Corinne Squire, "Narrative Genres," in *Qualitative Research Practice*, ed. Clive Seale et al. (London: Sage, 2004), 116.
11 Public places, such as cafes, which host regular, voluntary, and informal gatherings of individuals beyond home and work; See Ray Oldenburg, *The Great Good Place: Cafés, Coffee Shops, Community Centers, Beauty Parlors, General Stores, Bars, Hangouts and How They Get You Through the Day* (New York: Paragon House, 1989).
12 Some of the fieldnotes were made public in the form of blog-entries. See https://voicesoftheviaegnatia.wordpress.com, last accessed 24 October 2020.
13 Tim Ingold, *Ways of Walking: Ethnography and Practice of Foot* (Farnham: Ashgate, 2008), 3.
14 Pierre Bourdieu, *Outline of a Theory of Practice* (Cambridge: Cambridge University Press, 1977), 116.

about the reasons for one's decision to emigrate based on a person's everyday experience along the Egnatia, a cultural artefact that reaches beyond the creation of the nation state. Choosing to walk the Egnatia was, in other words, a conscious decision in our effort to avoid "methodological nationalism."[15]

3 National Symbolism and Symbolizing the National

The Roman Empire, according to Firmin O'Sullivan "lived on its roads."[16] We set out to discover one of these roads, the Egnatia, which served as an extension of the Via Appia. Ancient sources estimate the road to fall somewhere between 514 and 591 Roman miles, which amounts to a little under 800 kilometers.[17] We hiked 475 kilometers of this ancient *via militaris* the Romans had built sometime between 146 and 120 BCE to move military supplies and soldiers to the East. The road initially served military purposes, though soon turned into a *via publica*. Indeed, John Vanderspool has stated that the Egnatia supplied present-day Thessaloniki with a steady stream of travelers.[18] Margret M. Mitchell, too, describes the Egnatia as a "major thoroughfare from the East to Rome […] [where one] would have encountered a great range of artisans, peddlers, slaves, sailors, traders, farmers, and civil servants, alongside the formidable presence of the Roman military."[19] With the onset of the mid-fifth century CE and the subsequent collapse of the Roman Empire, the Egnatia suffered through invasions and consequently fell into disrepair. The road nevertheless remained important since it served Western incursions into the Balkans between the eleventh and the thirteenth centuries.[20] In the fifteenth century, the rising Ottoman Empire used and relied heavily on this same artery to move its army, goods, and cultural traditions westwards. As a result, markets, amphitheaters, charitable kitchens, *ha-*

---

[15] Nina Glick Schiller, "A Global Perspective on Transnational Migration: Theorizing Migration without Methodological Nationalism," in *Diaspora Transnationalism: Concepts Theories and Methods*, ed. Rainer Bauböck and Thomas Faist (Amsterdam: Amsterdam University Press, 2010), 110–29.
[16] Firmin O'Sullivan, *The Egnatian Way* (Exeter: David & Charles, 1972), 9.
[17] John Vanderspoel, "Provincia Macedonia," in *A Companion to Ancient Macedonia*, ed. Joseph Roisman and Ian Worthington (Oxford: Blackwell, 2010), 264.
[18] Ibid., 272.
[19] Margret M. Mitchell, "1 and 2 Thessalonians," in *The Cambridge Companion to St Paul* (Cambridge: Cambridge University Press, 2006), 51.
[20] O'Sullivan, *Egnatian Way*, 9.

*mam*s, mosques, and churches that variously date back to the Byzantine, Roman and/or the Ottoman Empire are still visible along this route, some derelict, others partially renovated. The Egnatia connected Rome with Byzantium, and then subsequently Istanbul with the West. Yet the route evolved into a road of greater importance. The Egnatia allowed for goods, ideas, and cultural practices to travel back and forth between the East and the West, thus preserving a whisper of a common history in the Balkan region.

To be sure, national belonging cannot be wished away by the mere will of an ethnographer who stumbles around a historic route for one month. National symbols, including the very existence of manned borders, flags, and a localized understanding of historiography are as present along the Egnatia as are the Ottoman and Roman architectural relics amongst which locals live their lives. The town of Meliti in Greece serves as a case in point.

Meliti, a village within the Florina regional unit along the Via Egnatia, was "a centre of fierce fighting between Greek Government and Greek Communist troops as late as 1949," according to O'Sullivan.[21] The civil war was, as we learned that afternoon, still a hotly debated topic. After we had reached the first bar-café in search of food, we encountered a group of middle-aged men who deliberated about the civil war between the communist and governmental forces vociferously, and in playful earnestness. We tried our luck again and started a conversation in BCSM. The men, all sitting around a table with heaps of half-eaten meals, beer bottles, and *rakija* glasses, immediately invited us to join their table at which the discussion about communists and fascists continued in both Greek and Macedonian at once.

One of the men, Davor, invited us to stay at his house that evening. During our tour through his beautifully renovated house, we learned that Davor had refurbished his late parents' place in cooperation with an architect as well as using material that came from North Macedonia. Davor, a self-described Macedonian, visits Meliti twice a year, though he now lives in Western Europe with his two kids. He likes to bring his children along to introduce them to both the Greek and Macedonian culture and language. Both of his kids learned to speak Greek in addition to some Macedonian. *I want to teach them Macedonian,* Davor explained, *but I never learned the language in school, and so don't know the proper sentence structure. But I speak Macedonian with them, and that is how they learn the language.*[22]

---

21 Ibid., 77.
22 Fieldnote, Sandra King-Savić and Joshua King, Meliti, Greece, 5 August 2016.

The North Macedonian state formation as well as the Macedonian language were both recurring themes that evening. Davor later introduced us to his friends who own an eatery in town. While at their house, the two of them told us about the local population's diversity, and about the Hellenization efforts by the Greek state—a circumstance that had become more than evident in the bar-café earlier that afternoon. Especially older people in town, according to Davor and his friends, identify as North Macedonian despite state efforts to homogenize this border region. As we prepared to leave, one of Davor's friends disappeared, and returned with a CD in hand. *Here you go, Kostas Theodorou is a great musician. Listen to the CD,* he said and added, *look up Rousilvo.*

Rousilvo is, according to the CD booklet and Kostas Theodorou's website, an old Slavic name for the present-day village of Xanthogeia that is located in northwestern Greece.[23] The village, according to the song booklet:

> [...] fell victim to the policy of the Greek state to forcibly 'Hellenize' the land and its people. At the end of the Greek Civil War (1946–49) most of the women in the village were left alone for the rest of their lives; their husbands either killed or exiled. Since 1986 the village has been uninhabited as a result of long-lasting social marginalization. [...] Ten compositions, alternating with location recordings of the surviving elderly residents of the village (sometimes singing, at times narrating their stories) salvaging and transforming a treasure trove, an elegy, of a vanishing poetry.[24]

Kostas Theodorou mirrors local sentiments about the North Macedonian question as encountered in Meliti afternoon. Fig. 1 is perhaps telling as to the Greek refusal to recognize North Macedonia prior to 2019.

Narratives of belonging trace political boundaries along the Egnatia. Dimitar most clearly situated belonging within a national, even a genetic frame, while Davor and his friends celebrate North Macedonia as their natural homeland. Davor, one might argue, practices a variant of long-distance nationalism,[25] in view of the renovation of his ancestral (vacation-) home in cooperation with an architect and material coming from North Macedonia. Like Davor, moreover, the two owners of the local eatery mourn the loss of, as well as identify with North Macedonia notwithstanding their being citizens of a Western and Southern European state, respectively. National boundary making, however, does not prevent locals from interacting, even in their preferred languages. Earlier that after-

---

23 Dine Doneff and Kostas Theodorou, official website: https://www.ecmrecords.com/catalogue/1516108852/rousilvo-dine-doneff, last accessed 7 March 2019.
24 Ibid.
25 As defined by Nina Glick-Schiller, "Long-Distance Nationalism," in *Encyclopedia of Diasporas*, ed. Melvin Ember, Carol R. Ember and Ian Skoggard (Boston: Springer, 2005), 570–80.

Fig. 1: A street sign near Meliti, Greece, indicating the distance to SFRY. Joshua E. King took this picture in 2016, 24 years after the dissolution of SFRY.

noon, Davor debated history in both Greek and Macedonian with a large group of men, while all the above interlocutors either had family members or had themselves migrated to Central and Western Europe to find work, or else for educational purposes. Experiencing the Egnatia from the perspective of the local population illustrates that belonging and cultural traits blur and shift as locals not only come to terms with their national histories, but also their experience with migration.

4 The Egnatia and Urban Settings

Dyrrachium, or present day Durrës, is located at an ancient crossroads that connected Italy with Greece, the Porte, and Byzantium, respectively. Goods and people came from Bari across the Mediterranean and into the port of Durrës, just the way we had come on the Rhapsody. Kim Bowes and Afrim Hoti called Durrës "[an] important Adriatic port and one of the western termini of the Via Egnatia, [it] served as a nodal point binding Italy to the Balkans and Greece to Dalmatia."[26] Vjolca, a woman we met outside the Museum in Durrës, affirmed this point of view and added that *Durrës was just as important as Apollonia in present day Greece, in terms of trade, ideas and culture. The big difference between the two ancient cities,* she explained, *was cultural development. Whereas Durrës welcomed everyone and was a city of merchants and traders from all backgrounds and classes, Appollonia was an aristocratic city,* she said.[27]

Vjolca, an educated, attractive lady dressed in a sheath dress and perfectly coiffed hair was not only proud of, but also clearly knowledgeable about the history of this region. The conversation, however, soon turned from history to more personal topics, and specifically her desire to move to the United States. *I already registered with the Green Card lottery,* she said. *Maybe I will win a Green Card, otherwise I will find another way to get a work permit.* Vjolca is one of many people in the Western Balkan region hoping to be among the 50,000 annual winners of a Green Card. I have met people in all parts of the Western Balkans who either hope to win, succeeded in winning, or have relatives who won a Green Card. *I am an educated professional; I work 56 hours a week, but I get paid for only 40. I long for a life where the working hours merit a standard of living that includes enjoying a vacation.* Vjolca has no overblown expectations. *I don't need to go on a holiday abroad,* she explained, *a weeklong vacation on the southern coast of Albania, known as the Albanian Riviera, would be enough. But I struggle to make a living, how can I afford to go on a vacation? This is why I applied for the lottery. I am not alone,* she said, *many Albanian professionals, including doctors, nurses, engineers and accountants apply for visas to go to the United States, Canada, and especially Germany. Albanians used to go to Greece and Italy,* she explained. *But since the 2008 financial crisis, fewer Albanians desire to migrate to Greece and Italy. Some Albanians even returned home during that time. But they have either left or are trying to leave Albania again.* Vjolca explained that coming back was especially difficult for the children who had grown up elsewhere.[28] Yet, Vjolca appeared torn.

While unmistakably planning to leave Albania, Vjolca also emphasized how much she treasured her country. She reiterated several times her fear of leaving her aging parents, the wonderfully fresh food, her friends, and the life she is ac-

---

26 Kim Bowes and Afrim Hoti, "An Amphitheatre and Its Afterlives: Survey and Excavation in the Durres Amphitheatre," *Journal of Roman Archaeology* 16 (2003): 381.
27 Fieldnote, Sandra King-Savić and Joshua King, Durrës, Albania, 19 June 2016.
28 Fieldnote, Sandra King-Savić and Joshua King, Durrës, Albania 19 June 2016.

customed to in Durrës. Time and again we met people who sought to leave whilst emphasizing their love of country. Edin Osmić, better known under his alias Edo Maajka, is an established hip-hop artist with residence in Zagreb, Croatia, who expressed this very sentiment on his record called *Savske Meduze:*

[...] Visa in hand, [...]
[...] [A feeling of] bliss and agony at the same time
Me, my wife and our child – my family and hers
[...], we sing, me and [all] those people I will miss
I am going to one, and leave behind another world
[...] tomorrow is my flight
[...] I smile at the stewardess, but feel wistful inside
But then, here is America
The language is tough, and the air is heavy
But I sleep well, and my [blood] pressure is low
Every new beginning is difficult, it will get easier
[...] The other day my son called me *daddy*
[...] I told him I am your *babo*, and not your daddy or your father
But he is a nice kid, aren't you *sine*
He downloads folk music from the computer for me
[...] He does not understand why his *babo* cries when listening to the *Indeksi* [...][29]

Osmić echoes many of the themes that our interlocutors addressed during interviews and casual conversations on the Egnatia. As was the case with the elderly gentleman in Mesochori who moved back to Greece without his children, so too does Osmić describe the fictitiously diverging microcosms experienced by father and son following their emigration to the U.S.

Vjolca, like many emigrants and migrants to be, often regretted having to leave family members and friends behind and having to leave to have a "better life" and a steady income at all. Leaving one's home behind is never a simple act. This became more than evident during our walkabout. It was no different for Vjolca who longed to leave with every fiber of her being, knowing full well that leaving was not an easy undertaking. Steering the discussion back to history, Vjolca implored us to visit the amphitheater before continuing along the Egnatia.

The amphitheater in Durrës was buried underneath a local settlement near the center of the city until 1966, when Vangjel Toçi, a local archeologist, discovered it.[30] Amphitheaters, however, were not commonly located at the center of

---

29 Edo Maajka, *Savske Meduze*; lyrics available in BCSM at http://www.tekstovipjesamalyrics.com/.
30 Bowes and Hoti, "An Amphitheater and Its Afterlives," 381.

Roman towns, but situated somewhere near the edge of a settlement. Gutteridge, Hoti and Hurst state: "[T]he amphitheater occupied something of a liminal zone in the Roman townscape, at the blurring between the civilized urban and the more uncontrolled areas beyond. In the early Roman town, it was not culturally central to the socially defined notion of 'urban'."[31]

In Dyrrachium, however, the amphitheater came to be located at the center due to fluctuating sea levels that moved the city-core to the northeast. Another factor was the construction of a wall in late-Antiquity that again moved the city-core to the south.[32] Following the post-Roman era, the amphitheater served as a site for Christian worshippers. Gutteridge, Hoti and Hurst have dated the St. Stephen chapel to the seventh century, and stated the amphitheater might have been an expansion to a previously constructed martyrium.[33]

Archaeological excavation sites are visible in most of the bigger cities we encountered along the Egnatia, with streets, antique walls, and former caravanserais having been renovated accordingly. Elbasan in Albania, too, illustrates this point. Situated between the Shkumbi river and the Albanian highlands, Elbasan lay directly along "the only transverse road at all practicable for wheeled traffic [that] enters the mountains," according to Ernest Nowack.[34] Writing about Elbasan in 1921, following his being stationed there during WWI, Nowack notes that people in Elbasan traditionally traded in oil, tobacco, and/or herded sheep thus connecting the Albanian high- and lowlands. Elbasan, also referred to as Scampa castle in the literature, was thus situated in an opportune location for trade and the protection of Durrës further down the valley. Maria Grazia Amore confirmed Nowack in 2005, stating that "Scampa castle occupies a strategic location for control of the Via Egnatia and also served as an advanced fortification of Dyrrachium."[35] The Egnatia itself runs from East to West through the historical city center of Elbasan, a municipality with a fortified center, fully restored (Fig. 2 and 3).[36]

Durrës and Elbasan are, of course, cities to which local and regional tourists flock to vacation. Renovating, restoring, and excavating significant landmarks,

---

31 A. Gutteridge, A. Hoti and H.R. Hurst, "The Walled Town of Dyrrachium (Durres): Settlement and Dynamics," *Journal of Roman Archeology* 14 (2001): 392.
32 Ibid., 407.
33 Ibid., 392.
34 Ernest Nowak, "A Contribution to the Geography of Albania," *American Geographical Review* 11, no. 4 (1921): 530.
35 Maria Grazia Amore, Lorenc Bejko, Ylli Cerova and Ilir Gjapali, "Via Egnatia (Albania) Project: Results of fieldwork 2002," *Journal of Roman Archaeology* 18 (2005): 352.
36 Fieldnote, Sandra King-Savić and Joshua King, Elbasan, Albania 23 June 2016.

Fig. 2: Fully restored Via Egnatia in Elbasan, Albania, leading to an old Mosque dating to Ottoman times. Photo by Joshua E. King, 2016.

Fig. 3: Street sign naming the Rruga Egnatia (Via/Street Egnatia) in Elbasan, Albania. Photo by Joshua E. King. 2016.

including the amphitheater in Durrës, or the Egnatia itself in Elbasan, serve to illustrate a historic continuity to the visitors. Another example for this phenomenon is the area around the Church of St. Kaneo in Ohrid, North Macedonia. We have both been to Skopje many times, though had never arrived at this enigmatic lake by foot. Ohrid is most famous for Kyril and Methodius who translated the bible into the Glagolitic script, as well as Kliment and Naum who continued the work of Kyril and Methodius by using the bible as a means to teach people how to read in the ninth century. Today, one can visit the Literary School that was established by Kliment in 886.

Ohrid is also famous for the *Ohridski biseri*, Pearls from Ohrid. This is a one of a kind pearl, handmade using fish scales from the Plasica, a fish species native to lake Ohrid, and covered with ground shells, also from lake Ohrid. We met Jozef, a middle aged, tanned, and fit looking man with a smoky voice in one of the stores that sells the pearls, and quickly began talking about the town, history, and migration. *You know, the Via Egnatia passed right through this very town, and connected Rome with the East*, he started right after we told him about our walk along the Egnatia. Gesticulating with his arms to the east and west, he clarified that:

Constantinople used to be an important seat, back in the day. Constantinople then, Istanbul now. It was good for us, since this road passed right through this town. This means that a lot of people came through here to trade... all this left historical traces here. One probably met and talked with so many different people... that's a source of wealth. Ohrid was a center back then, and at that time, the Egnatia was an important travel route. This means that people must have known about Ohrid. You can compare this to Yugoslavia where Belgrade was the node through which you had to travel. This means, Belgrade was the center of Yugoslavia. When you compare this to the Egnatia, you can say that Ohrid was sort of a center back in the day. People had to travel through Ohrid on their way to other places.[37]

Indeed, Ohrid was not only an important archbishopric and vital for the spread of the Cyrillic alphabet, it was also a center for trade, as confirmed by O'Sullivan: "The Romans seized (the city) [Ohrid] during their struggle with the Illyrian king Gentius. Its importance has been manifested again and again right down to recent times [...]. [...] The staple exports of this city have always been fish, wine, grain and furs. Even in ancient times fish was sent salted and frozen as far as Rome."[38] But Ohrid did not only, according to Jozef, export goods. Ohrid and neighboring towns also exported labor:

> People here have migrated as merchants and craftsmen from ancient times. This is called *pečalba*,[39] you understand. There were empires back then, the Austro-Hungarian empire. People went there, because it was more developed. They went to work, attended the University, studied... they went for a short period of time, and then returned. It was the men who left most often, the women and children stayed here. This goes back hundreds of years, but it is still like this. People used to migrate to find work in the past, and they still migrate to find work at present. [...] In the Balkans, all the Balkan countries were part of the Ottoman Empire... for 550 some years. This means they all have a similar mentality; they have come closer together. That is why people from all the Balkan countries leave. That was how it was done here. People leave to make money, but not only for themselves, because people live together with their families. They leave to make money to give it to their children, to build a house, to have a better life.[40]

It is interesting to note here how Jozef collapses the time-space continuum perhaps in his effort to make sense of the present. Jozef, in other words, seems to

---

37 Jozef, interviewed by Sandra King-Savić, Ohrid, Macedonia, 30 June 2016, Atlas.ti transcript/quote no. 7:2.
38 O'Sullivan, *Egnatian Way*, 62.
39 Seasonal migration of merchants and craftsmen, also known as *kurbet*.
40 Jozef, interviewed by Sandra King-Savić, Ohrid, Macedonia, 30 June 2016, Atlas.ti transcript/quote no. 7:3.

superimpose the past onto the present, perhaps in an effort to forge the future?[41] It is evident, for instance, that Jozef connects his perception of the Egnatia with ancient, *but also current* migratory patterns.

Ohrid is a town of in- as well as outmigration. As is the case with other holiday destinations that are popular in the region, including Budva, Kotor, or Split, for instance, people migrate to Ohrid to find work during the high season when visitors populate this "gem on the lake." Then, the sheer volume of tourists becomes excruciating, as was the case when we arrived on foot. Tourists sipped cold Skopsko beer wearing swimsuits. Tourists dined in fancy restaurants with suited waiters. Tourists were paraded around town by guides apologizing for all the stairs going up and down. Tourists shopped for handmade Ohrid pearls, which did not bother Jozef, who kept on gesticulating and talking about Ohrid and the Egnatia all the while serving his customers. Clearly, Ohrid is on the map, and rightly so, according to Jozef:

> Ohrid is one of the oldest towns… so that… the Egnatia left here traces, how can I explain this to you… This is a very special town, it is unique. During the existence of the Kingdom of Yugoslavia… they did not… how can I say this… they knew about the town of Ohrid, but that was it. Then, king [Aleksandar] sent his messenger, I believe this was during the 1920s… sometime during the 1920s, probably… sends his messenger to see Ohrid, so that the messenger could tell the king that this town was culturally significant, that this town has a special spirit, that this town is good, that it looks nice… that is how the king sent his messenger, to report back to him. And, the messenger was here for three weeks, and when he returned, the king asked him, 'What did you see? Can we use it for tourism?' 'No,' said the messenger, 'this town is not good for tourism, it is good for enjoyment!'[42]

People, such as Jozef and Vjolca, who live along the Egnatia in urban centers are not only proud of the heritage amongst which they live their lives, they also pride themselves in being knowledgeable about the history that continues to shape their city. This comes as no surprise, given that municipal authorities spruce-up historic landmarks to emphasize a historical continuity and connection with the ancient Romans, the Illyrians, and/or the Macedonians, for instance.

---

41 See also: Sandra King-Savić, *Thriving Markets in Times of Crisis: Forging Transnational Belonging through Informal Trade* (London: Routledge, 2021).
42 Jozef, interviewed by Sandra King-Savić, Ohrid, Macedonia, 30 June 2016, Atlas.ti transcript/quote no. 7:1.

5 Walking the Back Roads: Tracing Pre-Industrial Pathways

Leaving urban centers such as Durrës, Edessa, and Bitola behind, walking the Egnatia can feel like going back in time. Although older tractors are used, many of the farmers work the land with animals (Fig. 4). Donkeys are common. Sitting down in the shade under one of the many pockmarked olive trees, one can often hear the cicadas giving their best performance in the afternoon, their electrical buzz standing in stark contrast to the call to prayer in the distance. To be sure, landmarks are still common, and one can even identify and walk on actual remnants of the ancient road. Any purposeful sprucing up of landmarks, however, is nearly non-existent in the backcountry (Fig. 5). This is also the case with the Roman bridge just outside Peqin, Albania (Fig. 6).

Fig. 4: Joshua E. King in conversation with a young man near Durrës, Albania. Photo by Sandra King-Savić, 2016.

Peqin, we learned from Ilir, does get a few visitors seeing that even though the town is small, it nevertheless is a major stop along the Via Egnatia. In 2015, more than one hundred people from several countries traveled the route and stayed in the town. Some visitors came by foot and others behind a windshield.

Fig. 5: Original traces of the Via Egnatia near Dardhe, Albania. Photo by Joshua E. King, 2016.

Fig. 6: Roman bridge near Peqin, Albania. Photo by Joshua E. King, 2016.

In 2016, the year we walked the route, only nine tourists had stopped by Peqin while en route along the Via Egnatia.[43] Ilir, a young wiry man with excellent English skills explained that he learns about the life of the tourists who come through Peqin, their jobs, and their culture. *They show me how they live when they get here.*[44] *But people usually don't stay very long, maybe one or two days, then they leave. Some people don't know anything about Albania before walking the Egnatia*, he added shrewdly. Ilir might be described as a local gate keeper. Used to seeing a trickle of tourists on a regular basis, he talks to people as they come and leave. Clearly ambitious, Ilir, too, plans to leave Albania. He is studying medicine because he sees a medical degree as a means to leave Albania. This is a narrative we heard repeatedly on our walk along the Egnatia, often by way of chance encounters.

One such chance encounter transpired near Broshke, Albania, as we walked along the tracks, together with our newly purchased donkey. *Hey!* we heard someone shout in the distance, *come here! over here!* We soon spotted two

---

43 Fieldnote, Sandra King-Savić and Joshua King, Peqin, Albania, 20 June 2016.
44 Ilir, interviewed by Sandra King-Savić and Joshua King, Peqin, Albania, 21 June 2016, Atlas.ti transcript/quote no. 6:1.

women who gazed over the fence, one young the other elderly, waving us to their house. The three of us, Joshua, *Gomar*,[45] and I, trudged over to the see the women, who greeted us by exclaiming, *my mother-in-law said, 'Those must be Albanians, they have a donkey', but I said no! Look ... they have walking sticks, they must be Americans!*' Majlinda and her mother-in-law invited us into their spacious and wonderfully cool home where we drank water and ate plums from their garden. We learned that this home belonged to Majlinda's fiancé, and that she was a medical student. Although the young woman emphasized her passion for medicine, she added that she also had chosen her subject of study based on her chance to emigrate from Albania to a Western European country, or else the United States. Like Ilir, this young woman had researched her options before embarking on her studies, all with a view toward leaving Albania. I later learned that this is a common route chosen by young Albanians during my subsequent trips to Albania.[46]

How do people here feel about all this? I asked Ilir back in Peqin. *So many people are leaving the country, especially young people like yourself.*

> Ilir: Well, yes. It is a problem. Everyday, people are leaving this country. I remember, my father told me the population of Peqin was about 30,000 maybe 20 years ago. Now, there are maybe 10,000 people in Peqin, including all the villages around Peqin.
>
> Me: Yes, we walked by so many abandoned houses yesterday...
>
> Ilir: Yes, that is common. There are villages with just one old lady as the only inhabitant there. I know a lot of people here from Peqin who have left, and now live in different European countries. They work... some of them live there, they have passports, some of them come back to live in Albania again. People leave because of the bad economic situation. They want to improve their options, also for their family. You can find Albanians in every European Union country.[47]

Ilir's impressions corresponded very much with the views of other individuals we met along the Egnatia. Majlinda (introduced above), a dainty young woman with long, black hair, emphasized her hope to make something out of her life, for instance.

From Majlinda's perspective, this would be impossible if she stayed in Albania. *I want to study, work, and earn money. I want to get married, and have a fam-*

---

[45] We had named our donkey Gomar, which translates into donkey in Albanian.
[46] DAAD Summer School in 2017, and a University of St. Gallen Study Abroad course I taught together with Dr. Yves Partschefeld in 2018.
[47] Ilir, interviewed by Sandra King-Savić and Joshua King, Peqin, Albania, 21 June 2016, Atlas.ti transcript/quote no. 6:2.

ily... I just want to be happy. Life is very short!, she maintained over and again.[48] From there, our conversation turned to the economic situation in Albania, the lack of perspectives young people face, and the political corruption which, as the young woman said, facilitates the career chances of those with connections:

> Majlinda: I was born into a poor family, but I have a wonderful family. We are three children, two sisters and one brother. I am studying at the university. I am studying medicine. It's a very pretty school, but there are problems. It's not very easy to go... in this country, in Albania. Here, we can find a lot of love, a lot of friendship, hospitality and all that, but we cannot find a lot of work. Here, we can find corruption. It's very important to say. I can say that. I know that we have corruption, because I can see it every day with my family. I see that every day with my friends.
>
> Me: How do you see that?
>
> Majlinda: If my father needs work, for example, he will ask someone who is not in the same party as he is. Then, this person will say: no, you are not in my party, I will not give you the job. That is corruption. They take money that is ours. [But,] on the other side, it's... umm... quiet [here]. There is a lot of love here in this country. It is tranquil, it's not noisy here... it's nice here.[49]

It is important to emphasize here that all interviewees highlight their wish to work upon emigrating, many of the interlocutors had even researched what types of jobs are needed in Central Western Europe to fit a specific niche. European Union member states are looking to find caretakers due to the aging population. The EU 28 reported a "record high old-age dependency ratio" in 2017 with 29.9 per cent, and trending upward.[50] Albania's and North Macedonia's elderly dependency ratio, by comparison, hovers around, 18.1 per cent, and 17.7 per cent, respectively.[51]

Individuals are propelled to emigrate not simply for economic reasons. Sure, Ilir, Dimitar's sister, and Majlinda seek to go abroad to earn money. Yet, people also strive to study, work, and to have a family uninhibited by party-politics. In short, they seek to fulfil their dreams. Like Vjolca who hopes to move to a country where working hours merit a standard of living that includes enjoying a va-

---

[48] Majlinda, interviewed by Sandra King-Savić, (between Peqin and) Elbasan, 23 June 2016, Atlas.ti transcript/quote no. 2:1.
[49] Majlinda, interviewed by Sandra King-Savić, (between Peqin and) Elbasan, 23 June 2016, Atlas.ti transcript/quote no. 2:2.
[50] Eurostat: "Record High Old-Age Dependency Ratio in the EU," https://ec.europa.eu/eurostat/web/products-eurostat-news/-/DDN-20180508-1, last accessed 5 April 2019.
[51] CIA Factbook, https://www.cia.gov/library/publications/resources/the-world-factbook/, last accessed 5 April 2019.

cation; so too does Majlinda who does not know how to envisage a future in Albania due to the political corruption. This is a widespread sentiment. According to Doris:

> [People] want to leave because they don't like to be humiliated, by having to go to these crazy counter-protests,[52] or by liking really, really messed up stuff [on Facebook]… or just kind of like stepping all over their dignity and their integrity. They don't like that. Their salaries are minimal. They are barely making it. They want out because of that. Now, the intellectuals who actually do have money, they want out because they don't want their children to grow up in such a system. Maybe they have a nice business, they made it, but they don't want their children to have to go through the same thing. They want freedom, freedom to be who they want to be, to work hard at their job, but be remunerated for what they are doing. They don't want their children to grow up in such a system. The only people that do want to stay here are people in the higher echelon of the political parties, who are cashing in billions of dollars.[53]

Doris is a very resolute, though warm lady we met near Kičevo.[54] She states in no uncertain terms that people seek to move to preserve their dignity, to be free from the oftentimes suffocating party politics through which people find employment or not, as stated by Majlinda earlier. Albania and Macedonia rank 99th and 93rd on the corruption perception index, out of 180 states.[55] Doris, in particular, was talking about what is now the ousted Internal Macedonian Revolutionary Organization-Democratic Party for Macedonian National Unity (VMRO-DPMNE) which had turned Skopje into an Alexander the Great Disney park.[56] Though describing

---

[52] Doris refers to the protests following the wiretapping scandal in 2015. The recordings exposed the VMRO-DPMNE's track record of human rights violations and corruption as documented by Amnesty International at https://www.amnesty.org/download/Documents/EUR6517682015ENGLISH.pdf and Al Jazeera: https://interactive.aljazeera.com/ajb/2015/makedonija-bombe/bos/grafika.html, for instance. As a response to the exposure, government employees and individuals close to the VMRO-DPMNE ministry were made to stage counter-protests in support of the party, as well as the then sitting Prime Minister Nikola Gruevski.
[53] Doris, interviewed by Sandra King-Savić, Kicevo, Macedonia, 28 June 2016, Atlas.ti transcript/quote no. 1:5.
[54] Please note that this is not a stage along the Egnatia. We visited Kičevo to see the doctor, and recorded an interview while there.
[55] Transparency International, https://www.transparency.org, last accessed 5 April 2019.
[56] The VRMO-DPNE launched the "Skopje 2014" project in 2008 so as to imbue the North Macedonian capital city with a European identity. The architectural style and suitability of the newly erected buildings and renovations of existing structures are a much-discussed topic among locals in the capital (fieldwork and participant observation of the Colorful Revolution taking place in 2016). Yet, the exorbitant cost and accompanying corruption were of greater worry to many citizens I talked to over the course of the protests. The Balkan Investigative Reporting Network

the Albanian and North Macedonian context respectively, both women identify dignity, freedom, and their desire for a good life when asked for their reasons for emigrating. And yet, individuals are conflicted about their decision to emigrate. Like so many others, Ilir explained he would miss *the food and the weather, and, of course, my family* when leaving Albania.[57]

Nearly everyone we met on the Egnatia lamented the quality of the food in Central and Western Europe. One interlocutor, Estevan, explained, *the food in Germany... potatoes, meat and coleslaw. I liked living in Germany very much*, he assured us, but *could not get used to the food there. The tomatoes taste like cardboard... you might as well eat the chair, or this tablecloth. I think it would taste the same. Here, when you grill a steak, the whole village smells good! When you grill a steak in Germany, there is no smell. No smell. Not good, not bad. Just no smell*. As was the case with the elderly gentleman in Meschori, Estevan had moved to Germany after his compulsory military service. He shared a flat with a bunch of colleagues and worked in the nearby Mercedes factory between 1968 and 1970. His recollections of his time spent in Germany conjured up mixed emotions as he spoke of the girlfriend he once had, the steady and safe work schedule, and the tasteless vegetables. With the money he had earned in Germany, he returned to Greece and opened a little restaurant near Edessa. It is a little family-run restaurant where he employs his daughter in law. She, in turn, had come from Albania to earn a living picking fruit until she met Estevan's son.

The food is indeed, remarkable. More than once we were invited to share a meal with locals on the Egnatia as was the case near Dardhe in Albania. Enjoying the weather as much as the views around us, we wound our way across pastures, over ridges, and through small hamlets until a family hollered at us that we ought to seek shelter from an approaching storm, and that we should come to their house. Dark clouds and thunder rumbled above our heads so that we happily accepted this family's offer. We stayed with the family for quite some time, and the invitation to coffee soon turned into a lavish meal. During our time with the family, we learned more about the Enver Hoxha regime, the

---

(BIRN) uncovered that the state spent an estimated 684 million Euros on the project. It must be added here that many of the renovations and new buildings are of poor quality. For more information on the "Skopje 2014" project see, for instance, "Skopje Uncovered," *Balkan Investigative Reporting Network*, http://skopje2014.prizma.birn.eu.com/en, last accessed 5 January 2019; Florian Bieber, "Macedonia on the Brink," *Open Democracy*, at https://www.opendemocracy.net/en/opensecurity/macedonia-on-brink/, last accessed 9 April 2019; Ilka Thiessen, "Life among Statues in Skopje," in *Everyday Life in the Balkans*, ed. David W. Montgomery (Bloomington: Indiana University Press, 2019).

[57] Fieldnote, Sandra King-Savić and Joshua King, Peqin, Albania, 20 June 2016.

transition period, as well as the family's personal stories concerning questions of migration. We learned that one of the brothers had left the family at the age of fourteen to find work in Greece. The boy, Antigona explained, had gone to Greece over a green border, sleeping and hiding in the bushes to avoid the law. Once in Greece, the boy started to traffic marijuana until he was caught by the Greek police. He was sentenced to jail for seven years, but the family bailed the boy out with borrowed money. Ever since then, the family has been indebted to the other villagers, and the son is no longer allowed to travel to Greece. Other members of the family now continue to travel to Greece on a regular basis to bring back money for the family as well as to pay off the debt the family incurred.[58]

> Antigona: My brother went to Greece when he was 14 years old. He stayed in Greece for six years, then he came back. He went there to work, and to earn money for us. He went there with his friends. That is normal, everybody does that. He just left over the mountain... just the mountain. He walked for two weeks to get to Greece. It took him about ten days. He slept on the road, stuck to the mountains. There were about five guys who walked to Greece to find a job there then. Five guys from two villages. It was hard, I mean, he had to hide in the trees and in the bushes to hide from the cops...[59]

This was a stark reminder that jerked us back to thinking about our positionality. To us, outsiders, the Via Egnatia resembled a bucolic stroll with stunning views. For Antigona, a young woman whose home is located directly along the Via Egnatia, the road symbolizes an avenue that leads to Greece across the green border. Antigona, who translated the conversation between us, her two brothers, her mother and her father, stressed that there was nothing strange about her family's story. *Like I said before*, she repeated, *Albania is poor. There is no way for us to make any money. Life is very hard [up] here. We can work in the garden here, but we don't save any money. We can be sure to have enough food for the winter, but we don't earn money. Going out, going to another country to make money is an opportunity [to save money].*[60]

---

[58] Fieldnote, Sandra King-Savić and Joshua King, Dardhe/Mirake, Albania, 5 August 2016.
[59] Antigona, interviewed by Sandra King-Savić and Joshua King, Dardhe/Mirake, Albania, 25 June 2016, Atlas.ti transcript/quote no. 5:13.
[60] Antigona, interviewed by Sandra King-Savić and Joshua King, Dardhe/Mirake, Albania, 25 June 2016, Atlas.ti transcript/quote no. 5:8.

6 The Via Egnatia: For some Bucolic, for Others a Means to an End

This, said Dimitar, the man with the long white beard near Sopotsko, *is the very spot where the Via Egnatia passed through. We are standing on history.*[61] Dimitar confirms Arja Kariveri's findings by which "the local people have always been aware of the ancient ruins in the surrounding area and have been used to finding ancient coins, roof tiles, pottery and other material on the slope."[62]

> Listen *Devojko*,[63] you could dig a hole with a pickaxe right here where we stand, and you would immediately find some artifacts. I dug a hole a while back, and found some plumbing pipes. Perhaps they were Roman, they sure were dirty, full of mud! I cleaned them, and now they are so clean that you can drink water out of them again. Only God knows about all the people who have come through here... who built what is here. That is why I tell you that we could find artifacts right where we stand. We know exactly where the Egnatia is.[64]

Dimitar is more than aware of the significance of the Egnatia. The road, however, is not sacred to him. To the contrary. He, like so many others we met along the way, lives along the ancient road, and incorporates the materiality of it into his life, as he did with the pipe he had cleaned and repurposed.

To us, the Egnatia promised to grant us a glimpse into the past before embarking on the ethnographic journey on foot. For locals, the Egnatia is a place they call home at present. For those who are unable to make a living along the ancient road, migration is the only answer while others transform the region to deem it fit for the twenty-first century. This is especially the case in Greece. Following the Via Egnatia in Greece means getting an inside glimpse into the world of large-scale fruit and crop cultivation. Noticeably different from the Albanian and Macedonian rural landscapes, the Greek countryside showcases more capital with modern tractors and expensive irrigation systems.

On our last day on foot, we started the morning in the city of Giannitsa and paid homage to Alexander the Great's birthplace in Pella. On through vineyards

---

[61] Fieldnote, Sandra King-Savić and Joshua King, Sopotsko, Macedonia, 5 August 2016.
[62] Arja Karivieri, "Along the Via Egnatia: A Pastoral Economy, Religious Space and Military Presence in Arethousa in the Early Byzantine Period," in *From Ephesos to Dalecarlia: Reflection on Body, Space and Time in Medieval and Early Modern Europe*, ed. Elisabet Regner et al. (Stockholm, 2009), 31–3.
[63] "Girl," form of addressing women and girls.
[64] Dimitar, interviewed by Sandra King-Savić, (in the vicinity of) Sopotsko, Macedonia, 5 August 2016, Atlas.ti transcript/quote no. 8:1.

and cotton fields splattered with yellow and purple flowers, orchards, dilapidated buildings, and abandoned factories, we walked on a dyke where we were spotted by one of the farmers on the field. From the farmer's field, we could see a vast plain dominated by agriculture. The farmer only spoke Greek. *Helvetia*, we said, explaining that we came from Switzerland. This caught his attention. He rubbed his thumb and forefinger together, indicating money. Then he pointed at himself and shook his head. We got the message. He pointed towards a nearby hillside where ripe watermelons grew in abundance. He made a cutting gesture, and strode with us among the melons, picking out an enormous specimen, far too large to carry on a pack (Fig. 7). Without hesitating, he cut the watermelon from the plant and then split the fruit in half. He handed over the watermelon and gave us his knife before walking away. So, the two of us sat down in the field and gorged ourselves on the watermelon under the midday sun. Juice ran down our chins. A couple hours later we arrived in Thessaloniki. We strolled through the city, marveling at Aristotle's Square, and remnants of the ancient Greek, Roman, and Ottoman civilizations along with hundreds of other tourists.

7 In Search of Employment: Leaving the Via Egnatia

Walking along the Egnatia in Albania, North Macedonia, and Greece allows for a nuanced consideration about how locals interact with the multilayered history they inhabit. Locals along the more remote passageways of the Egnatia appear to *inhabit* the material world the Roman, Byzantine, and Ottoman Empires left behind. No significant veneration surrounds the Ottoman bridge or remnants of the original Via Egnatia outside Peqin and Elbasan. Sometimes individuals salvage artifacts to renovate their homes, as did Dimitar who replaced a pipe in his house with one he had dug-up in town. *We are standing on history*, he emphasized. Yet, instead of worshiping the materiality that represents a distant past, he repurposed his discovery. Larger cities differ markedly from these more remote backroads. Spaces such as the Durrës amphitheater or the St. Kaneo Church in Ohrid, excavated and restored respectively, serve as tourist attractions one ought to visit, and perhaps venerate. These sights serve the purpose of illustrating to potential visitors and locals alike a specific historicized continuity and connection with the past. Traveling the backroads on foot was therefore especially illuminating because doing so allowed for our emphasizing the Via Egnatia itself—a material artifact that reaches beyond nationally-bounded cultural signifiers. This was especially evident near the (formerly) con-

Fig. 7: Farmer picking a watermelon for us near Pella, Greece. Photo by Sandra King-Savić, 2016.

tested border region between Bitola in North Macedonia and the Florina regional unit in Greece. Electing to emphasize our walk across the Egnatia was therefore a methodologically productive decision that decentered discussions around the divisive nature of drawn and redrawn borders.

What emerged as a result of the above methodology was a common thread about the often-trying living conditions across the region. A high level of unemployment, potential destitution, and low average salaries indeed contribute to driving local outmigration. Yet, this is only half of the story. Equally important is the wish to live a life in dignity. Individuals such as Vjolca, Ilir and Majlinda seek to study, work, and have families that are uninhibited by party-politics and corruption. Perhaps Doris said it best when she stated that people *want to leave because they don't like to be humiliated*. They do not like politicians to step *all over their dignity and their integrity*.

Employment based on merit, without having to enlist as a party member, and having a job that warrants taking a vacation were central aspects in numerous discussions along the Egnatia. It may therefore come as no surprise that migrants-to-be "play the long game." Not only did potential emigrants research what types of laborers Western and Central European employers seek, they also prepare accordingly. Ilir and Majlinda serve as a case in point here. Both of them study medicine because they, as many others do, plan on working upon arrival in Central and Western Europe.

Florian Riedler and Nenad Stefanov
Balkan Transit: Conclusion and Outlook

The contributions to this volume have addressed a wide range of topics concerning historical routes in the Balkans, most prominently the route from Istanbul to Belgrade. They have focused on infrastructures and places such as caravanserais, villages, towns and cities; they have included the experience of both travelers as well as those living alongside the road; and they have also examined the role of the route in different imperial and national settings as to its symbolic value and its function for structuring space. In these concluding remarks, instead of reviewing the results of the individual contributions, we want to reflect on a common issue, i.e., the way in which all of them address different geographical and temporal scales in examining the route. Seen from the microperspective of the local as opposed to the macro-perspective of a transcontinental system of circulation, the route appears very differently. The same is true for different temporal scales: while the route may be dysfunctional in certain periods, it appears very stable when a long-term perspective is taken. In the following, we will reflect on the tension between these different perspectives. We will argue that routes call for a multi-scalar examination and thus are also an ideal subject for a global history of connections.

In order to approach the issue of scale, let us start by problematizing the boundaries of our object of research, the route. The present volume has taken for granted the Istanbul–Belgrade route as a more or less stable conduit for traffic, trade, and migration with a fixed beginning and end. The two cities at either end of the route were conveniently chosen to bracket the places in between on which the contributions were focusing. From an imperial point of view, the beginning of the route seems to be clearly marked by the *milion*, the monumental milestone in the heart of Constantinople. When Constantine the Great rebuilt Byzantium as the New Rome at the beginning of the fourth century CE, he erected this milestone in imitation of the *miliarium aureum*, the Golden Milestone in Rome.[1] Although the *milion* disappeared at the beginning of the sixteenth century, it is quite obvious that for the Ottoman Empire, the city remained the center of a network of roads that radiated out to the provinces, as the chapter by Florian Riedler discusses in detail. As was the case for all its imperial predecessors,

---

[1] Iris von Bredow and Georgios Makris, "Constantinople," in *Brill's New Pauly*, first published online 2006, consulted online on 6 June 2020. Also see Fig. 4 of Matthew Larnach's chapter in this volume.

these roads were essential for the Ottoman domination of the territory. However, the notion of Constantinople/Istanbul as the imperial center, the starting point of roads in all directions, also suggests a broader perspective. Particularly in the case of the Ottoman Empire, we can think of the Istanbul–Belgrade road as just a part of a larger diagonal axis that connected Belgrade with Damascus and in this way integrated the core of the empire. From such a perspective, it is not the image of the spider web that describes imperial mobility, but rather that of a transcontinental line of connection.

Likewise, the endpoint of the route is hard to determine. For pragmatic reasons we have chosen Belgrade, because for a long time the city marked the border of both the Byzantine and Ottoman states. But this is quite an arbitrary choice. For the Byzantines, Belgrade was the extreme end point of their sphere of influence in the Balkans. As Matthew Larnach has shown in his chapter, in many respects the section of the road connecting Constantinople with the Thracian center of Philippopolis was much more important. Conversely, for the Ottomans, the road did not stop at Belgrade. At the peak of Ottoman power, in the second half of the sixteenth and into the seventeenth century, it continued on through Ottoman territory to northern Hungary where the Ottoman-Habsburg border was marked by a line of fortresses. Even beyond this border we can still meaningfully speak of the same route. As this volume has demonstrated, routes and borders are reflexively linked to one another in regulating mobility and only in exceptional cases blocking it. As a consequence, the route should not be understood as an infrastructure belonging solely to one state or empire. Although it evidently thrived on the investment and attention it received in certain imperial contexts, and therefore is remembered as an imperial infrastructure, it was more than that. At all times, it was a route connecting cities, regions, states and even continents across multiple borders.

Many travelers, their purposes and destinations, attest to this border-crossing and transitional dimension of the route. Some of them had fixed destinations, such as the crusaders in the late twelfth century, the Austrian and Ottoman ambassadors shuttling between Vienna and Istanbul between the sixteenth and eighteenth centuries, and the Turkish migrant workers of the twentieth century on their summerly journey from their homes in Europe to their holiday destinations in Anatolia. Others were mobile on yet a larger scale, like the truck drivers for whom the road was only a part of their transit from Western Europe to Iran, or various dropouts and adventurers on their way to India. While on a field trip in Dimitrovgrad, one of the authors encountered the most recent and most incredible of these transcontinental travelers: Rosie, who was running from London to Kathmandu as part of a humanitarian project.²

The large groups of migrants and refugees who used the Balkan Route in 2015 in order to get away from their war-torn home countries in the Near and Middle East (such as Afghanistan, Pakistan, Iran and Syria) seem to belong to both categories. With Western Europe they had a clear destination, but this particular route was not their own choice, but rather was determined by the available transport facilities and the border regimes along their way. Regarding the issues of refugees and migration, we hope that our long-term historical approach could support the view that the contemporary rhetoric of crisis employed by Western European politicians and publics is not appropriate.³ The demand for controlling and tightening of borders on which this rhetoric rests, underestimates mobility and its effects on both a local and a transcontinental scale. In the context of the present volume, the events of 2015 only add to the long list of historical examples for the obstinacy of mobile actors.

Also, in a temporal dimension it seems difficult to give the road a fixed beginning and end point. A lot of the fascination for the route derives from its seemingly unbroken continuity from Antiquity to the present. However, this is only one side of the story. As is shown for the late medieval period in Vladimir Aleksić's chapter, or for the early nineteenth century in Florian Riedler's chapter, periodically traffic on the route was disconnected or relevant for only certain regions at best. Especially in the nineteenth century, there was a strong link between technological innovations such as steam shipping and the decline of the route, and only the introduction of the railway reversed the decline. So, the route as a conduit on a large geographical scale was a transient phenomenon. Time and again it turned into a phantom route, only then to resurface in a different form under different technological, political and societal circumstances a few decades later. In this sense, the route resembles other spatial entities such as boundaries and regions, for which continuity also includes periods of a phantom-like existence.⁴

---

2 Cf. https://phaseworldwide.org/get-involved/rosieruns/, last accessed 24 October 2020.
3 Manuela Bojadžijev and Sandro Mezzadra, "'Refugee Crisis' or Crisis of European Migration Policies?" *FocaalBlog*, 12 November 2015, www.focaalblog.com/2015/11/12/manuela-bojadzijev-and-sandro-mezzadra-refugee-crisis-or-crisis-of-european-migration-policies. Also see Igor Ž. Žagar, Neža Kogovšek Šalamon and Marina Lukšič Hacin, eds., *The Disaster of European Refugee Policy: Perspectives from the 'Balkan Route'* (Cambridge: Cambridge Scholars, 2018).
4 Béatrice von Hirschhausen et al., "Phantom Borders in Eastern Europe: A New Concept for Regional Research," *Slavic Review* 78, no. 2 (2019): 368–89.

In view of this, it becomes clear that as a mobility network the route stretches across and connects spatial units on different geographical scales. It is beyond the scope of this concluding chapter to determine the relation of a network such as the route with these units or the process of scalar structuration of space in general. There is an ongoing discussion among human geographers about scales as a concept to describe the hierarchization of spatial units as a special form of the social production of space.[5] Here we rather want to refer to a more playful approach, the *jeux d'échelles* (games of scales).[6] French historian Jacques Revel coined this expression for a new approach to social history which seeks alternative viewpoints for its objects of research, e.g., by putting them into different micro- and macro-contexts. In this sense, the contributions in this volume have used the route very successfully as a device to change scales for their analysis of social life. At the same time, this special dimension of the route offered the contributors a way to question the rigid classifications of conventional scales, e.g., the local, the regional, the national, the imperial, the global. Moreover, the volume has demonstrated how historical actors themselves were also "playing with scales" by placing themselves into various social contexts, which affected their social strategies and experiences. Thus, "playing with scales" can also be used as a descriptive category for the historical actors interacting along and around the route.

The tensions between the geographical scales of the local, interregional and transcontinental and between the temporarily phantom-like character as opposed to the overall continuity of the route are visible in all the contributions. These tensions are productive in the extent to which the scales are not exclusive; social networks and their effects move across scales. A good example is Tatjana Katić's chapter, which addresses the concrete social effects of the imperial Ottoman road management. It shows how the social order and division of labor in the villages along the route were established by their interaction between the imperial center in Istanbul and the local populations living alongside the route. In a similar manner, Nenad Stefanov's chapter develops this topic of the tension between center and periphery: the border regime, which defined the local situation

---

5 Neil Brenner, "The Limits to Scale? Methodological Reflections on Scalar Structuration," *Progress in Human Geography* 25, no. 4 (2001): 591–614.

6 Jacques Revel, ed., *Jeux d'échelles: La micro-analyse à l'expérience* (Paris: Gallimard, 1996). Id., "Microanalysis and the Construction of the Social," in *Histories: French Constructions of the Past*, ed. id. and Lynn Hunt (New York: New Press, 1995), 492–502. Also cf. Nikola Tietze, "Jeux d'échelles: Reflexionen über ein methodisches Prinzip und eine analytische Beschreibungskategorie," *Migration, Mobilität, räumliche Neuordnung* (blog), 16 October 2019, https://rm2.hypotheses.org/1046.

in Tsaribrod/Dimitrovgrad, was designed far away in national capitals, but it became a social reality in the concrete local circumstances. At the same time, the route also affected the border and turned its crossing points into places that were governed by a transnational rather than a national logic. In these as well as in other contributions, it has been the micro-perspective that has yielded fascinating results regarding the connection between state power, mobility and borders. In consequence, many contributions zoom in on particular parts of the route, most prominently on the middle part between the cities of Niš and Sofia. Rather than using the local as case studies for proving a larger trend, the micro-perspective focuses on the interaction of contexts on different scales that co-constitute each other.

We can see the entanglement of scales not only in the organizations and social institutions which structures historical mobility, but also in transport infrastructures when conceptionalized as socio-technical systems. The railway was able to connect societies over large distances and channel ideas and practices (for example, about modernity) as the contribution of Dobrinka Parusheva shows. However, with a gap in this infrastructure, certain places could also become breaking points in the connectivity of the whole route. A case in point is the passage south of Niš, which was opened only in 1888 for rail traffic. Also, in the realm of ideas and discourses, the different scales overlapped and influenced each other. For example, the seemingly immobile locals living in the small town of Tsaribrod, as analysed in Nenad Stefanov's chapter, could imagine themselves as part of a transcontinental route. This can be seen in expressions in the local newspaper calling the town a "gate to the Near East" and in the stories about Iranian drug smugglers.

Also, at a temporal level, the route structures the interaction between scales. Frequently, new versions of the road reused older material or parts of the infrastructure, in this way creating a material palimpsest. Often, the long continuity of the route is acknowledged and is made part of the cultural heritage. The archaeological remains from Antiquity, which were found while building the present motorway as the newest infrastructural expression of the route, are a case in point. As Sandra King-Savić shows in her chapter, locals frequently compare such a heritage of mobility with their present practices of mobility, which they consider a principal part of their identity. As it turns out, such an understanding of continuity is not a new phenomenon; already in early modern times, European travelers were highlighting in their accounts the Roman remains they encountered along the way.

The issue of scales has become particularly urgent in global studies where one of the core questions is the boundaries of and the interaction between the local and the global. Despite diverging scholarly approaches to this question, there seems to be a consensus that both spatial units can only be determined relationally.[7] Studies on historical globalization have addressed this question by focusing on topics such as migration, trade or transcultural exchanges to show the interaction between different localities. We propose that such a study of routes can form a valuable addition to historical studies of globalization within the growing attention being given to the connectivity within and among land empires such as the Ottoman Empire, Persia, Russia or Poland-Lithuania.[8] Especially for this larger region the focus on road connections, of which the Balkan Route is but one such route, promises new insight into the hitherto neglected topic of historical mobility.

---

[7] Angelika Epple, "Lokalität und die Dimensionen des Globalen: Eine Frage der Relationen," *Historische Anthropologie* 21, no. 1 (2013): 4–25.
[8] Florian Riedler and Stefan Rohdewald, "Migration and Mobility in a Transottoman Context," *Radovi: Zavoda za hrvatsku povijest* 51, no. 1 (2019): 201–19; Stefan Rohdewald, Albrecht Fuess and Stephan Conermann, eds., *Transottomanica – Osteuropäisch-osmanisch-persische Mobilitätsdynamiken: Perspektiven und Forschungsstand* (Göttingen: V&R unipress, 2019).

List of Contributors

Vladimir Aleksić teaches Serbian medieval history at the University of Niš, Serbia. He still vividly remembers short trips from Niš to his grandparents with a cowboy style regional train he frequently took a few decades ago. These days, he switched to the personal car or buses when traveling to Sofia.

Tatjana Katić is a Senior Research Associate at the Institute of History in Belgrade. Her scholarly interests revolve around the social and economic history of Serbia under Ottoman rule in the fifteenth to seventeenth centuries. Her favorite resting place on the Tsarigrad Road is a small inn near the Lisine Waterfall.

Sandra King-Savić is a postdoctoral researcher at the University of St. Gallen. As passionate hiker, she strives to combine her enthusiasm for wandering with fieldwork whenever possible.

Matthew Larnach is an independent researcher who completed his PhD in Medieval History at the University of Sydney. His research interests include the Historical Geography of the Balkan Peninsula and medieval military logistics. Whilst employing a variety of means of transportation whilst conducting field research along the Via Militaris he found by far the most enjoyable, and enlightening, was to hike sections of the route by foot.

Dobrinka Parusheva is Associate Professor in Theory and History of Culture at the University of Plovdiv and Associate Professor in Modern and Contemporary History at the Institute of Balkan Studies with the Bulgarian Academy of Sciences in Sofia. Her academic interests are in the field of modern and contemporary history of South-East Europe and history and anthropology of everyday life. She has no preferred means of transport while moving from the South-East to the North-West of Europe and back, for in her opinion it is the shape of mind which matters and not practicalities.

Florian Riedler is scientific coordinator of the priority program Transottomanica at the University of Leipzig. His research interests include Ottoman urban history as well as the history of infrastructure in the nineteenth century. In summer 2017, he enjoyed traveling with his family from Sofia to Istanbul in an air-conditioned bus.

Nenad Stefanov is scientific coordinator of the Interdisciplinary Center for Border Research at the Humboldt Universität zu Berlin. His preferred means of transportation during field research on the route is a small red automobile.

Index

abdal   88, 90
Adrianople   31, 37
Adriatic   10, 14, 54, 77, 105, 107, 109, 111, 210
Aegean   2, 75, 77, 118, 129
Afghanistan   1, 231
Albania   6, 35, 176, 202, 205, 210, 212–4, 217–21, 223–4, 226
Aleksinac   113
Alexandroupoli   118, 129
Anna Comnena   37–8
antemurale christianitatis   3
archaeology   21, 29, 37, 39, 48, 61, 74–5, 79, 83, 103–4, 212, 233
Australia   201–2
Austria   15, 176, 181
– Austria-Hungary   151–2, 161
– Habsburg Monarchy   112–3, 184
Autoput   146, 175, 179, 189–91

Baghdad Railway   125
Balkan mountains   25, 41–3, 49, 82
bandits   62, 93, 97, 106, 110–2, 114, 120
Bari   202, 210
Basil II   30, 39–41, 49, 51
Bela Palanka   83, 87, 91–2, 94, 99–100, 143, 146
Belgrade   1, 4, 31, 37, 56, 67, 72–3, 76–7, 112, 139, 152–3, 155, 157, 170, 215, 230
Bertrandon de la Brocquière   67, 71
Bitola   141, 144, 184, 201, 217, 221
Black Sea   75, 77, 107, 116, 118, 127, 131, 156, 183
border region   181, 187, 208, 228
border town   112, 109, 139–41, 155–7
borders   3–5, 8–9, 139–41, 181–2, 231
– Albanian-Greek border   9, 224
– Danubian border   48
– Eastern Rumelian-Bulgarian border   129, 131
– Greek-North Macedonian border   3, 201–2, 207–9
– Greek-Turkish border   4

– Habsburg-Ottoman border   112–3, 230
– Hungarian border   78
– Inner German border   162, 164
– Phantom border   5–6, 184–5, 231
– Serbian-Bulgarian border   1–2, 12, 17, 63, 139–41, 149–51, 155–61, 180, 184, 195, 197
– Serbian-Ottoman border   113–114, 151
– Yugoslav-Bulgarian border   146, 161–80, 188–9, 193–4
Bosnia-Herzegovina   118, 127, 142, 190
Bosporus   36, 81
Boué, Ami   16, 115
Braničevo   57, 64, 66, 71, 73, 75–6
bridge   8, 45, 54, 71–4, 84–5, 95, 101, 106, 109, 111, 120, 178, 205, 217, 219, 226, 46
bridge-building   28, 32, 146
Bulgaria   1, 2, 4, 12, 17–8, 40, 103, 113, 119, 122, 127, 140–2, 150, 152–6, 159–65, 168, 171, 173–8, 180, 182, 184, 186, 188
– People's Republic of Bulgaria   146, 188–89, 191, 193–4, 197
– Principality of Bulgaria   128–9, 131, 135, 138, 149
Bulgarian Empire   30, 39–40, 49
Burel   144–5, 150
Byzantine Empire   13, 21–50, 60, 63, 81, 105, 230

camels   91, 70
camps   32, 40, 53, 62–4, 71
Canada   202, 210
caravans   63, 69, 77, 91, 106–7
caravanserais   85, 87–8, 91–2, 106, 108, 120, 212, 229
carriages   70–1, 115, 163
cars   1, 17–8, 146, 175, 188–91, 194, 196–97, 203, 217
carts   36, 42, 86, 116
citizenship   158–60, 180, 203
coaches   115–6

Codex Theodosianus   27–8
Cold War   3, 165, 175, 179, 180–181
compulsory labor   28, 44, 146
Congress of Berlin (1878)   128, 131, 140, 149
Constantinople   9, 16, 23–4, 26, 31–2, 35, 37, 39, 41–4, 46–50, 82, 106, 124, 127, 153, 168, 215, 229–30
Croatia   2, 190, 211
crusades   10, 13, 16, 34–6, 39, 45–8, 59–60, 70–1, 73, 106, 230
Ćuprija   74
cursus publicus   44
customs   113–4, 129–31, 150–1,153, 156, 175, 177–8, 182, 188, 193, 197

Damascus   2, 107, 230
Danube   16, 22, 25, 29–30, 41, 57, 64, 66, 71, 76–8, 81, 109, 113, 115–6, 118, 124, 127, 140, 145–6, 151
Dedeağaç.   See Alexandroupoli
derbencis/derbentçis   15, 87, 94–100, 106, 111
derbend/derbent   93–5, 97–101, 111
dervishes   87–90, 101
Dimitrovgrad   1–2, 11–2, 56, 75, 83, 86, 140, 143, 171–2, 174–81, 184, 189, 230, 233
donkeys   70, 217, 219–20
double owners   163, 166
Dragoman   82, 85–6, 92–102, 105, 115, 144, 168, 170, 174, 193
Durrës   202, 209–12, 214, 217, 226
Dyrrachium   209, 212

E-80 motorway   1, 12, 178, 183, 188–9, 195
Eastern Rumelia   113, 122, 128–32, 135
Edirne   4, 106, 108–9, 111, 114, 116, 118, 127, 129
Egypt   42, 86
Elbasan   212–4, 226
endowment   84–5, 90–2
engineers   15, 18, 28, 114, 121, 127, 145, 183, 204, 210
epidemics   111–2, 120
Europeanization   122, 124, 136

everyday life   1, 17, 54, 79, 122, 137, 166, 181, 184

ferries   57, 71, 74, 84, 191, 202
Filibe.   See Plovdiv
forests   22, 31, 36, 65–6, 86–7, 93, 130
fortress   27, 33, 62, 65, 73, 76, 83, 85, 89, 96, 109, 230
Frederick Barbarossa   36, 47, 59, 71
frontier   25, 157

Gates of Trajan   34, 40–2, 45, 51
geography   73, 108, 110
Germany   1, 8, 18, 171, 174, 188–9, 194, 201–2, 210, 223
Godeč   82, 14
grain   42–3, 106, 215
Greece   2–4, 6, 68, 72, 140–1, 174, 176, 191, 201–5, 207–11, 223–8
Guest workers.   See labor migrants

halting place   63, 105–6, 108
han.   See inn
Harmanli   108, 115
Hellenzation   208
Hirsch, Baron Maurice de   118, 122, 124, 127, 129–31, 154
Horeum Margum   57, 72
horses   25, 44, 68–70, 89, 92–3, 95, 100, 105–6, 116, 168
Hungary   1, 4, 75–8, 91, 108–9, 111–2, 176, 191, 230

Ihtiman   105, 115
imaret   88–90, 101
immobility   5, 104, 233
infrastructure   6–8, 13–5, 18, 22–7, 33, 45, 49, 53–4, 56, 60, 72, 74–5, 79, 82, 87, 92, 103–7, 109–12, 114–5, 121–2, 125–6, 128, 132, 137, 143, 145–6, 153, 157–8, 169, 175, 178, 183–4, 188–9, 191, 194, 197, 229–30, 233
inn   8, 24, 91–2, 96–7, 106, 109, 146, 157–8, 172, 189, 197
Iran   1, 178–9, 230–1, 233–4
Iron Curtain   8, 146, 164–5, 171, 173, 179–82

Iron Gate   113
Istanbul   82, 84, 100, 107, 109–11, 113–5, 118–9, 127–8, 130–1, 137, 148–9, 151, 153, 169, 172, 180, 186–7, 215, 230, 232
Istanbul Express   171, 174, 176, 179
Italy   24, 27, 35–6, 77, 105, 170, 176, 181, 191, 201–2, 209–10
itineraries   10, 15, 24, 67, 108
Izvor.   See Bela Palanka

janissaries   71, 100
Jireček, Konstantin   9–10, 13–4, 16, 56, 81, 119, 136–7, 154
Justinian   21, 28, 31, 33

Kalotina   82, 86, 93, 95–6, 98, 194
Kanitz, Felix   16
Katib Çelebi   109–10
kaza   88, 94–5, 143–6, 148–9, 171
khan.   See inn
Kinammos, John   60–2
Konstantinov, Aleko   167
köprücüs   94–6, 98–9
Kosovo   77, 97, 118
Kosovo myth   194–5
Kovin   67, 71, 76

labor migrants   8, 19, 179, 189–91, 194, 201, 203
landscape   17, 24, 54, 60, 65, 82, 87, 144, 160, 183, 193, 225
Laveleye, Emile   150, 153, 156, 168
limes   25
Lom   145

Macedonia   112, 116, 128, 152–4, 156, 161–2
– North Macedonia   2–4, 141, 201–3, 205, 207–8, 214, 221, 226, 228
Manastır.   See Bitola
Mandeville, John   72–3
mansion   24, 56
Manuel I Komnenos   60, 75
Manuel II Comnenus   44

maps   5, 24, 104, 108, 110, 142
– mental maps   3, 15, 104, 108–10, 120, 178, 182
Maritsa   22, 31, 41, 43, 45, 81, 105, 134
Marmara Sea   46, 114, 118
Matrakçi Nasuh   108–9
menzil   87, 92, 106, 116, 143, 156
Midhat Pasha   115–6, 145–6, 149, 168
migration   2–3, 5, 9, 15, 18, 22–3, 29–30, 37, 54, 99, 105, 155, 158, 166, 169, 186, 203–4, 209, 214–5, 224–5, 229, 231, 234
milestones   10, 52, 229
mining   67, 77
mobility   1, 4–5, 7–9, 15–9, 82, 101, 104, 111, 120, 140, 149, 151, 158, 160–1, 163, 166, 169, 171, 173, 175, 179–82, 184, 193, 197, 230–4
modernity/modernization   15–6, 103, 110, 114–5, 119, 121, 123–5, 132–3, 135–8, 143, 153, 233
monastery   28, 66–9
Monastir.   See Bitola
Morava   13, 31, 55, 57, 59–61, 63, 65–8, 71, 73–4, 76, 81, 101, 105, 151–2
mountain pass   8, 15, 34, 36, 40–3, 51, 82, 86–7, 93–5, 105–6, 115
Murad I   88, 194–5
Musa Pasha Palanka.   See Bela Palanka

Naissus   30–1, 37–8, 45,47
nationalism   2–3, 5, 141–3, 153, 155, 168, 183,194–5, 204, 206, 208
Niš   6, 9, 55, 58–60, 62–4, 70, 72–3, 75, 77, 83, 85–92, 95, 112, 115–6, 139, 141–2, 144–5, 161, 167, 170–1, 175, 188–9, 197, 233
Nišava   31, 43, 55, 72–4, 81–6, 89, 94, 96, 101, 105, 144–5

obstinacy   150, 156, 160–1, 163, 166, 181, 185, 188, 194, 231
Ohrid   214–6, 226
Orient Express   16, 119, 127, 166, 169–71, 174
Oriental Railway   118–9, 122, 127, 130–1, 154

Ottoman-Russian War (1877–78)   113, 118, 127
pack animals   31, 35, 40–1, 91
padalište   63
Pannonia Express   170, 173–4
Paraćin   56–7, 60, 65, 67, 112
Paulicians   38–9, 43
pavement   22, 31, 33, 42, 45, 81, 85–6, 104, 120
Pazardzhik   115, 118, 167
pečalba   169, 215
Pechenegs   43, 72–3
Philippopolis   13, 22, 30–1, 37–9, 41, 43–4, 51, 230
pilgrims   33–6, 49, 59, 79, 107, 111
Pirot   1, 6, 83–8, 90–2, 94–6, 98, 112, 115, 143–7, 149, 151, 153, 155–6, 158–63, 166–8, 170–1, 180, 183–9
Plovdiv   113, 116, 118, 122, 125, 127–38, 151, 170
post riders   92, 106
post station   8, 24, 56, 92, 106, 116, 143, 156
post system   44, 116
Procopius   29, 31

quarantine   112–3, 116

Ragusa   77, 111
railway   6, 16–7, 83, 114, 116–20, 122, 124–31, 134, 140, 148, 152–7, 161–3, 166–70, 174–5, 177–9, 181, 186, 190, 197, 231, 233
Ravno   57, 72–3, 74
refugees   1–5, 29, 163, 178, 231
Rhodopes   127
roads   15–8
– asphalted roads   175
– macadamized roads   114–5, 119, 145, 147, 175
– motorways   12, 17, 146, 179, 183, 188–9, 233
– Roman roads   1, 9–13, 24, 27–9, 41, 46, 56, 75, 79, 86, 104–5, 201, 206

– remnants of Roman roads   10, 12, 16, 50–1, 55–6, 74–5, 79, 86, 103, 105, 217, 226
Roman Empire   10–1, 13–4, 23, 25–7, 32–4, 41, 45, 49, 57, 72, 81, 104–5, 107, 206, 215–6
Romania   127, 136, 140, 176, 191
Rome   24, 37, 201, 206–7, 214–5, 230
Rusçuk.   See Ruse
Ruse   113, 116, 167
Russia   15, 124, 197, 234

Salonica.   See Thessaloniki
Şehirköy.   See Pirot
Serbia   2, 4, 12, 17, 34, 36, 60, 62–3, 67–70, 77–8, 99, 103–4, 118–9, 140–2, 150–4, 159–62, 167–8, 180, 183, 186, 190, 194, 195, 197, 201
– Principality of Serbia   113–4, 145–6, 149
Serbian-Bulgarian War (1885)   150, 156
Serdica   28, 30–1, 37–41, 45, 51, 72, 103–4
Shopi   142, 157
Singidunum   10–1, 56, 104
Skopje   109, 154, 214, 222
Slavs   29–30, 38–9, 69, 82, 195
– Slavic migration   29–30, 54–5, 59
Smederevo   67, 76–7, 89
smuggling   3, 163, 166–7, 172–3, 184, 233
Sofia   2, 9, 103–5, 109, 112–3, 115, 118, 127, 138–9, 141–2, 144, 148, 151–7, 159–60, 162–4, 167–71, 173, 175, 193, 233
Soviet Union   162, 164, 170–1, 178
Stalin, Josif Visarionovič   141, 164, 178
Stara Planina   144–5, 148
steam shipping   16, 114–6, 127, 231
straža   93, 101
Struma   29, 43
Süleyman I   63, 108, 111
Šumadija   66–7, 151
Suva Planina   83
Switzerland   201–3, 226
Syria   1–2, 107, 231

tabor/wagenburg   70–1
Tabula Peutingeriana   10, 24

Tanzimat   114–5, 124, 139
Tapchileshtov, Hristo   148–9
Tatarpazarı.   See Pazardzhik
taverns   92, 96–7, 157, 187
taxes   84–5, 93, 95, 97, 100, 130–1, 155
Tekirdağ   114, 118
Thessalonica   29, 37
Thessaloniki   107, 109, 118, 151–2, 167, 202, 206, 226
Thrace   27, 38, 42–4, 49, 77, 230
Tito, Josip Broz   141, 164, 171
Torlakians   82, 99, 101
trade   4, 9, 14, 43, 63, 66–7, 74–9, 82, 86, 91–2, 100–1, 110–155, 1, 113–4, 116, 120, 127–9, 131–2, 146–9, 151–3, 158, 155–6, 158–9, 162–3, 165–6, 168, 174, 184–6, 206, 210, 212, 215, 229, 234
Treaty of Passarowitz (1718)   113
Trieste   16, 115, 171–2, 179–81
Trn   94, 144–6, 156–7
truck drivers   179, 183, 191, 193–5, 197, 230
Tsaribrod   17, 83, 85, 91–2, 139–41, 143–4, 155–60, 162, 164, 166–71, 178–81, 184, 233
Tuna/Dunav Vilayet   143–5
Turkey   1–2, 4, 8, 119, 171, 174, 176, 178–9, 188–9, 191, 193–4, 202

United States   202, 210, 220
urbanization   67, 128, 132–3, 135, 137
Üsküp.   See Skopje

Varna   127, 151, 167,
Via Appia   206
Via Egnatia   10, 15, 18, 27–8, 34–6, 47, 81, 105, 107, 191, 201–28
Vidin   109, 116, 145
Vienna   103, 112, 115, 125, 127–8, 154, 230
vigla   93
Visok   144, 150, 160
Vlachs   69, 99, 101
voynuk   95–6, 99–100
VZRO Vrtop   162–3

wagons   27, 31, 35–6, 45, 47, 70–1, 86–7, 107
waqf.   See endowment
wheeled vehicles   35–6, 50, 212

Yugoslavia   3, 18, 140, 146, 162, 164–5, 170–3, 175–6, 178–82, 184, 188, 190–1, 194, 203, 215–6

zaviye   88–90
Zirojević, Olga   14, 56, 93–4

Bei Fragen zur Produktsicherheit wenden Sie sich bitte an:
If you have any questions regarding product safety,
please contact:

Walter de Gruyter GmbH
Genthiner Straße 13
10785 Berlin
productsafety@degruyterbrill.com